TRANSFORMING
THE **SKIES**

TRANSFORMING THE SKIES

PILOTS, PLANES AND POLITICS IN BRITISH AVIATION, 1919–1940

PETER REESE

The
History
Press

To those men and women who blazed
the aerial trail between the wars.

First published 2018
The History Press
The Mill, Brimscombe Port
Stroud, Gloucestershire, GL5 2QG
www.thehistorypress.co.uk

British Library Cataloguing in Publication Data.
A catalogue record for this book is available from the British Library.

ISBN 978 0 7509 8410 2

Typesetting and origination by The History Press
Printed and bound in Great Britain by TJ International Ltd

CONTENTS

ACKNOWLEDGEMENTS

I am extremely grateful to many organisations and people for their immense help.

Above all I required a specialist aviation collection, which I found in the National Aerospace Library at Farnborough with its world-class collection of published and unpublished sources. There I have enjoyed the ready assistance of Chief Librarian Brian Riddle with his noted enthusiasm and encyclopaedic knowledge. I have also received immense help from Christine Woodward and latterly the kind and utterly professional Tony Pilmer, including his work on the index.

As on many other occasions, I have also worked in the Prince Consort's Library at Aldershot with its fine military collection, including aviation, where the staff are my firm friends of long acquaintance.

Further help has been received from the National Archives, the RAF Museum at Hendon, the Farnborough Air Sciences Trust Museum and the Royal Aeronautical Society (in particular for its original illustrations).

With regard to notable individuals, I am indebted to Mrs Jennifer Prophet for her early reading of the book and editing its text along with technical help from her son, Charles Prophet; Paul Vickers, historian and author, for ideas with titles and much more besides; Linda Mansell for her valued computer skills and great patience with my scrappy longhand; Tim Winter for illustrative sources; Frances Bean for additional typing; Stewart Davis for aerodrome maps; Dave Evans for other written material; and the late Nigel Legge for extensive discussion and valued advice.

As for the invaluable contribution of a publisher, I wish to acknowledge the faith and support of The History Press and in particular its commissioning editor, Amy Rigg and project editor Rebecca Newton.

Finally, my indefatigable wife Barbara, for being what she is, for organising our complex home affairs while I have been absent in libraries and for listening and then giving her acute reactions to my early drafts.

I alone remain responsible for any errors and deficiencies.

Ash Vale, autumn 2017

PROLOGUE

After my recent book[1] about the pioneering figures and events that shaped British aviation from the beginning of flight to the movement in 1914 of the Royal Flying Corps detachments to France, I felt I was almost predestined to consider what followed.

Predictably I found that the First World War had its official and unofficial histories, biographies and pilots' accounts (from both sides) about their aircrafts' performances and their tactics in attempting to gain command of the air. Following such tales of high adventure, sacrifice and loss, I never expected the period between the wars to have been capable of attracting comparable attention or of being of equal or greater interest to the pioneering years of aviation prior to the war. It was therefore to my considerable surprise that, although it has drawn little literary attention so far, I found it packed with graphic incidents of genuine significance to the development of aviation and the survival of the British state during the Second World War. In short I discovered it was a magnificent story waiting to be told.

At first, I doubted whether anything could equal the advances made by the early aviators from their first flights measured in feet and seconds to the genuine cross-country performances of the aircraft that flew across to France in 1914. Yet, I quickly came to realise the far greater technological achievements of the interwar period. Although in its initial stages the disinterest shown towards British aviation prior to 1914 was repeated, with the role of the air force again questioned and the British aircraft industry shrinking in both size and capability, it could not last. By the mid 1930s the Royal Air Force faced likely attacks from a formidable new opponent and was compelled to enter into a breakneck race in which aeronautical developments went beyond the imaginings of the earlier pioneers. For such reasons I began to understand that this was indeed the time where British aviation came of age.

I also learned that the events of the interwar years went far beyond jostling for military advantage, including as they did such issues as the birth and expansion of British civil aviation, the building of huge airships before their final rejection, and the familiarisation of aeroplanes to ordinary men and women in Britain. Even so, it was the country's involvement in the Schneider Trophy competitions, bringing major advances in both airframe and engine technology, that enabled Britain's Royal Air

Force to develop from a threatened and backward service to one whose balanced forces could meet assaults from a country that viewed air power as a major weapon of war.

Such was the speed and extent of the technological advances during this time that eminent scientist Sir Harry Garner called them discontinuities rather than the result of gradual improvements.[2]

While he acknowledged that much of the progress was due to a steadily growing knowledge of materials, structures, aerodynamics and engine design, he identified other inventions bringing radical alterations (discontinuities) to the design of the aeroplane, such as unbraced monoplane construction that replaced the heavily braced biplane, and the gas turbine (rather than the piston engine) invented in Britain by Frank Whittle and tested in 1937 – although this would not play a substantial role until late in the Second World War.

The piston engine shouldered the lion's share of wartime missions and among the regular advances that Garner saw as transforming its performance and reliability were improved air-cooled radiators, superchargers and constant speed propellers, together with improved fuel that gave its bombers an increase of up to 70 per cent in the ratio of power to weight compared with those in the First World War.[3]

Such advances became ever more significant when the weight of airframes was reduced by using improved materials, e.g. alloys with stressproof qualities (compared with the previous wood and canvas) leading to dramatic increases in wing loading. Speaking after the war as an expert on aircraft engines, Roy Fedden maintained that aviation 'had and will continue to have a more far-seeing effect in other fields of material endeavour than any other previous single development'.[4]

While Fedden's supreme confidence was by no means shared by everyone, during the interwar years there were service leaders who, too, understood and exploited such fast-moving technological developments to bring RAF strategy more into line with what was possible. One was Air Marshal Wilfrid Freeman with his widespread responsibilities for aircraft design and production. In the British democratic system, however, there were bound to be others of high rank who were far less astute and whose actions would have malign consequences. Among them was Freeman's chief of staff, Edward Ellington, who floundered due to his unease with and misunderstanding of such technological advances.

The same applied to civil aviation that in Alan Cobham had someone who, before its establishment in Britain, envisaged airports for every major British town and airlines that would fly regular services to the ends of the earth. In contrast, Sir Eric Geddes, chairman of Imperial Airways, the nation's favoured airline, sought fiscal soundness above all else and thereby missed a host of opportunities for his formidable company.

The widespread advances in British aviation during the interwar years were bound to bring contrasting assessments. Guy Halford-MacLeod, writing about British civil aviation, emphasised its contrasts and complexity, leading to 'an ordered incoherence, an endearing story of muddle; heroic pioneering, lost opportunities, determined entrepreneurs, extravagant waste, commercial reality'.[5]

In contrast, test pilot and aviation author, Harald Penrose, viewing it from a pilot's point of view, emphasised the pioneering elements 'whether trail-blazing air routes that did not become established until years later, extending the boundaries of power and speed, conquering greater heights or making aeroplanes and even airships, their engines and equipment more efficient and reasonably reliable'.[6]

Political commentator Montgomery Hyde approached it with Britain's strategic requirements in view, although he too emphasised its contrasts, writing that 'British Air Policy in the years between the two World Wars is marked by inconsistencies and changes which were dictated by the recurrent need for economy in national expenditure and also in the second decade by the growing menace of Germany's rearmament'.[7]

All, however, acknowledged how the rollercoaster pattern of such years was exacerbated by the contrasting attitudes between the 1920s and '30s. In Britain during the earlier period, for instance, memories of the recent loss of life were still raw and many looked to the ideals of pacifism and universal peacekeeping through international bodies rather than the use of standing armies or air forces. This was to change with the rise of the dictators, when British politicians were soon compelled to acknowledge a world of sovereign states pursuing their own self-interest and protected by national armed forces. Parallels can, in fact, be found with the time of the English Civil War with its repeated questioning of such issues as individual and state morality, the structure and use of armed forces and the legitimacy of making war.

However one considers the interwar period, during it British military aviation gained equal status with the other two armed services, and civil aviation rose from nothing to become a means of faster communications between both near and far-flung countries that offered almost unimaginable potential.

As such, it appears as a time of intriguing contrast and change manifesting a unique stage in the story of British aviation.

PART 1

BACKS TO THE WALL
1919–26

1

FREDERICK HANDLEY PAGE AND THE GREAT SELL-OFF

In his summary of the first year after the war, Charles Grey, editor of *The Aeroplane* and self-appointed voice of the British aircraft industry, observed that:

> 1919 has been one of extremes in aeronautics. It has seen the Aircraft Industry reduced from one of the greatest and most important in the country to one of the smallest as regards output and one of the least important as regards the present existence of the Empire. It has seen firms which made hundreds of thousands of pounds out of building aeroplanes during the war shut down their aircraft departments and dismiss their skilled staff and it has seen other firms which struggled gamely through the bad times before the war spending their hard-earned and over-taxed war profits in perfecting aircraft for peaceful purposes.[1]

Turning to the nation's air force, he wryly observed that due to the scale of the rundown it did not seem that many more people remained to be eliminated.

He ended his editorial with the heartfelt comment that we have finished with 1919, for which the Lord be thanked.

Whatever Charles Grey's opinions, aviation at this time was no place for the faint-hearted, with John Seely, the former Under-Secretary for Air, concluding that 'the air industry in this country is dying, it is withering away, and it is most sad it should be so, and it is also very dangerous. Of the great firms which were producing aircraft and which had large design staffs – and it is on them that our future in the air depends – nearly all have gone out of business.'[2]

On the other hand, Winston Churchill, as the serving Secretary for War and Air and future Chancellor of the Exchequer, was sure that some robust figures remained, and the best solution lay in ending subsidies and for Government to get out of the way and let the aeronautical industry and nascent civil aviation fly by themselves.[3]

However contrary these standpoints, the challenges of post-war conditions were immense for a young industry that had started in the early twentieth century on a semi-amateur basis led by gentlemen enthusiasts working in competition with the Royal Aircraft Factory, and progressed to one that had met demands for more advanced aircraft in unheard of numbers, where in spite of many of its trained men enlisting into the services, design departments of real strength were created.[4]

Some idea of such vastly increased production can be seen by comparing the period between August 1914–May 1915 with that from January 1918–October 1918. In 1914–1915 530 aircraft were built (fifty-three per month) compared with 26,685 aircraft (2,669 a month) in 1918.[5]

During the war, Winston Churchill, speaking as Minister of Munitions, emphasised the amazing progress: 'We are now making in a single week more aeroplanes than were made in the whole of 1914, in a single month more than were made in the whole of 1915 and in a single quarter more than were made in the whole of 1916.'[6]

The companies involved in such precipitate advances were fully aware that such conditions were unlikely to last, and in 1916, under the leadership of Holt Thomas from Airco, they banded together to form 'The Society of British Aircraft Constructors' in an attempt to support their common concerns both in and out of Government.

Its forty founding members were joined later by Armstrong Whitworth, British and Colonial, Gloster Aircraft Co. Ltd and Fairey. Although it represented all the major firms, at the end of the war the society found itself powerless to prevent a major collapse in its members' fortunes, when contracts for 25,000 aircraft were cancelled. With RAF manpower falling by 90 per cent in fifteen months, it simply did not need new aircraft, and the numbers of civil aircraft built would drop from a by-no-means impressive 240 in 1920 to a minuscule ninety-seven in 1922. As a result, the aircraft

A four-engined Handley Page V/1500, the civilian version of which carried passengers. (Author's collection)

firms attempted to diversify into whatever products they thought might sell: Westland made pianos and milk churns, A. V. Roe produced a small monocar, Gloster turned some of its hangars over to pig rearing and mushroom growing[7], while Vickers commercialised its Vimy bombers for the Chinese Government.

To make matters worse, the companies faced instant demands for an excess tax on profits 'in excess of a stipulated peacetime standard', which by 1917 were levied at a punitive 80 per cent. 'This hit the aircraft industry especially hard for during the war the firms had regularly put the majority of their profits into their expanding undertakings, before at its end, when tax demands (requiring immediate payment) were still coming in, the requirement for aircraft abruptly ceased.'[8]

Finally, a huge quantity of spare aircraft and equipment was about to flood the market whose sales, after early haphazard arrangements, were coordinated through the so-called Aircraft Disposal Co. Ltd, where leading constructor Frederick Handley Page acted as managing agent. The firm succeeded in acquiring this role after Handley Page raised the very large sum of £1,080,000 through debenture shares charged to his company's property, with which he purchased the entire stock of aircraft assembled by the Government Disposals Board for £1 million plus 50 per cent of all profits on the future sale of the stock.

After producing an impressive brochure, the Disposal Company held its initial launch on 23 April 1920 at the Savoy Hotel, where the Under-Secretary of State for Air, the Marquess of Londonderry, voiced his official support: 'The Government as the dispenser of property is always in a difficult position. In my official capacity, therefore, I welcome the advent of an organisation which is prepared to carry on the best interests of private enterprise, the undertaking we are recommending today.'[9]

He was followed by Handley Page himself who, after listing the stunning amount of stock that he estimated was worth upwards of £100 million, including 100,000 different aeroplanes, 350,000 aero engines and vast quantities of other spares of all descriptions, told his listeners it could all be purchased at 'a cost which is only a small proportion of the original cost to the British Government.'[10] The aircraft came with the necessary adjuncts of spare parts for both engines and machines but 'after these stocks are exhausted it will be impossible to replenish them or obtain material except at three or four times the cost'.[11]

Handley Page shrewdly pointed out the benefit of such low-cost machines for civilian air transport, which he said made great development possible that under rigid Government control of sales would have been out of the question.

Whatever use was made of such machines, the sales proved so successful that Handley Page was soon able to remit £500,000 to the Government as its share of the profits (while earning the same himself) although so much stock remained that the Disposal Company still had plenty for sale ten years later.

The success of the Disposal Company was less advantageous for other constructors because it further reduced the requirement for new planes and led them to face three

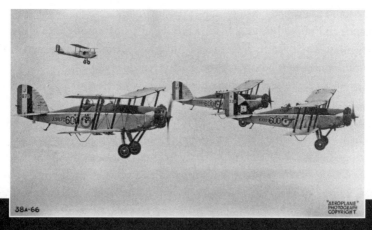

RAF Wapiti fighter patrol planes. (Author's collection)

stark choices: the need to slim right down, restructure – in order to avoid the full force of the excess profits tax – or close down altogether.

In the event Airco, the largest of all, was forcibly amalgamated with Birmingham Small Arms (BSA). Sopwith Aviation disappeared to re-emerge as Hawker Engineering Co.; Bristol and Colonial Aeroplane Co. was wound up to reappear as Bristol while Grahame-White Aviation Co. lost its independence altogether.

In the process, the number of aircraft constructors fell to sixteen and the few military orders that came through during the early 1920s were in the main for modifying and improving existing models. The RAF for instance found that its operations in the Middle East against insurgent tribesmen could be fulfilled by continuing with semi-obsolescent aircraft such as the Westland Wapiti, itself designed to use many components from the earlier DH.9a.

This plane would continue in production from 1927 until 1932[12] and its successor, the Wallace, came from a Wapiti conversion for which orders continued until 1936 with eighty-three Wallaces still on RAF strength at the beginning of the Second World War.[13]

So desperate were the constructors for new business that when an RAF requirement promised to lead to a significant production order, it would attract a clutch of venture prototypes. An example was W21/26 – the last two figures related to the year in which it was issued – for a single-seater fighter to replace the 6/22 Fairey Flycatcher. This attracted no fewer than ten competing designs for a single contract, all of which had to be built, flown and tested.

In such a climate, aircraft constructors needed special qualities. Along with technical know-how and immense self-belief, they required nerve and determination, if not ruthlessness; qualities that were invariably united with a hearty dislike of the civil servants who doled out the few contracts available. Such attributes were undoubtedly possessed by the swashbuckling and formidable Frederick Handley Page, the constructor involved in the Aircraft Disposal Company but still in the market for new contracts.

Handley Page's lower middle class origins were not that unusual in the aircraft industry of the time. He was the second son of a master upholsterer and proprietor of a small furniture business, and an ardent member of the Plymouth Brethren. Frederick was given the opportunity to attend Cheltenham Grammar School, following which – in 1902 – against his family's wishes – he enrolled at Finsbury Technical College for a three-year course in electrical engineering under Professor Sylvanus Thompson. Ever ambitious, he chose this course because he was convinced that the electrical industry had good prospects for expansion.

Frederick proved himself a clever pupil and after graduating at 21, the London firm of Johnson and Phillips appointed him as their chief electrical designer. Even so, he soon developed what would become a lifelong interest in aviation. After joining the Aeronautical Society he consulted the aviation press and made contact with French landscape painter and aeronautical enthusiast José Weiss, uniting with him in developing an advanced glider and crescent-winged monoplanes in his spare time.

In 1908 Handley Page went over to France to see the Wrights flying at Le Mans and on his return was so anxious to press ahead with constructing a machine of his own that he took the risk of doing some experimental work at his employers' factory 'without their authority'.[14] When they found out they straightaway accused him of embezzlement and he was dismissed.

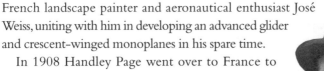

Frederick Handley Page in 1914. (Royal Aeronautical Society/National Aerospace Library)

Undaunted, Handley Page set up a business of his own near Woolwich Free Ferry, where he obtained a commission to build a tandem biplane for the inventor Deverall Saul, after receiving permission from Weiss to incorporate some of his aircraft patents.

The plane never flew, even when towed by a motor car, but on 17 June 1909 Handley Page turned his aviation business into a limited liability company, reputedly the first of its type, although from an authorised total of £10,000 capital only £500 was subscribed. Rumour had it that Handley Page raised his initial sums from his winnings at poker on the commuter trains in and out of Fenchurch Street Station but the truth was probably more prosaic since he lived very frugally and earned money from manufacturing components, including propellers, for the Willows No. 2 airship of 1910.

Calling upon his boundless energy, in the evenings he taught at Finsbury Technical College, and by 1911 he had progressed to the Northampton Polytechnic Institute at Clerkenwell (the forerunner of the City University), where he lectured on aerodynamics. He installed a wind tunnel there and set his students practical coursework to investigate design problems connected with his own airframes.

By now his aerodynamic skills were advancing quickly and from Weiss he developed a belief in building larger planes. In July 1911 one of his crescent-wing monoplanes (nicknamed the Yellow Peril because of the extreme colour of its dope) was piloted across London by Edward Petre to Brooklands, a distance of 55 miles,[15] and in the following year another two-seater plane (whose construction had been made possible by a loan of £500 from his uncle) took part in the military trials held on Salisbury Plain, where it flew satisfactorily before crashing. In 1913 he moved his work premises to a larger 11-acre site at Cricklewood where he built his first biplane, which featured in the Hendon air show of that year.

Ever the opportunist, when the brilliant George Volkert became one of his students he made him the company's chief designer for a salary set at an undemanding 15s a week.

By now Handley Page was becoming well known among constructors not just for his academic and practical skills but as a good salesman and an effective public speaker, where his knowledge of the Bible acquired from his father proved valuable. While not averse to using others' ideas, he kept abreast of current aeronautical research and design and became recognised as a legendary hard worker, with a natural self-confidence and a determination not to become downcast from adversity.

Gustav Lachmann worked closely with Handley Page during the interwar years and believed his personality contained three heady archetypes: 'the circus director representing the ebullient entrepreneur, the scientist, and in his personal encounters that of the Indian goddess Durga, multi-armed with ambivalent qualities of destruction and benevolence'.[16]

Whatever his personality, before the war Handley Page's company had designed small aeroplanes, including ones offering notable stability, and his breakthrough came in late 1914 when he was summoned by Captain (later Rear Admiral) Murray Sueter to consider making planes that could both bomb the German High Seas Fleet in its base at Kiel and the Zeppelin sheds along the Friesian coast. Handley Page produced drawings for a two-engined aircraft with a 100ft wingspan that delighted Sueter, who drew from his desk a signal from Commander Samson in France saying 'what we want here is a bloody paralyzer to stop the Hun in his track'. 'That,' Sueter repeated (pointing to the drawings) 'is what we want.' Handley Page's design was to become the 0/400, which flew about eighteen months later and was the forerunner of large bombers in Britain.

The experiments conducted in the Northampton Institute's wind tunnel moved Handley Page far ahead of most other designers, although Geoffrey de Havilland took advantage of his association with the Royal Aircraft Factory with its own wind tunnels. In 1915 Charles Grey affectionately described Handley Page's august relations with his small design team as 'that benevolent autocracy which is known as Handley Page'.

By the end of 1916 Handley Page had delivered forty-six of his 0/400 bombers before being asked to build a new four-engined derivative, the V/1500 with a wingspan of 126ft and a range of 1,200 miles capable of bombing Berlin. Because his factory at Cricklewood was fully committed to building the 0/400, he decided the new bomber should be constructed at the Harland and Wolff factory in Belfast. There George Volkert, assisted by weekend visits from Handley Page himself, set the shipwrights to work twelve hours a day, six and a half days a week, but although the plane first flew in May 1918 this was too late for it to enter operational service before the war ended.[17]

With his affinity for large aircraft that were capable of carrying passengers, it was fully understandable that Handley Page should be one of the first constructors to turn his attention to their commercial possibilities. As early as 1919 he formed Handley Page Transport Ltd to promote civil aviation in Europe and such was his enthusiasm that he sent 0/400 rebuilds – with fitted interiors including seats and tables for passengers – to potential customers in South Africa, Argentina, China, Greece, India, Peru, Poland, Scandinavia, Spain and the USA.

The pattern of British civil aviation during its early years is considered more fully in Chapter 3, but Handley Page's bold initiatives in this field soon resulted in him suffering massive losses amounting to £130,000 in 1920 alone.[18] This was particularly serious because of his other heavy financial commitments. The year before, he had attempted to raise extra capital by turning his manufacturing complex into a public company by issuing 500,000 £1 cumulative shares, most of which he was forced to take up himself. He also incorporated his airline company, Handley Page Transport Ltd, with £200,000 capital and bought his Cricklewood premises from the Ministry of Munitions with further money borrowed from Barclays Bank.[19]

In a praiseworthy attempt to retain his full workforce he entered into a further agreement with the motor car firm Eric Campbell and Co. to build car bodies.

Within a short time Campbell and Co. went bankrupt and this cost Handley Page a further £150,000. If this were not enough, his trade missions to sell converted bombers still did not bring the orders expected and by the end of 1920 they had accumulated a further £286,492 of debts.

Such liabilities gave him ample grounds for going into receivership but this was not Handley Page's way, and by using the proceeds from his Aircraft Disposal Company he succeeded in wiping off both his debts and his overdraft. The company proved itself as a cash cow and by 1939 it was estimated to have earned him an amazing profit of £3 million, but this also brought its problems. During its early years it threatened his managing directorship of the parent company where, due to a lack of orders, the value of its ordinary £1 shares had slumped to 1s. His solution was to channel some of the Disposal Company's funds into his own company – as a likely temporary measure – with the predictable result that he found himself accused by its shareholders of spending £400,000 of their money in promoting new transport services across the globe.[20] The seriousness of this can well be imagined when at the time he owed the Bank of Scotland a similar amount.

In the end the bank agreed that Handley Page could remain on as managing director providing the Disposal Company and the bank nominated new directors to the Handley Page board, including Lieutenant Colonel J. Barrett-Leonard to act as chairman for no fewer than six years. This agreement cost Handley Page royalties of £179,000 – although characteristically he considered it far more important to remain as managing director. While in Handley Page's case his laudable if overambitious plans to sell airliners were responsible for many of his debts, the root of his problems, like those of other constructors, came from a chronic lack of orders. This was especially the case following the world financial crisis of 1921, when for a time the RAF ordered no new aeroplanes and Handley Page's works foreman, William MacRustie, was left to supervise just eight apprentices and five workmen. It forced Handley Page into even more drastic reductions to his workforce, including the release of George Volkert, his chief designer, who went to Japan to help set up an aeronautical industry there.

However deep their cuts, without income from orders, neither Handley Page nor his fellow constructors could hope to solve their financial problems. In 1924 Barrett-Leonard, who by this time had also joined the board of the Disposal Company, demanded that Handley Page settle debts totalling £242,477. In a Herculean effort including using his profits from the Disposal Company, selling off land at Cricklewood and negotiating a fresh loan with Barclays Bank, he managed to do so.

It had been the closest thing for, although in July 1924 Handley Page was finally awarded a contract to build fifteen Hyderabad bombers based on his 0/400s, such had been the rundown of his company that he had to borrow more money to buy the necessary materials. The Air Ministry made things even more difficult by never ordering more than fifteen planes at a time and although he built seventy-nine in all, he had to sack his workmen after each order for fifteen was completed.[21]

Remarkably by 1926, the indefatigable Handley Page had not only paid off all his debts but was able to carry out a further capital reconstruction of his firm due to fresh expectations from an important technological breakthrough arising from his earlier work with George Volkert at Cricklewood in developing automatic slots on planes' upper and lower wings, for which he had lodged patents in October 1919.[22]

When such slots were fitted to the leading edge of wings they increased an aircraft's range of speed, enabling it to be controlled at lower speeds and to be free from spinning. On being informed that another patent had been registered by a German designer, Gustav Lachmann, Handley Page went straight to Germany and recruited him into the company to make further wind tunnel experiments at Gottingen University (and safeguard his own patent). Far from Lachmann being aggrieved, this started a lifetime association between them.

During the 1920s the slot system was fitted to aircraft in forty-three countries and the Air Ministry specified that slots should be fitted to all RAF models, thus earning the Handley Page Company some £750,000 from the invention. He personally received £100,000 from the British Government and £200,000 from the US[23] for his technical breakthrough.

By the late 1920s Handley Page had come through the worst of his troubles and before the start of the Second World War his company built a number of aeroplanes, both airliners and bombers, although the extent of the problems experienced by one of the industry's most innovative and indomitable figures illustrates the immensely difficult conditions for the British aeronautical industry during the first decade after the war.

Aviation commentator Peter King believed that only two constructors, Tommy Sopwith and Geoffrey de Havilland, came through with their aims untarnished[24] and that this was because both found special and idiosyncratic ways of survival.

Sopwith was not only a brilliant leader but also possessed rare business acumen. Although at the war's end he believed as strongly as others in the growth of civil aviation, he directed his company into manufacturing motorcycles and car bodies despite realising it could not survive for long that way. When in 1920 the Treasury duly lodged an enormous claim for excess war profits and refused to place it against the firm's heavy losses during 1919, he decided he could go on no longer. After effecting stringent economies, including mortgaging the company premises, Sopwith placed his firm in voluntary liquidation[25], thus enabling him to meet the Treasury's claim in full and pay all his creditors at 20s in the pound.

This accomplished, he started again in a small way with three of his 'originals', Harry Hawker, Fred Sigrist and Bill Eyre, who joined him in investing £5,000 each for a firm dedicated to building relatively small aeroplanes. Although Harry Hawker died tragically in 1921, the knowledge and enthusiasm of the remaining three meant Hawker Aircraft was very likely to succeed, especially when after 1926 it began to produce fighter aircraft designed by a young Sydney Camm.

Geoffrey de Havilland took another route towards survival; after demonstrating advanced design skills at the Royal Aircraft Factory and at Airco (before that company closed down on 25 September 1920) he founded his own company, de Havilland Aircraft Co. Ltd, helped by capital supplied by Airco's Holt Thomas. Like Hawker Aviation, it started on a small scale but its particular strategy was to tender for non-governmental work both in Britain and overseas in the form of airliners and smaller passenger carriers – until in 1927 it brought out the outstanding Tiger Moth light aircraft. Although some work was subsequently undertaken for the Air Ministry, this was generally confined to reconditioning de Havilland aircraft and by the end of 1925 de Havilland was so confident in his design ability that he did not 'submit a competitive military prototype until the late 1930s.'[26]

Another company that survived because of its owner's outstanding business acumen was Fairey Aviation. It was formed in 1915 by Richard Fairey, who like Sopwith swiftly took it into voluntary liquidation before re-forming it in 1921. A man of almost unassailable self-belief, Fairey steered his company through the stormy passages of the early 1920s helped by the Navy's loyalty to his designs and by producing biplanes that were capable of going through a succession of models over a comparatively long period. He also showed a capacity to act quickly, as shown in 1930 when his Fox bomber lost out for RAF orders to the Hawker Hart. He went over to Belgium and sold satisfactory quantities to the Belgian air force, including one contract totalling £300,000.[27]

Geoffrey de Havilland. (Royal Aeronautical Society/National Aerospace Library)

Whatever such achievements, the 1920s were extremely difficult years for the British aircraft industry. The previous war's insistent demands for greater numbers of planes for both the Army and Navy resulted in massive expansion and the creation of a first-class airframe and engine industry. However, such rapid growth caused many firms to be undercapitalised and dependent on Government orders. The total cessation of these brought immediate losses and gross uncertainty, and while some companies attempted to switch over to new products, demands for Wartime Excess Profits Tax, allowing no latitude nor concession for the losses made during 1919, brought on a massive crisis. Things were made worse still when the belief that opportunities for exports and an expanding civil market would carry the industry through also quickly evaporated.[28]

With the likelihood of another war ruled out for a full decade at least and by 1918 the RAF reduced to just ten per cent of its peak size, the Air Ministry expected it to be able to make do with wartime planes, of which it held a three-year supply. In any case, Hugh Trenchard, Chief of the Air Staff, was far more concerned with building up the RAF's infrastructure than spending his small budget on new planes. Any remaining prospects for new aircraft orders were hit by the vast quantities of existing planes, engines and the other spares available at knockdown prices from the Aircraft Disposal Board.

Although from 1922 there was a measure of official assistance through the granting of subsidies to civil aviation and with the Air Ministry's decision to no longer purchase front-line aircraft made from wood, in the absence of a clear strategic doctrine (demonstrated by the number of multi-purpose aircraft favoured at this time) and the strictly limited numbers of contracts that had to conform to both rigid and uninspired Air Ministry specifications, the industry was prevented from achieving the massive technological leaps that were already beckoning.

In the circumstances it was lucky the industry had the leaders it did, many of them self-made men whose extra qualifications had been acquired through part-time study. Most of them were not natural businessmen – although they could hardly have avoided making money during the war – nor were they the best employers – as self-made men they were not only heavily demanding but often martinets to their staff. Yet as a group they possessed two common beliefs that helped them through, namely their continuing mission to conquer the skies and their deep-held scorn of the Air Ministry's civil servants. When speaking in his accustomed biblical fashion in 1959 at the memorial address to his friend Richard Fairey, Frederick Handley Page recalled the struggles during the 1920s with the condemnatory words of St Paul that: 'We wrestle not with flesh and blood but with the spread of wickedness in high places.'[29]

'Brab' Moore-Brabazon, who knew the pacesetters so well, emphasised their vulnerability during the dire struggles of the early 1920s following the years of plenty. 'They were my friends, I lived with them, I knew them as brothers … but it was not their fault, believe me, it was not their fault that it has all gone a little mad,

Tommy Sopwith (right) talking to P.W.S Bulman, chief test pilot at Hawker Aviation. (Royal Aeronautical Society/National Aerospace Library)

we were all suffering from dreams of such a wonderful future. No one really thought of money in connection with it.'[30]

For many of the construction pioneers, even more than their opposite numbers in the more traditional industries, the early 1920s were years when the highly exciting and seemingly unending progression since 1908 ended, when a heavy cull of their numbers took place and when survivors such as the Shorts, although deprived of their brilliant eldest brother, Horace, continued in business but would never recover their former ascendancy.

Fortunately the indomitables such as de Havilland, Handley Page and Fairey were still there and, in a more detached role, so was Tommy Sopwith. While these and brilliant new constructors were still prepared to meet different but no less important challenges, some of the early blithe spirit had been lost forever.

HUGH TRENCHARD AND THE FIGHT FOR A SEPARATE AIR ARM

The creation of the Royal Air Force from the Royal Flying Corps (RFC) and the Royal Naval Air Service (RNAS) just seven months before the end of the First World War was undoubtedly one of the most important events in the history of British arms. It therefore seems all the more surprising that by the beginning of 1919 the British Prime Minister, Lloyd George, should have decided to dismantle the Air Ministry and with it a separate Royal Air Force.

Against such a powerful Prime Minister any defence was bound to be difficult and it was made even more so by the exceptional circumstances that had brought about the creation of the Royal Air Force, namely the degree of national anger at the then current bombing attacks on the British capital that appeared to signal that henceforth they would become a new means of waging war.

To avoid possible party rivalries, Lloyd George appointed former Boer general Jan Christian Smuts to join him on a two-man committee to consider the air defence of Britain and the higher direction of air operations. The Prime Minister left the practical work to Smuts and the resulting reports that went to the War Cabinet were in his name, the first appearing on 8 July 1917. It was relatively straightforward and involved the setting up of a unified command to defend London, comprising observers, anti-aircraft guns, a balloon barrage and fighter squadrons. This was accepted by the Cabinet without delay.

David Lloyd George in 1916 shortly before he became Prime Minister. (Author's collection)

Smuts's second report of 17 August was far more sweeping. This proposed the creation of a separate Air Ministry to control and administer all matters in connection with air warfare and plan arrangements for the amalgamation of the existing two air services (the Royal Flying Corps and the Royal Naval Air Service) into a single organisation.

Smuts (supported by Sir David Henderson, Head of the Royal Flying Corps at the War Office) sketched out a grandiose role for future British air power:

> The Air service ... can be used as an independent means of war operations. Nobody who witnessed the attacks on London on 11 July could have any doubt on that point ... As far as at present can be foreseen there is absolutely no limit to the scale of its future independent war use. And the day may not be far off when aerial operations with their devastation of industrial and populous centres on a vast scale may become the principal operations of war, to which the older forms of military and naval operations may become subordinate.[1]

This hyperbolic – and unproven – forecast of future capability came at a time when the German raids were about to become much reduced and transferred to night-time, and when the future Allied Independent Bombing Force (formed in June 1918 under General Trenchard) would prove capable of mounting little more than nuisance attacks on German border targets such as Metz and Cologne. Smuts's expectations were fuelled in part by inflated forecasts of future aircraft production – far in excess of the current Army and Navy requirements – and during the remainder of the war (which had been expected to last for some further years) the RAF had little chance of achieving even part of Smuts's overarching hopes. Even so, by the war's end it was the largest air force in the world with more than 27,000 officers and almost 300,000 airmen and airwomen.[2]

These strength levels were soon to be massively reduced: by 3 January 1920 no fewer than 26,087 officers, 21,259 cadets and 227,229 other non-commissioned ranks had been discharged from RAF service.[3] With the Air Force yet to prove itself a war-winning instrument and with the Air Estimates just a quarter of the Navy's and less than 20 per cent of the Army's, it was near inevitable that the two older services should start pressing for it to revert to its two original portions and be returned to their control. With Lloyd George's negative attitude, powerful opposition from the other two services and without a strong political champion of its own, the chances of the RAF keeping its separate identity seemed hopeless.

That their attacks failed were largely due to an exceptional defence put up by Hugh Trenchard (1873–1956), arguably the greatest figure in RAF history, who after being re-appointed Chief of the Air Staff on 11 January 1919, held the post for almost the whole of the 1920s. Such an achievement did not seem likely from his early service record and even after joining the Royal Flying Corps in 1912 he seemed a most unlikely figure to reach high rank, let alone successfully champion a separate air force. Born into a family of six children whose solicitor father went bankrupt, Trenchard showed little ability for the armed forces' entrance examinations. He eventually succeeded – at his third attempt – in passing the less demanding tests for the Army militia, coming eighth from the bottom of the 169 successful candidates. Commissioned into the Royal Scots Fusiliers, he was far from an immediate success, with an aggressive attitude that made him unpopular while acquiring the reputation as something of a loner – although he quickly distinguished himself as a good organiser.

At the outbreak of the Anglo–Boer War, Trenchard took the opportunity to raise a company of irregular cavalry and quickly shone as their gifted, if headstrong, leader before he was seriously wounded conducting a rash attack. Following his recovery he became an acting lieutenant colonel with the colonial South Nigeria Regiment, but when the war ended and he returned to his parent regiment in Londonderry he reverted to the substantive rank of major. There he unwisely locked horns with his commanding officer, who told him the town was too small for both of them.

By 1912 Trenchard was still a major and on entering his 40th year he was understandably discontent with his lack of progress. Upon the advice of a friend he decided to attempt a flying career, for which he had to pass a flying course before his 40th birthday. He was granted three months' leave and after paying £75 (returnable on passing) for lessons at the Tommy Sopwith School of Flying at Brooklands he succeeded in gaining his pilot's certificate just in time, although his flying skills did not over-impress his instructor.

The Royal Flying Corps was formed during the same year and as one of its older officers he was sent to its Central Flying School at Upavon in Wiltshire. At Upavon, Arthur Longmore (later Air Chief Marshal Longmore) found

Viscount Hugh Trenchard, defender of the RAF. (National Portrait Gallery)

Trenchard's flying suspect, judging that he was overconfident and lacked finesse – but this did not appear to hamper Trenchard unduly for he was soon appointed adjutant and then assistant commandant of the school due to his undoubted administrative ability. At Upavon he became known for requiring instant obedience but despite a booming voice and an imposing presence, it was soon apparent that he experienced difficulties in conveying his messages clearly, either on paper or directly. However, he came to exert a strong hold over those under him, not least because of his genuine conviction in the aeroplane's vast potential.

As a senior figure among a small pool of regular officers, the war brought Trenchard rapid advancement. In 1915 he was promoted to major general to replace Sir David Henderson as head of the Royal Flying Corps in France, where he served under Douglas Haig in command of the British forces there. On his appointment Trenchard was particularly lucky to inherit the brilliant Maurice Baring as his private secretary, who became invaluable to him and to whom he reputedly said during their first meeting: 'I can't write what I mean … I can't say what I mean, but I expect you to know what I mean.'[4]

During Trenchard's time in France he tirelessly pressed for better aircraft, although his chief concern was to develop an aggressive spirit among his fliers that he believed would enable them to gain air supremacy over the battlefield and go on to attack

Lord Rothermere, short-lived Secretary of State for Air. (Flight, 29 November 1917)

enemy lines of communication, and even industrial centres beyond the defence lines. It was a costly stance for, although after 1916 British aeroplanes increasingly outnumbered their German opponents and came to match them in performance capability, they suffered up to four times their casualties.

The creation of the RAF brought Trenchard to the pinnacle of power when he was offered the post of Chief of the Air Staff (CAS) despite still being less than enthusiastic about it becoming a separate service. Predictably, before the RAF's official birthday on 1 April 1918 serious dissension had broken out among its leaders, with Trenchard directly involved. The dispute originated with Prime Minister Lloyd George's wish to favour the Harmsworth brothers, who as press barons had much influence over public opinion and shared his antipathy to Douglas Haig, the Commander-in-Chief in France. The elder, Alfred, Lord Northcliffe, publicly refused the Prime Minister's offer to appoint him Secretary of State for Air in the columns of his *Times* newspaper, before his younger brother Harold, Lord Rothermere, accepted. It is highly debatable whether he was well served by his Chief of the Air Staff, for on his appointment Trenchard proved very reluctant to leave Haig when the climactic land battles of the war were about to start. In any case, he utterly disagreed with the political attacks being mounted against his former chief and it was only after the strongest pressure from both Harmsworth brothers that he accepted the post as Chief of Air Staff – but it quickly became apparent that Trenchard and Rothermere were fundamentally incompatible. In fact, Trenchard quickly lost all faith in someone he believed was an intriguer by nature (although Trenchard himself never hesitated to make use of his own powerful supporters). More importantly, he believed Rothermere was patently out of his depth when it came to the necessary discussions regarding the new service. Whatever his shortcomings, Rothermere undoubtedly had major problems of his own, not only with his health but also from the devastating loss in action of his second son that quickly followed the death of his first. This counted for little with Trenchard, who felt compelled to ask to be relieved of his duties and be allowed to tender his resignation (serving officers had no right to resign).

Trenchard's decision triggered the departure of Sir David Henderson as vice president of the Air Council, with Major Baird, the department's Parliamentary Under-Secretary, likely to follow. Such losses among his senior staff triggered Rothermere's resignation just four months after assuming office and caused the arrival of Lord Weir (former Minister of Munitions and as Secretary of State for Air a strong champion of air power and strategic bombing), with the post of Chief of the Air Staff going to Trenchard's long-term rival, Major General Frederick Sykes. Weir confirmed Sykes in the appointment but, as an admirer of Trenchard, gave him command of the Independent Bombing Force that Trenchard had formed earlier in France. Trenchard attempted to build this into a force of formidable proportions, but during its early raids it suffered greater casualties at the hands of defending aeroplanes than he had anticipated.

As the intensity of the air war over the western battlefront increased, Trenchard criticised the duplication of staff required by his bombing force, and on Armistice Day declared with typical forthrightness, that 'a more gigantic waste of effort and personnel there has never been in any war'.[5] Even so, it was while he was directing the Independent Force, that Trenchard came to believe in the utility of heavy bombing and its particular effects on civilian morale (a conviction expressed earlier by Smuts and wholeheartedly supported by Weir). In justification of the tactics used by the Independent Force Trenchard wrote:

> By attacking so many centres as could be reached, the moral effect was first of all very much greater as no town felt safe and it necessitated continual and thorough defensive measures on the part of the enemy to protect the many different localities over which my force was operating. At present the moral effect of bombing stands undoubtedly to the material effect in a proportion of 20 to 1 and therefore it was necessary to create the greatest moral effect possible.[6]

How Trenchard reached this proportion of 20:1 was never explained, and not everyone was as convinced as Trenchard, Smuts and Weir about the effects on morale. In a memorandum sent at the time of Weir's appointment as Air Minister, Winston Churchill had written that:

> It is not reasonable to speak of an air offensive as if it were going to finish the war by itself – it is improbable that any terrorism of the civil population which could be achieved by air attack would compel the Government of a great nation to surrender. Familiarity with bombardment, a good system of dug-outs, or shelters, a strong control by police and the military authorities should be sufficient to preserve the national fighting powers unimpaired … therefore our air offensive should consistently be directed at striking at the bases and communications upon whose structure the fighting power of his armies and his fleets of the sea and of the air depends.[7]

Weir was unlikely to have been convinced by Churchill's arguments against air attack, and in any case he had planned to resign by the end of the war. When in January 1919 he handed over his keys of office to the more sceptical Churchill, his ambitions for air remained at the highest, and in his farewell speech to the Air Staff at the Hotel Cecil he reminded them that the Air Ministry's responsibilities were twofold, namely 'the administration of the young Air Force with its great traditions, and the development of civil aviation with all its vast possibilities'.[8]

At this point Churchill not only had reservations about the effects of bombing, but neither did he take civil aviation all that seriously. Weir took pains to impress on him (as he was due to become Secretary of State for both War and Air) that if the RAF was not to disappear, its Chief of the Air Staff had to be a man 'with a mind and will of his own'. Weir believed the truculent Trenchard rather than Sykes possessed the required force of character not only to meet opposition from the other two services but also create a new service from the wreckage of wholesale demobilisation and the sale of all surplus aircraft. 'Trenchard,' he said, 'can make do with little and won't want to be carried.'

Churchill, who had had a genuine belief in the need for a separate air arm since before the First World War, sent for Trenchard and offered him the post of CAS (despite the fact it was presently held by Sykes), while at the same time asking him to submit brief plans concerning the reorganisation of the Air Ministry and, more crucially, the RAF. Churchill already had in his possession the ambitious plans that Sykes had submitted to Weir for a post-war air programme, including proposals for the formation of a multi-national Air Force (with standardised equipment) operating from permanent air bases across the Empire, supported by a standing striking force that Churchill knew the Cabinet had rejected on grounds of expense.

Trenchard's proposals to Churchill covered just two sheets of foolscap paper, on which he suggested that a future Air Ministry should be as small as possible with an Air Council of just three branches and no more than a dozen senior officers.

In anticipation of the expected attacks from the other two services, he also made proposals for a small Air Force, with only a limited number of its officers holding permanent commissions. Others would be offered short service commissions and a further group of officers would be seconded from the other two services for a period of four years. (Whatever their type of commission, Trenchard was adamant that all officers had to learn to fly.)

Trenchard's second main proposal was that the RAF should have specialist and thoroughgoing training units quite separate from its operational ones. By these means he hoped to establish foundations with nothing much else on show – but ones that would be hard to destroy.[9] Trenchard also made clear that the infant RAF needed a demonstrable part to play in the nation's security.

Churchill approved Trenchard's proposals and brought him back as CAS after gaining Sykes's agreement to head civil aviation, which that officer naively and wrongly hoped the Government would immediately support financially.

Trenchard hoped his modest proposals might appeal to the political establishment but, during September, he became convinced that Churchill himself was weakening over the RAF's continuing existence in the face of the strong arguments being brought by the other two services. So strong was Trenchard's belief and such was his temperament that he burst into Churchill's office and, after a blazing row, Trenchard undertook to write an additional short statement outlining the strategic case for an independent RAF. Recognising that: 'There is still a great deal of discussion going on now as to whether it is justifiable to retain a separate air force,' he went on to affirm confidently that:

> the consensus of expert opinion would be that the power of the air will be an increasing power in years to come – which is right. It seems to me there are two alternatives:
>
> 1. To use the air simply as a means of conveyance captained by chauffeurs weighted by the navy and army personnel, to carry out reconnaissance for the army or navy, drop bombs at places specified by them immediately affecting local operations or observe for their artillery.
> 2. To really make an air service which will encourage and develop airmanship, or better still, the air spirit, like the naval spirit, and to make it a force that will profoundly alter the strategy of the future.[10]

While making a strong plea for an independent air force, this still did not make the new organisation's strategic role clear. Even so, Churchill considered it sufficient to form the basis of a white paper that he submitted to Parliament on 11 December 1919. This contained Trenchard's additional suggestion that the new force should have parts specially trained for work with the other two services, 'these two small portions probably becoming in the future, an arm of the older services.'[11] This was in fact a sop to the other two services, which he came to bitterly regret later.

However short on strategy, the white paper gave details of the force's disposal and training arrangements. In the case of the twenty-five-and-a half operational squadrons (whose planes were, of course, still the models used during the war), nineteen were scheduled to be based overseas 'to defend the Empire' (although here his intention to remove them from covetous eyes was equally important). With no mobilisation considered necessary for at least ten years, the remaining squadrons were considered enough to form a reserve in the United Kingdom. From these, two army co-operation squadrons would be based at Farnborough and Stonehenge and three Navy co-operation ones at the Firth of Forth and at Gosport, leaving a tiny reserve for emergencies. The way in which Trenchard allocated such minimal figures made it virtually impossible for critics to raise any queries about extravagance or any squadrons being surplus to establishment. The paper proposed spending the bulk of the RAF's small £15 million budget – a fraction of that allocated to the other two services – on building training facilities (where the essential traditions of the new service could be driven home). The highest possible standards of performance would be required and there were three main aims: one was to train officer entrants at a cadet college at Cranwell where two-thirds of them would be offered engagements for three, four and five years' service only; senior officers would be trained at a staff college set up at Andover and aircraft apprentices in a school to be established at Halton, where boys would undertake a three-year course.

The white paper proposed transferring the vital functions of supply and research from the Ministry of Munitions to the new Air Ministry, although with such a small overall budget only £2 million could be spared for this purpose (of which £500,000 would be for civil aviation). The required facilities for aeroplanes would be provided at Farnborough, Biggin Hill and Martlesham Heath, and for airships at Cardington and Howden.

As Trenchard remarked of his proposals, 'I have laid the foundations for a castle. If nobody builds anything bigger than a cottage on them it will at least be a very good cottage.'[12] Parliamentary approval was still needed and this came on 15 December 1919, after Churchill had presented the Air white paper to a generally unenthusiastic if not actively hostile House of Commons. In such fashion and against the odds, Trenchard succeeded in having the RAF endorsed as a separate service, however small and poorly funded.

His next vital success came when the other two service leaders undertook to give him a year's grace in order to get his service under way – subject to him meeting their requirements in the meantime.[13] It was a decision that the Navy in particular came to regret bitterly, for Trenchard seized the opportunity to move the RAF on to a stronger organisational and administrative footing and – most important of all – to prepare his justification for its role in a future Continental war.

While working towards this aim he enjoyed a large slice of luck when an opportunity arose to use his aeroplanes in a novel role. In 1920 the need came about for a campaign against the so-called Mad Mullah in Somaliland, a chief who had for more than twenty years harassed and pillaged tribes supporting the British administration, and had resumed his attacks. In the past the response had been to send a punitive expedition to restore order at the cost of millions of pounds and many lives, but Trenchard proposed using a single bomber squadron for the same purpose. To considerable surprise, within three weeks of making twice-daily attacks on the Mullah's camps and forts from the air, he was overthrown and his dervish followers dispersed.

All this was achieved at the declared cost of £77,000, which Leo Amery, the Parliamentary Under-Secretary for the Colonies, called 'the cheapest war in history'.[14] As a result Trenchard was able to establish the principle of substituting RAF squadrons for large Army contingents, particularly in the event of trouble among the Middle Eastern territories held under British mandate. The fruits of this were seen in Iraq during October 1922 when Air Vice-Marshal John Salmond was made general officer commanding *all* forces in the area.

Trenchard laid down rules of procedure for such countermeasures. Arab villages or camps, for instance, 'were never to be bombed or strafed until the inhabitants had received at least twenty-four hours' notice by air-dropped leaflets. But if they persisted the punishment must be severe, continuous and even prolonged'.[15]

Trenchard must have been fully aware that bombing primitive tribesmen, however measured and controlled – and however good the results – was bound to raise moral questions about such use of air power, although this did not seem to trouble him unduly when it was far more important to establish a clear raison d'être for his RAF, not only in the colonies but in the likelihood of European hostilities. By such means during the three-year period from 1920 until the autumn of 1923, Trenchard waged an epic struggle with the other two services over the RAF's strategic role and its continued existence. He not only showed near endless endurance but also remarkable skills at fighting his corner, and by proposing the highest responsibilities for air power he succeeded in raising the level of his own position on to a par with the other two commanders.

In December 1920 for instance, Trenchard faced a direct challenge from Admiral Earl Beatty (seen by the public and politicians alike as the perfect embodiment of the fighting captain),[16] who pressed for the allocation of funds for his future naval programme in preference to air. To counter this, Trenchard wrote a new paper about the RAF's role in imperial defence, which he sent to Churchill. By now Churchill had his own visionary belief in air power when writing:

> We are sure that if, after a prolonged spell of peace, war on a grand scale suddenly broke out again, the power which had made the most intensive study of aerial warfare would start with an enormous initial advantage, and the Power that neglected this form of active defence might well find itself fatally situated.[17]

Churchill, who was now Colonial Secretary, had Trenchard's propositions circulated as a Cabinet paper, in which he made three specific claims, namely that:

a) The primary function of the Air Force in the future would be the defence of the British Isles from invasion by air from the continent of Europe. This defence would largely take the form of a counter-offensive from the air assisted by a ground organisation co-ordinated by the Air Ministry.

b) Certain responsibilities at present assigned to the Navy and the Army could be more economically and just as adequately carried out by air units.

c) Under present conditions the strength of the RAF at home was absorbed by its functions as an auxiliary to the Navy and the Army, and while the proper discharge of these functions was of vital importance *'there should be more use made of the Air Force as an independent arm used not as an auxiliary but as a substitute for naval and military forces.'*

The claim of being able to mount an aerial counter-offensive against a Continental enemy was a remarkable one for the commander of a small air force whose aeroplanes and bombing systems were not undergoing any marked technological advances.

Nevertheless, despite the practical limitations of the RAF's strategic capability at the time and Trenchard's highly theoretical and over-optimistic doctrine of precision bombing, that he maintained would undermine the will of an enemy populace to carry on the war,[18] his arguments had undoubted effects in Parliamentary circles. When Arthur Balfour, chairman of the Government's Standing Defence Sub Committee, issued his report on the relationships between the three services, it surprisingly concluded that the Air Force must be autonomous in matters of administration and education, and in the case of air raids the other two services must play a secondary role. Trenchard also came to enjoy the approval of Brigadier-General Groves, one time Director of Flying Operations at the Air Ministry, who had become a correspondent for *The Times* and wrote on 21 July 1922 that 'The original conception of a separate Air Ministry was founded upon the assumption now universally admitted to be correct, that henceforth Britain's first line of defence must be in the air.' The corollary to such an assumption was that in any future struggle without adequate air defence Great Britain and the British Empire must almost certainly fall through a knockout blow on the heart.

Such support helped Trenchard better to survive the enquiries of the Geddes Committee, intended to further large financial savings, which found in his favour and pointed out that dividing the Air Force between the other two services would bring duplication and extravagant waste.

Trenchard enjoyed another piece of luck when his arguments for the RAF's strategic role benefitted from the continual arguments taking place between Britain and France over such questions as the occupation of Germany, post-war reparations, and a string of competing colonial issues. Although Trenchard's staff knew he did not believe war with France was likely, he was not averse to encouraging the Government's fear. RAF intelligence reports, for instance, disclosed a great and growing imbalance between the two air forces, with France not only having 123 squadrons totalling 1,000 aircraft, but plans to double this total, and they came to the highly alarmist conclusion that in case of war with France that country was capable of delivering 100 tons of bombs in the first twenty-four hours and causing more than 20,000 casualties in the first week of the war.[19]

As a consequence, Parliament agreed to expand the RAF by adding fifty-two more squadrons by 1928, specifically for the air defence of Britain.[20] Budget shortages prevented them being formed that quickly but Trenchard was able to consider publically how best to use them. A vital component of his preserving and extending the role of a separate RAF was the assertion that air superiority was essential to military success and that air power was an offensive weapon capable of inflicting significant material and morale damage upon a would-be enemy. To achieve such results Trenchard favoured bombers over fighters in a ratio of at least 2:1, which in practice was greater still when the bombers' larger size and more numerous crews were taken into account. He justified this because of his belief that the nation that would stand being bombed longest would win in the end – and because of its people's traditional phlegm this could only mean Britain.

Trenchard made sure his ideas were fully supported within the Air Force by means of Air Staff memoranda, lectures at the RAF Staff College and through senior staff meetings. At a senior staff meeting held on 19 July 1923 where the delegates included the Air Commander for India, Trenchard told them that 'fighters should be limited to short range interceptors while bombers should constitute the offensive arm for they were capable of defending themselves well and evading air defences and dropping a greater weight of bombs on the enemy than he could on the United Kingdom.'[21] Never mind the over-optimistic tactical assumptions and the fact that the numbers of British bombers had already fallen so far as to make this unattainable against other major powers!

By 1928 Trenchard had been CAS for nearly nine years and as the senior member of the Chiefs of Staff Committee was by now confident enough to emphasise the unique advantages of air over the other two services in its ability 'to paralyse from the very outset the enemy's productive centres of munitions of war of every sort and to stop all communications and transportation.'[22]

He went further, 'Air power ... can pass over the enemy's navies and armies and penetrate the air defences and attack direct the centres of production, transportation and communication from which the enemy's war effort comes.'[23] To make such assertions with the planes currently available to the RAF was quite unjustifiable and that this could be achieved by daylight raids with bombers that would always get through ignored the lessons of his Independent Bombing Force of 1918 as well as the possibility of an effective air defence.

Notwithstanding, more than 100 years after the commencement of the First World War, Trenchard retains his place as the seminal figure of the Royal Air Force. He undoubtedly deserves it, for with invaluable help from Churchill and to a lesser extent from Sir Samuel Hoare when Secretary of State for Air, he constructed a strategy for the RAF as a separate service and ably defended it against determined attacks from both the Navy and the Army during his long term as CAS. At the same time he built facilities for training his apprentice tradesmen and his trainee and senior officers that helped to develop a tradition of loyalty to the RAF that would prove invaluable during the expansion prior to and during the Second World War.

On the debit side, and perhaps due to his early educational difficulties, was his lack of enthusiasm for revolutionary developments, like early radar, his contentment with the rigid procedures of the prevailing contract system for new planes, his failure to develop much-needed systems for direction-finding and target identification, and above all his neglect of fighter planes at the time of him leaving office which rendered his country extremely vulnerable in a future Continental war.

Following his resignation in 1929, successive Chiefs of the Air Staff (many of whom Trenchard had identified and sponsored), in conjunction with their political masters, would have a bare decade in which to drive through much-needed reforms and tackle the fallibility of the Trenchard strategic doctrine in a further mortal struggle. Yet without Trenchard's brilliant defence the RAF would have surely been split between the two older services and could not have responded as it did in 1940.

BRITISH CIVIL AVIATION: THE UNLOVED CHILD

When in February 1919 the newly established British Air Ministry created a Department of Civil Aviation (that would stay under its control until 1945) there was as yet no definite concept about the full nature and scope of its activities. The department's first announcement on 1 May 1919 was to authorise non-military flying to take place, although the first instances of regular air services to destinations outside Britain had occurred during the previous November when the Royal Air Force flew members of the British Government to Paris for the Peace Conference and carried airmail for the Rhine Army of Occupation.[1]

From the beginning there was concern about whether civil aviation was too important to be left in private hands. Lord Weir, the former Secretary of State for Air, speaking in Manchester on 20 December 1919, maintained that the best interests of civil aviation would be met by it being a government monopoly – and (somewhat confusingly) that it should 'strive to acquire the best qualities of a private business, for a public end'.[2]

During the same month Winston Churchill, the incumbent Secretary of State for Air, had obviously envisaged the potential of passenger planes when he appointed a standing committee to consider the best method of organising air routes across the British Empire. This recommended routes to India, South Africa and Australia that had already been pioneered by ex-Service flyers, and acknowledged that a provider could either be a state-organised company, or one that combined state and private capital, or a private enterprise that had the benefit of state aid. Such

George Holt Thomas. (Royal Aeronautical Society/National Aerospace Library)

options were felt necessary due to the expense of setting up the necessary facilities, and because with few being likely to use air transport at this time, some form of central subsidy would be required.

At this early stage, Britain already possessed a figure in entrepreneur and air enthusiast George Holt Thomas, who deserved to be called the father of civil air travel, and whose aircraft construction company (Airco) was the largest in the field. In 1916, three years before the official establishment of a Civil Aviation Department, when the air war was still growing in intensity, Holt Thomas had shown his regard by registering his own international airline, Aircraft Transport and Travel (AT&T) with a capital of £50,000. Three years later AT&T was the first British company to enter the field of civil aviation.

Unlike other noted aircraft constructors A.V. Roe, Geoffrey de Havilland and Frederick Handley Page, for whom money was always short, the tall and distinguished-looking Holt Thomas (with his well-known resemblance to King George V) benefitted from his father's economic success as founder of the daily and weekly *Graphic* newspapers. When, after attending King's College School, George was sent to Queen's College Oxford, he stayed for only two years without taking a degree for he was anxious to enter his father's newspaper business, where he soon made his own fortune by successfully founding two more illustrated weeklies, *The Bystander* and *The Empire Illustrated*. These championed the production of British goods and he went on to found the Association of British Motor Manufactures that advocated an import duty on foreign cars.

By 1906 Holt Thomas had abandoned Fleet Street and fully committed himself to the cause of aviation, which he believed had far-reaching military and commercial prospects. As a strong patriot he believed Britain had a duty to become a world leader in aviation but by April 1909 he realised that instead of taking up its responsibilities it was badly neglecting them, with Germany spending £400,000, France £47,000 and his home country (just) £5,000 a year.[3] To remedy this he developed an association with the early French aero constructors Henri and Maurice Farman, convinced that their aircraft could help move British aviation forward. Holt Thomas also encouraged Britain's leading press baron, Lord Northcliffe, to take an interest in aviation and to offer massive prizes for air races. Northcliffe's £10,000 prize for the first aeroplane to fly from London to Manchester was in fact won by a Farman, and the main reason for Holt Thomas setting up his company Airco was to build Farmans, large numbers of which entered service with the Royal Flying Corps during the early stages of the war. When his London factory developed into the premier production unit in Europe he also manufactured French Gnome and Le Rhone engines under licence.

In 1914 Holt Thomas persuaded Geoffrey de Havilland, the leading aeroplane designer at the Royal Aircraft Factory, to join him at Airco where de Havilland's director Mervyn O'Gorman was a firm friend.[4] De Havilland would go on to design 30 per cent of the British warplanes, which were distinguished by the prefix

DH – this de Havilland believed should actually have been DHT, in recognition of his enlightened employer who at Airco installed a wind tunnel and the latest metal-working machinery.

While there was massive demand for aeroplanes during the war, Holt Thomas anticipated the industry's likely vulnerability afterwards. In 1916 he therefore sponsored the Society of British Aircraft Constructors to give them a common voice against the anticipated demands of Government agencies. His founding of the airline AT&T during the same year not only represented his faith in post-war British Aviation but his hopes that Airco would be able to switch some of its manufacturing resources to civilian aeroplanes.

In 1917 he also told a large audience at the Aeronautical Society that so far military aviation should have been taken more seriously, and after victory was won the same mistake should not be made over civil aviation. By then he had already visualised airlines flying between British cities and every European capital before their extension across the Empire and to the United States.[5]

Six months later, on 28 November 1917, Mervyn O'Gorman gave a lecture on Holt Thomas's behalf to a large audience at the Society of Arts that emphasised the need 'to prepare for the cataclysm of peace by avoiding restrictive legislation and remembering that our mercantile marine fleet before the war did not cost a third of what our air fleets were costing during the war so we must provide for future air fleets.'[6] O'Gorman also drew their attention to Holt Thomas's firmly held fears about a reduction or cessation of production after the war and that anyone could believe that restricting production would make him wealthy.[7]

It was therefore unsurprising that from 25 August 1919 Holt Thomas's AT&T should be the first company to begin a regular scheduled service that included passengers, mail and parcels. From Hounslow's grass airfield it offered a daily flight – whether there were passengers or not – to Le Bourget in France, and with the aircraft then available such arrangements represented an act of faith. AT&T operated with more than forty-five different aircraft, almost all converted military types, including a DH.4 that carried just two passengers in cramped conditions and a DH.16 carrying four passengers, until the next year when the company introduced its first civilian-designed aircraft, the DH.18, with a capacity of eight passengers flying at a speed of 121mph. It was, however, very difficult to maintain a regular and reliable service with such wooden-framed, fabric-covered aircraft whose engines required frequent maintenance and when weather forecasting was still in its infancy.

In any case, Holt Thomas's airline faced formidable rivals: in addition to the emerging British ones, a German airline service had already begun linking Weimar to Berlin and the French followed shortly afterwards with heavily subsidised flights from London to Paris and Paris to Brussels.[8] However, the British Government felt quite differently and Winston Churchill declared in the House of Commons that:

Civil aviation must fly by itself; the Government cannot possibly hold it up in the air. The first thing the Government have got to do is to get out of the way, and the next thing is to smooth the way … any attempts to support it by floods of state money will not ever produce a really sound commercial service.[9]

Without Government support all the British civil airlines found themselves at a serious disadvantage with their Continental rivals and as a direct result by February 1921 all were forced to suspend or close down their services.

By this time, with so few orders for new aircraft, Holt Thomas's parent company, Airco, had suffered heavy losses and by March 1920 he was forced to sell it to Birmingham Small Arms, which promptly closed down its aeronautical activities.

This was especially sad for a man who had played such an influential part in considering the steps needed 'for the development and regulation of aviation for civil and commercial purposes from a domestic, imperial and international standpoint'.[10]

During the war as a member of the Civil Aerial Transport Committee Holt Thomas had worked with outstanding figures including the aeronautical constructor Lord Montagu and Sir Richard Glazebrook, the director of the National Physical Laboratory, where he was recognised as 'one of the outstanding figures in aeroplane manufacture and commercial aeronautics'. His influence can be detected in the committee's belief that after the war the aircraft industry needed to be kept vigorous in order to respond to any possible war emergency of the future and that 'the development of civil aerial transport services will not at present be sufficient to keep the industry alive unless it receives substantial support from the State[11] either in the form of State ownership or participation'. However, without legislative powers, the committee could not ensure that Government support for civil aviation would be forthcoming with Churchill initially refusing subsidies.

Apart from his work on the Civil Aerial Transport Committee, Holt Thomas played a central part in the vital work of creating a working framework for civil airlines. On 25 August 1919 – the day of the AT&T's inaugural flight – he assembled a group at the Hague that came to be called the IATA, the International Air Transport Association, committed to establishing a free union of interested companies to create the standards and procedures required to smooth the flow of international travel. All such members were to be anonymous and non-political, and the rules few and flexible enough to meet situations as they developed.

Holt Thomas's influence was apparent when the IATA's first meeting was chaired by Major General Sir Sefton Brancker, a subsequent inspiring Director of Civil Aviation who was his friend, business partner and chair of the AT&T. At its first meeting Brancker presided over twelve members representing six companies, some of whom had not yet started flying operations.

The IATA's detailed concerns were essentially commercial; flying schedules, conditions of carriage, procedures for paying accounts, insurance, air mail, conditions of contract, taxation, transport of newspapers and technical standardisation, without which the aviation industry could not have developed as successfully as it did. By 1938 it had twenty-nine member companies and in 2009, 230 members accounting for 93 per cent of all scheduled traffic.[12]

———————— • ◆ • ————————

Although Holt Thomas's airline AT&T was the first to be registered, it had two early British rivals in the shape of Handley Page Transport and The Instone Air Line.

Frederick Handley Page incorporated his airline on 1 June 1919 and its main purpose was to make use of the firm's converted 0/400 bombers. The first flight from Handley Page's aerodrome at Cricklewood to Paris took place on 22 July 1919, although regular services were not offered until 31 August, six days after Holt Thomas's AT&T, following which on 23 September an additional route was added.

Sir Sefton Brancker, Director of Civil Aviation, at Croydon on 13 April 1925. From left to right: Brennan, a news correspondent; Frederick Handley Page; Air Cdre Samson; Harry Harper (*Daily Mail*); Sir Sefton Brancker, C.C. Turner (The Observer); Charles Grey (The Aeroplane). (Royal Aeronautical Society/National Aerospace Library)

Vickers Vimy third prototype B9954. (Royal Aeronautical Society/National Aeronautical Society)

Fares were not cheap; the cost from London to Paris was £10 single and £18 18s 0d return, and by 11 October the company was offering the first aircraft meals made up of six sandwiches, fruit and chocolate for 3s.

In practice, although Handley Page's converted 0/400s offered seating for eight to ten people they did not always prove reliable. During one of the company's early trips from London to Paris, the pilot, Captain Gordon P. Olley recalled that he made as many as 'seventeen forced landings after leaving London and before I got to Paris: while by the time I neared the French capital it was so dark that I could not find a proper aerodrome and had to finish up eventually in a football field'.[13]

Under such circumstances the airline's clientele tended to be rich, adventurous and relatively few in number, for whom the airline produced a little booklet containing a weekly diary featuring London's social events that also included advertisements for All Breeds of Dogs, Debenham and Freebody's Furs and Cartier's jewellery (by appointment to royalty).

Speaking more than thirty years later, Handley Page remained fiercely critical of the unhelpfulness of British Government policy at this time:

All in all, in 1919 while the world was impatient to reap the benefits of the new air age the newly-formed air transport companies had neither the time nor the capital to indulge in the development of aeroplanes specially designed and built for the carriage of fare-paying passengers because the limited funds available for the air were mainly absorbed in meeting the urgent needs of military aviation.[14]

The second competitor to AT&T, The Instone Air Line, was established by the shipping company S. Instone and Co. as a private service to take the company's documents and staff from Cardiff to London and Paris. This went public on 18 February 1920 and on 30 April its one aircraft, a Vickers Vimy Commercial named *City of London*, entered service and immediately became popular with the travelling public. Even so, like AT&T and Handley Page Transport, it could not cope with the competition mounted by the subsidised European airlines and it ceased operating on 28 February 1921.

However imperative the need for subsidies at this time, the British Government continued to believe that a return to business as usual, free trade and the economies to be obtained by disarmament were the priorities of the day.[15] Fortunately during the Air Ministry's First Air Conference at the Guildhall, Churchill perceptibly softened his earlier attitude in the House of Commons by offering temporary subsidies, stating that: 'I trust the day has now come when it will be possible for us to increase to some extent the resources which are available to the development of civil aviation,' although he still repeated his mantra that 'in the main civil aviation must fly by itself'.[16]

During this time two voices came out powerfully for more financial support. Major General Sir Frederick Sykes, who as Controller of Civil Aviation was fully expected to defend his area of responsibility, declared that:

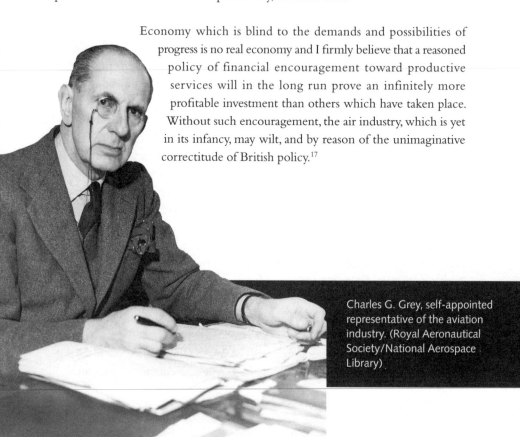

> Economy which is blind to the demands and possibilities of progress is no real economy and I firmly believe that a reasoned policy of financial encouragement toward productive services will in the long run prove an infinitely more profitable investment than others which have taken place. Without such encouragement, the air industry, which is yet in its infancy, may wilt, and by reason of the unimaginative correctitude of British policy.[17]

Charles G. Grey, self-appointed representative of the aviation industry. (Royal Aeronautical Society/National Aerospace Library)

The other was Holt Thomas who, supported by Sefton Brancker, put forward a proposal that 'the (income from the) carriage of all First Class mail to the Continent be handed over to the aeroplane transport companies and that an extra half penny postage should be charged for the rapid delivery which they should give'.[18]

He went further still, harking back to the wartime Civil Aerial Transport Committee's belief that there should be a national air transport company (with monopoly rights) able to meet foreign competition.[19] This was still a step too far for the British Government with its suspicion of subsidies.

Prior to the first air conference, Charles Grey, editor of *The Aeroplane*, in typical fashion had already warned those attending to take with them the philosophic state of mind of he who said: 'Blessed are they who expect little for they shall not be disappointed.'[20] He was proved right, for the air transport companies were not given a monopoly of the mail, nor were their rates of carriage raised like those across the Atlantic, where the US Post Office air services earned an amazing $22,234,000 from May 1918 to January 1920.

Contrary to Grey, *The Times* had far higher hopes for Churchill to 'be resolute in the cabinet about the funds needed for civil aviation'.[21] Whether such hopes were well founded or not, the continuing delays and uncertainties proved too much for Holt Thomas's AT&T, for following Airco's takeover by BSA he had to shut down his Air Transport Company. It was acquired (without its aeroplanes) by another potential carrier, Daimler Airways. However, Daimler did not begin service until 2 April 1922 and it came to rely on new passenger aircraft such as de Havilland's DH.34 and DH.18A.

The last of the early civil transport companies was the small British Marine Air Navigation Company that traded in just one year from 14 August 14 to 30 November 1923, during which it flew 180 passengers to and from the Channel Islands.

Despite the massive problems experienced by the first British airlines, in his book *Aerial Transport* published in 1920, Holt Thomas showed he retained his belief in the importance of air transport, for it 'was something the existing forms of transport cannot do',[22] 'it supplements, not supplants them for they cannot match its speed'. He was also certain that it could only succeed with Government support, 'a fact widely and openly acknowledged to be necessary for Civil Aviation in the interests not only of commerce but of prestige and long term standing'.[23]

As a result of Holt Thomas's and others' advocacy, the 1920–21 Air Estimates included a temporary subsidy for air transport that aimed to give the companies a profit of 10 per cent on gross receipts. Sadly it proved too late for Holt Thomas's AT&T, but in any event his health was beginning to give some cause for concern and he decided to turn his back on commercial aviation. However, he attended the Air Ministry's Third Air Conference of 1923 where he spoke strongly for 'a great national or imperial corporation working hand in hand with Government.'[24] He wrote other articles on aviation before he finally returned to his country home at Hughenden in

Buckinghamshire, where he took up the more straightforward challenge of breeding dairy cattle, before succumbing in 1929 to the throat cancer that had earlier begun to manifest itself.

Surprisingly, much of the responsibility for Holt Thomas's disillusionment and Britain's failure to become an early force in civil aviation (to match its wartime exploits) seemed to rest with Churchill who, after his earlier championing of air power, showed a strange lack of imagination where civil aviation was concerned. This was demonstrated by his decision to hand over its control to Major General Sir Frederick Sykes (who had by no means impressed him) as compensation for losing out to Hugh Trenchard, Churchill's friend and preferred candidate, as the RAF's Chief of the Air Staff. Although civil aviation was given little funding, it was unquestioningly one of the Air Ministry's major showcases, but after putting Sykes in charge Churchill largely ignored it.

In fact, Churchill spent much of his time on matters that he believed required higher priorities, namely the post-war Russian campaign and pre-eminently the struggle to retain a separate Royal Air Force, where he believed Trenchard was doing well against 'the assaults of the other two great military departments'.[25]

Had Churchill, for instance, used his influence to support the establishment of an Empire air service from Cairo to the Cape it might have advanced African civil aviation by a decade or more and the same could be said for British West Africa.

Churchill's public statements on civil aviation at this time contrasted with those of Sefton Brancker, who maintained that 'the war has bequeathed to us as a nation a great heritage in the air. Our pilots are the best, our designers the most efficient, and our industry the greatest in the world. Supremacy in the air is ours for the taking.'[26]

While supporting civil air transport with public funds was much more difficult than Brancker chose to make out, Churchill could undoubtedly have done more for civil aviation at the end of the war. Even when it faced extinction he restricted his renowned powers of persuasion over the Commons to approve a temporary subsidy of £60,000 for fiscal year 1921–22 – although this was subsequently increased to (a still miserly) £88,200. While this subvention breathed life into the airlines it was in the nature of giving limited rations to starving men, allowing them scarce opportunity to make any worthwhile plans for the future and contrasting, for instance, with the French airlines that during the same period received a massive £1,328,600.[27]

Air commentator Robert McCormack, for one, was heavily critical of Churchill, concluding that his twenty-seven months at the Air Ministry 'were indeed a time of missed opportunities in Great Britain, Africa and everywhere in the British air world'.[28]

While McCormack was undoubtedly a harsh critic, during the early post-war years British civil aviation never led the world nor did it ever look likely to do so, despite the replacement of the temporary subsidies by a revised scheme until March 1924 that, however niggardly, proved vital during its early small-scale operations.

In the period from March 1921 to March 1922, 5,804 passengers were carried at a cost of £20 15s 3d per passenger when the single fare was set at just £6 6s 0d, requiring a subsidy of more than 200 per cent.[29] For the period from 1 April 1922 to 31 March 1924 comparable figures are only available for one company, Daimler Airways, although they appear to show the level of subsidy to be on an even higher scale. From a total income of £113,939 the operating revenue was just £21,317 with the subsidies totalling £92,622, despite the company still making a loss of £17,303.[30] During this period almost 25 per cent of the total expenses were taken up with insurance, thus reflecting the difficulties of attracting people on to such novel and untried vehicles.

Subsidies were essential during the early years because of the airlines' relatively small numbers of passengers and because their converted military aircraft lost money even when, as Holt Thomas remarked, 'we were able to fill them with as much as they would carry'.[31] While this state of affairs improved when new machines came into service, aircraft productivity remained low with their reliability falling markedly in the winter months October–February. Safety constituted another problem: although the total of six passengers and eleven crew lost during the first four and a half years[32] was creditable enough for planes at this time, when this was combined with the relatively high number of forced landings, the public still viewed air as a relatively unsafe and expensive method of travel. This was illustrated by Handley Page Transport, which

Sir Samuel Hoare. (Bain Collection, Library of Congress)

during 1922 continued to charge 6 guineas (£12 return) to Paris compared with a first-class return fare by surface transport of £5.

Whatever the importance of subsidies for these early air companies, it made little sense for them to compete against each other and responsibility for changing this fell upon new Secretary of State for Air, Sir 'Sam' Hoare, whom Prime Minister Andrew Bonar Law appointed on 31 October 1922 and who, when Stanley Baldwin succeeded Bonar Law six months later, was admitted as a full member of the Cabinet. Following Churchill, Hoare acted as the political champion for aviation. He was Secretary of State up to 1926 (except for a short break in 1924 with the coming of the first short-lived Labour Government) and then until June 1929 when the second Labour administration was elected.

As Secretary of State, Hoare, like Churchill before him, rightly considered his primary responsibility was to support Hugh Trenchard in his struggles to preserve the RAF as a separate service, although he also aimed to reform and develop civil aviation – which in his eyes would continue to include airships – to fulfil his dreams of opening civil air routes to Africa, India and Australia.

Traditionally the Hoare family had always been in banking, with Sam's father breaking the mould by becoming a serving Conservative politician for more than twenty years. Sam, the fifth of seven children, had excelled at Eton both academically and in sport, despite being short and slight, and at New College, Oxford, he gained firsts in both classics and history while representing the university at rackets and tennis. In 1910, after three years on the London County Council, he was elected as Conservative MP for Chelsea (a seat he was to hold for thirty-four continuous years) before he married the well-connected Lady Maud Lygon, a union that would last until his death almost fifty years later. Hoare rapidly became an active and influential back bench MP and, although a recurrence of typhoid fever ruined any prospect of military service, during the war he headed a Secret Service mission in both Russia and Italy.

Following the war Hoare played a major part in bringing down the Lloyd George coalition, in the course of which he showed himself a skilled networker with influential connections and strong political ambitions. As a result he appeared to have good prospects for an important office in the new Conservative administration of 1922, but after a surprisingly long wait he was finally offered the portfolio for air, together with a warning from the Prime Minister that the position was soon likely to be abolished. It was therefore against expectations that he stayed on for so long in what could never be viewed as a crucial Cabinet post, although his broader ambitions contributed to his confident stance when Air Minister. This was seen in his selections for a three-man committee, to consider what 'could be gained at the least cost to the state of establishing air communications within the British Empire'.[33]

The committee was chaired by Herbert Hambling of Barclays Bank, Hoare's former business partner, who was assisted by Oliver V.G. Hoare, the Minister's brother, and Joseph Broadbank of the Port of London Authority, Oliver's close friend.

After fifteen meetings during which they consulted representatives from the Air Ministry, the operating companies, the aircraft construction companies and other large commercial organisations, the committee concluded that *only a large company with adequate finances* could eventually become self-supporting and undertake the expansion that was required for British civil aviation, and that this should be established as quickly as possible.

Crucially they believed that the proposed company should not come under Government control but exist as a commercial organisation run entirely on business lines. It should be financially responsible for the development of air routes both in Europe (including the Mediterranean and the Black Sea) and across the Empire but because the journeys from London–Paris and London–Brussels were too short to be economic the company would have to develop other and further destinations. It would require capital of £1 million (of which £500,000 needed to be subscribed before operations began) and a Government subsidy spread over ten years, with freedom to decide on the routes operated, the types of machines to be purchased and used, the number of daily services and the minimum allowance for point-to-point flights.[34]

Although a private company, the Government reserved the right to appoint two directors to help determine the subsidy payments needed and the degree of control exercised by the Department of Civil Aviation over civil flying. All its aircraft and crews were required to be British, the latter belonging to the RAF Reserve.

The committee further stipulated that when the company repaid the £1 million owing to the Government its interest would cease and all profits should belong to the shareholders.[35]

After nine months the Hoare-inspired recommendations were approved. With the establishment of Imperial Airways, Holt Thomas's dream for a single, monopoly company became a reality, whose first decision was the appointment of its senior staff.

By late October 1923 it was agreed that one of the Government's two directors would be the committee's ex-chairman Sir Herbert Hambling, with further appointees drawn from the aeronautical industry and the earlier air transport companies. Hoare personally selected Sir Eric Geddes, formerly general manager of the North Eastern Railway and a recognised expert on transport questions as its chairman. Geddes, who knew nothing about aviation, accepted the post on condition that he brought with him Sir George Beharrell, the chartered accountant on whom he always depended for financial advice. Colonel Searle from Daimler Airways was appointed managing director, with Major George Woods Humphery from Handley Page Airlines as general manager and Major H.C. Brackley also from Handley Page as air superintendent and the pilots' representative. Major Woods Humphery came with the disadvantage that when general manager at Handley Page Airlines he had acquired the unfortunate reputation of being hated by his pilots.

With its attempts to appoint representatives approved by both the Government and the former airlines, there remained the suspicion that the company might have missed the chance of appointing the fearless and dynamic leaders needed for such a pioneering organisation entering a highly competitive field.

Next came the question of its assets. Those of the original companies were valued with two-thirds returned to them in the form of shares in the new company.[36] Imperial Airways was established officially on 1 April 1924, although doubts about the first Labour Government's attitude to such a monopoly company delayed the start of its services until the 26th of the same month. The rapid progress of its rivals required it to make a major impact but the company faced immediate and pressing problems. It inherited a mixed batch of thirteen aircraft and a staff of about 260 (including sixteen pilots), most of whom were based at Croydon where sheep still grazed on its short grass runway. An initial bonus came when the Air Ministry assumed responsibility for improving the runway at a cost of £225,000 by 'smoothing' Plough Lane and incorporating 75 acres of adjacent Beddington, and this work was extended following a crash during take-off on Christmas Eve 1924 so that planes would no longer be required to take off uphill when further land was acquired to the west of the aerodrome.[37]

Difficulties were soon experienced with the staff when, after the company offered immediate posts to just sixteen pilots with the remaining twelve offered positions when they became available, they went on strike. This was resolved by 2 May but major problems remained with the aircraft, where there was an urgent need to rationalise the different types and standardise their maintenance and overhaul procedures. This proved more difficult than expected and at one time only two single-engined aircraft were operational. Charles Grey of *The Aeroplane* wrote mockingly: 'The Fleet of Imperial Airways has now been reduced to This and That and at any moment This may become That.'[38] Nonetheless, within its first year of formation the airline flew 800,000 miles in what was steady rather than spectacular progress.

At its second annual general meeting the company reported a loss of more than £20,000 and the ever-critical Charles Grey compared its number of passengers unfavourably with those of the German airline Lufthansa. He likened Imperial's traffic to that currently coming out of Penzance Railway Station while Lufthansa's was more like that coming from mighty Manchester. Grey could make such an unflattering analogy because in the year ending 31 October 1926 Imperial had carried 16,655 passengers, whereas during its first year of operations Lufthansa transported 56,268.[39]

This was not just due to German efficiency but because Imperial had experienced prolonged delays in mobilising its disparate aircraft stock and bringing in much-needed replacements while it continued to encounter powerful hurdles against developing its routes across the Empire.

To help publicise the airline and its new three-engined aircraft, in January 1927 'Sam' Hoare took the decision to make the journey by air to India, taking Lady Hoare with him. This dramatic gesture was intended to emphasise the feasibility and safety of such a

12,000-mile journey for ordinary passengers, although difficulties with Persia concerning overflying rights continued to delay a regular service between both countries.

In a subsequent book Hoare eloquently described the ancient cities they had overflown, while Lady Hoare took the more practical approach, describing how her flight wardrobe consisted of a stockinette coat and skirt with a crêpe de Chine jumper (worn most days) and a woollen jumper and tweed skirt as a change, then layers according to temperature – woollen cardigans, leather coat and fur coat.[40] The number of would-be travellers who would have sought out the book to follow such excellent advice was not likely to have been large.

As Air Minister, Hoare always believed the routes to India and South Africa were the key ones for an imperial airline and throughout his term he worked towards this end, finally securing agreement for the route to South Africa. Other initiatives included his support for the formation of the first University Air Squadron at Cambridge, and combatting what he saw as the public ignorance of everything to do with aviation[41] by encouraging the Royal Family to attend the newly formed Royal Air Force pageants and by routinely flying on official duties in order to make such flights appear unsensational. He also approached town clerks countrywide telling them that, although internal flights were not yet established, aerodromes would be needed for their inevitable development.

Notwithstanding these endeavours, the bulk of the Air Secretary's time and energy was inevitably spent in supporting the RAF against attacks from the other two services. With the heavy constraints on the Air Ministry's budget it was fully understandable that the service should also receive by far the lion's share of the funding. In 1924 from a total Air Estimate of £14,278,000 just £855,000 was devoted to civil aviation. In 1925 the figures were £15,570,010 to £357,010 and in 1926 £15,755,000 to £462,000.[42] Any chance of using such funds for a range of much–needed airport facilities was limited by the heavy demands of an ambitious Government Airship scheme, initiated by the first Labour Government and continued during most of Hoare's time as Air Minister.

In any event, despite his undoubted industry Hoare was no great apologist for civil aviation. He freely acknowledged he lacked the talent to paint sensational pictures (like Churchill) and arouse emotional audiences to his cause. Although he was astute, earnest and correct, he acquired a reputation as a sound performer rather than an inspired leader. Lord Birkenhead devastatingly called his bookish and prim colleague 'the last of a long line of maiden aunts'.[43]

For British civil aviation the years 1919–1927 were ones of struggle and no little confusion. Although its champions such as George Holt Thomas and Sefton Brancker worked tirelessly to persuade Governments wrestling with post-war political and economic turbulence to give financial support, such contributions were dwarfed by those of its Continental rivals. In any case, Imperial Airways' early days were spent tackling the problems bequeathed by the first British airlines.

At the highest level it has to be acknowledged that the Secretary of State's involvement proved somewhat disappointing. Churchill, whatever his unquestionable talent, had his eyes on what he believed were far more important matters, while 'Sam' Hoare, however conscientious, lacked the robustness and stature to attract the much-increased support that was needed. In this respect, Imperial Airways, the flagship company that he created and whose chairman he appointed, appeared to reflect his conventional personality. The company's shareholders undoubtedly deserved their dividends, but when these came from its capital resources they hampered the aggressive purchasing of new aircraft so urgently required at a time of such fierce opposition and unrivalled opportunity.

FLYING TO THE LIMITS

At the end of the First World War the ever-shrewd David Lloyd George returned to power in the so-called 'coupon' election on the platform of his promise to improve society and the country's living conditions. With such intended reforms and with Germany prostrate it was no wonder that both military and civil aviation should enjoy a low profile and a typically brash call on its behalf by the irrepressible Sir Sefton Brancker (who became Director of Civil Aviation in 1922) in the *Daily Mail's* Golden Peace issue seemed distinctly out of kilter. Brancker declared that the war had 'bequeathed us as a nation a great heritage in the air. Our pilots are the best, our designs the most efficient and our industry the greatest in the world. Supremacy is ours for the taking'.[1] With the attention of the Government elsewhere, the onus of taking on some of the long-standing aerial challenges dating to before the war would fall on the RAF's wartime airmen supported by private aircraft constructors now facing a rapid fall, if not widespread cancellation, of their future orders. The outstanding one was to fly non-stop across the Atlantic for which on 1 April 1913 press baron Lord Northcliffe had offered a massive prize of £10,000.

Northcliffe's aim was to stimulate long-distance flight and some indication of the interest he raised was seen in the preparations undertaken by indefatigable air pioneer Samuel Cody, who drew up specifications for a double-decked, twin-engined monoplane capable of carrying 1½ tons of fuel for which he ordered massive engines of more than 300hp from the German–Austro Daimler company. Following Cody's fatal air crash on 9 August 1913, a bill for £809 15s 10d for one of those engines was subsequently raised against his estate.

Whatever Cody's pre-war ambitions, during the conflict notable advances in both engine and airframe technology appeared to make the chances of achieving an Atlantic crossing more favourable, although in Britain with the political limelight on the results of the 'coupon' election, the lifting of the Royal Aero Club's ban on Atlantic flying seemingly attracted no interest from central Government.

The situation was different in America, where official plans were being made for a first crossing of the Atlantic, albeit with flying boats that would make intermediate stops and therefore not qualify for Northcliffe's £10,000 prize.

In Britain, where the aim was traditionally for a non-stop flight, any attempt needed the support of private constructors eager for the publicity they hoped would come with it. In such circumstances they considered it important to keep the details of their preparations from likely rivals.

While crossing the Atlantic was unquestionably the greatest flying challenge, in 1919 other significant plans were being made for long-distance flights. The RAF had already pioneered an aerial route to Cairo with intermediate landing places where fuel and other stores were available. This was subsequently extended to Calcutta before Brigadier (later Air Vice-Marshal) Borton went on to reconnoitre the route further eastwards as far as Timor, with Australia the ultimate destination.

Such work opened the way for the first flight over the 14,000-mile journey to Australia for which the Australian Government offered a £10,000 prize – restricted to Australians – to establish once and for all 'the aeroplane in long-distance transport, civil as well as military'.[2]

Nothing, however, could equal the feat of flying non-stop across the inhospitable and windswept waters of the Atlantic Ocean, which it was generally agreed should be from west to east to take advantage of the prevailing westerly winds across the minimum 1,880 miles from Newfoundland to Ireland.

Eleven manufacturers showed an interest, including two from America who, under the terms laid down by Northcliffe had a right to compete, although only four of the most resourceful British companies (Sopwith, Martinsyde, Handley Page and Vickers) actually sent teams to Newfoundland complete with their flying machines.

The Sopwith Company, which had rightly been acclaimed for its wartime planes including the 1½ Strutter and the Camel, designed a special plane for the purpose

Harry Hawker prior to his attempt at flying the Atlantic. (Author's collection)

within a remarkable six-week period. This was a two-seater biplane, appropriately called the Atlantic, powered by a single Rolls-Royce Eagle engine that had an endurance time of thirty hours when flying at an average speed of 100mph. Following take-off its undercarriage was designed to be jettisoned, thereby reducing wind resistance, with the top half of the fuselage being constructed in the shape of a boat in the event of it being ditched in the sea.

Their chosen pilot was Harry Hawker, Sopwith's famous Australian who, after being rejected by the Royal Flying Corps on health grounds, logged thousands of hours during the war as Sopwith's chief test pilot. Hawker was very enthusiastic even though his navigator had the major, if not the premier, part to play on such a journey. As Hawker generously wrote afterwards: 'One thing at any rate, is certain, that for navigating a transatlantic machine one wants a man whose dependability is of the very highest … I have no hesitation in stating that on a job of this kind, the pilot owes everything to the navigator.'[3]

Hawker's chosen navigator was Lieutenant Commander Mackenzie Grieve, who had served with the Royal Navy during the war as a navigation officer on the seaplane tender HMS *Campania*. When Sopwith asked Grieve to partner Hawker. he was seconded to the RAF for the purpose – a customary arrangement when the firms generally relied on service, or former service, personnel to crew their machines and when any pilot could accept Northcliffe's prize providing his 'flight was not directly sponsored by the Government'.[4] With its purpose-built aircraft, famed pilot and noted navigator, the Sopwith entry appeared to have a favourite's chance.

The 1919 entry from the Martinsyde Company was due to be piloted by another leading flyer in Hawker's friend and rival, Freddie Raynham, who had acted as chief test pilot for Martinsyde during the war. This was not Martinsyde's first attempt for in 1914 the company had already built a monoplane to cross the Atlantic with pioneer aviator Gustav Hamel as its chosen pilot. The project was abandoned after Hamel's death in the air, although they renewed their challenge after the war by constructing a new plane that they called the Raymor from the surnames of Raynham as pilot and Morgan, a former captain in the RNAS who was selected as his navigator. Like Sopwith's Atlantic, the Raymor was a two-seater biplane powered by a single engine – in this case a Rolls-Royce Condor. It was reckoned to be faster than the Atlantic and it needed to be, for it had a shorter endurance time of twenty-five hours at an estimated average speed of 110mph.

Some believed that both the Atlantic and Raymor aircraft were too small for a successful transatlantic flight, but this could never be said about Handley Page's entrant, the V/1500 giant bomber. This had four Rolls-Royce Eagle engines and at the end of the war it was the largest British plane with Berlin within its range, although the Armistice came before it could mount any raids. Even so, the V/1500 seemed the perfect machine for the protracted Atlantic crossing and Handley Page's attempt was directed by Admiral Mark Kerr, the first of his rank to gain a pilot's certificate, with Major H.G. Brackley, former commander of the Royal Flying Corps' 14 Squadron, as pilot. His navigator was the Norwegian Trygve Grass, who in 1914 had flown from Scotland to Norway and had previously been on Scott's last Antarctic expedition.

In the case of the fourth company, Vickers, there had been little enthusiasm for an attempted crossing before a visit from recently demobilised Captain John Alcock DSC, a flying 'ace' who had achieved seven 'kills' with the RNAS before joining the Royal Flying Corps. A brilliant long-distance pilot, he had endured months as a Turkish prisoner of war, during which he dreamed of flying the Atlantic. He convinced Vickers that its Vimy bomber could achieve this – provided he piloted it. Although smaller than the Handley Page V/1500, this twin-engined biplane with two Rolls-Royce Eagle engines had also been built to bomb Berlin, and it had a maximum range of 2,440 miles at an average speed of between 90 and 100mph. Alcock's main request for a custom-built Vimy was for its two cockpits to be combined so that the pilot and navigator could sit side-by-side.

When Vickers finally decided to compete it faced a seemingly impossible time lag, for Sopwith's Atlantic was almost due to make a test flight and the Raymor was in its final stages of assembly. Vickers still had no navigator until Lieutenant Arthur Brown came to the firm looking for a job. Although he had American citizenship he had enlisted in the British Army in September 1914 and was commissioned into the Manchester Regiment before transferring to the Royal Flying Corps. There he was shot down and suffered a serious leg injury before being made a German prisoner of war for fourteen months, following which he spent a further nine months in Switzerland undergoing 'medical' treatment. Brown acknowledged that it was then he first found time to begin 'a careful study of the possibilities of aerial navigation'[5], although it was pure chance that he became involved in the transatlantic competition. As he explained: 'One day I visited the works at Weybridge of Messrs Vickers. While I was talking with the superintendent, Captain Alcock walked into the office. We were introduced and in the course of conversation the competition was mentioned.'[6]

While Vickers finally had a flying team, by April the Sopwith and Martinsyde teams were well established in Newfoundland and rumours circulated that they would be able to fly the Atlantic on the 16th of the month.

It was not until two days later that the Vimy made its first test flight followed by several more, culminating with one of ten hours' duration, and it was the end of April before it was dismantled and packed up for its intended voyage. On 4 May the Vickers advance party, including Alcock and Brown, set sail on the *Mauretania* bound for Halifax. They were followed by their aircraft and its team in the freighter SS *Glendevon*, which was expected to dock a month after the advance party. Vickers not only lagged behind Sopwith and Martinsyde but Handley Page's machine had set off by sea for Newfoundland on 15 April, almost three weeks earlier, with Admiral Mark Kerr and the crew following by liner a fortnight later.

Meanwhile, on 11 April at St John's in Newfoundland, Hawker made an immaculate flight in the re-assembled Atlantic and declared himself ready for a full crossing attempt. Not to be outdone, the Martinsyde team had its aircraft ready for a test flight within a remarkable five days of arriving at St John's and on 16 April they made a successful flight, to come on terms with their rivals at Sopwith.

One can imagine both the teams' frustration and the bafflement of their colleagues back in England – where the weather was perfect – by continuous reports of severe storms in the mid-Atlantic.

While they were waiting they were joined by a small armada of Americans with their flying boats, who were due to make their own attempt, that included calling in at the Azores. The Americans brought with them a small airship, the C5, which they also planned to use for a first Atlantic crossing. On Friday, 16 May the three US flying boats set off for the Azores, with twenty-seven US destroyers spread out across the Atlantic beneath them and their objective. Harry Hawker characteristically called their attempt 'an unsporting aeronautical steam roller created by the US Navy', although they were not in direct competition with the British contestants.

The Sopwith and Martinsyde teams were now joined by Handley Page's contestant, which arrived in Newfoundland on 10 May, choosing to base itself at Harbour Grace, a small town some 60 miles along the coast from St John's where there was less pressure on accommodation and, most importantly, a possible site for another airfield.

Three days later the advance party from Vickers including Alcock and Brown finally docked at St John's, although their Vimy aircraft was still on the high seas. Hawker and Alcock quickly resumed their earlier warm friendship and Alcock rapidly came to appreciate the extreme difficulties of finding a site for an airfield in the rocky and swampy ground around St John's. Being so far behind the others, the Vickers team could only hope for the poor weather conditions to persist and keep their opponents grounded.

It was not to be, for at 3.48 p.m. on Sunday, 18 May, Hawker and Mackenzie Grieve finally succeeded in taking off – although the weather was still not that good. As promised, they alerted Raynham about their imminent departure, with Hawker generously inviting him to share a dinner in London the following evening.

One hour later Raynham also took off but within 200 yards disaster struck when his plane was caught in a crosswind, crashed and turned over. Both crew members were injured, but Morgan had the worst of it with a glass splinter entering his skull. Raynham immediately undertook repairs for a second attempt and sportingly offered Vickers the use of his flying field near Quidi Vici to assemble its Vimy, although it was too short for a heavily laden plane to take off for its transatlantic attempt.

Meanwhile, there was no news from Hawker and Mackenzie Grieve, who were to experience a most dramatic flight after releasing their undercarriage into the sea. For the first four hours things went well as they flew at a steady 105mph over a blanket of fog – although Grieve's wireless quickly proved useless when their engine's magnetos jammed all reception – but after five hours' flight 'rough air, cloud, fog and rain gripped the machine'[7] and Hawker noticed the temperature in the engine radiator was abnormally high. Its shutters were apparently fully open and Hawker attempted to lower the temperature by diving some 3,000ft to shift whatever was obstructing the radiator.[8] On reopening the throttle he saw that the water temperature had returned to normal but it soon rose and steam poured from the radiator. They flew on through the night, alternately diving and climbing before they met a mountainous mass of cumulonimbus cloud, which Hawker attempted to pass under. After a terrifying experience when their engine cut out before unaccountably firing again they were down to less than 20ft above the sea's surface before continuing their journey.

However, with little water remaining in their cooling system they knew they could never reach Ireland and turned south, looking for a ship that could conceivably pick them out of the sea. On sighting a small merchantman they succeeded in coming down nearby before releasing their small boat and climbing into it wearing their life-saving suits.

It was an hour and a half before the ship picked them up just in time, for very soon the rising seas would have made it impossible. Safe on board the Dutch steamer *Mary*, Hawker asked for permission to radio the British authorities that they were safe only to learn that the ship had no wireless.

During six days at sea before arriving off the Isle of Lewis the *Mary* did not sight another ship and in Britain Hawker and Mackenzie Grieve were presumed dead, although Hawker's wife was virtually alone in refusing to believe it. The King wrote to her with his and the Queen's condolences 'on your sudden and tragic loss', and the *Daily Mail* undertook to provide Hawker's and Mackenzie Grieve's kin with £10,000 each – the same sum as the prize money.

Everything changed when on the Sunday morning of 25 May the *Mary*, using flags, communicated with Lloyd's signal station on Lewis and within an hour the good news was telegraphed to London. After being carried by Royal Naval ship to Thurso the two men went south by train through crowd-packed stations until they were greeted at King's Cross by at least 100,000 people. They were awarded the Air Force Cross before recounting their story first-hand to the Royal Family.

On 27 May news was received that the American flying boat NC-4 had completed the first 2,400-mile crossing of the Atlantic, if by relatively easy stages since the adverse weather conditions caused it to spend eleven days on the journey.

While an undoubted achievement, a continuous crossing had still to be achieved and the British attempts gathered new momentum when on 26 May Alcock and Brown greeted the *Glendevon* at St John's, carrying their Vimy aircraft and its accompanying team.

Alcock arranged for the plane, still in its huge packing cases, to be drawn by dray horses to Raynham's airfield at Quidi Vici, where in its hangar Martinsyde's mechanics were working on repairing the Raymor. There the Vickers team faced the challenge of assembling their much larger aircraft under temporary tarpaulins that offered only limited shelter from the persistent wind and rain.

In spite of its mechanics' best efforts the Raymor remained a very doubtful starter and, although another take-off was finally made with a new navigator on 17 July, the plane crashed again and with it Martinsyde's attempt ended.

With the Raymor so doubtful and Sopwith's Harry Hawker back in England, the race appeared to be between the Handley Page V/1500 and the Vickers Vimy. The odds strongly favoured the V/1500, whose assembly at Harbour Grace was far more advanced than that taking place under adverse conditions at Quidi Vici. At this stage Vickers was still without an airfield of its own but Alcock received an unexpected bonus when Lester, the contractor who had transported the Vimy to Quidi Vici, offered him one free of charge. Initially unpromising, they worked furiously to level it by removing a stone dyke and blowing up and dragging away large boulders until Alcock pronounced it good enough – although he said he hoped he would only need to take off from it once!

By now the Handley Page V/1500 was flying, although the Vickers team was relieved to learn that there were still many faults to be straightened out, and on Monday 9 June the reassembled (and lightly loaded) Vimy flew off from Quidi Vici just thirteen days after the first crate had been opened to what had become known as Lester's Field about 3 miles away. This, Alcock predicted, would become famous as the first transatlantic aerodrome. During the plane's first short fifteen-minute flight Alcock described it as absolutely top notch. At this point the weather deteriorated and for the next forty-eight hours there were winds of near gale force. On Thursday the 12th the wind dropped appreciably and Alcock and Brown took the Vimy up to prove its wireless and test the small corrections that had been made after the first flight. This proved so satisfactory that Alcock wanted to set off the very next day – because he was sure the Handley Page team was close to solving its problems and thirteen was his lucky number!

Dawn on Friday the 13th saw heavy rain and gusting winds that prevented any attempt to fly, while a further problem occurred when the heavily loaded plane carrying 870 gallons of fuel and 40 gallons of oil developed a problem in one of its axle shock absorbers. Work on fixing this took much of the night but just before dawn on the 14th the wind dropped and the attempt seemed possible. To Alcock's disappointment the gusts resumed, and one was so strong that it clattered the Vimy against a rope stay and broke a petrol pipe.

This was soon repaired and, despite continuing crosswinds at the airfield, Alcock was encouraged by reports from their local RAF meteorological officer, Lieutenant Clements, who forecast moderate westerly winds throughout their journey. Crosswinds still made take-off impossible but these eventually died down and at 1.45 p.m. (4.13 GMT) the wheel chocks were removed and the irrepressible Alcock called out to the Vickers team: 'Good-bye. See you all in London. Don't worry, it's Alcock in front and Brown behind!'

At Lester's Field the Vimy began its take-off into a wind blowing at a steady 30mph. Alcock pushed the throttles wide open and the heavy plane gradually gained speed along the bare uneven field until finally, with less than 100 yards remaining it rose into the air, clearing the boundary dyke and its neighbouring woods by inches.

After moving inland to gain height the pair flew once more over St John's before, at 4.28 GMT, they crossed the coast to begin their perilous journey.

In spite of their madly cheering team and a crowd of local supporters, following the dramatic rescue of Hawker and Mackenzie Grieve, the British public's interest in transatlantic flight had dropped in the face of other more dramatic events such as the banning of Germany from the new League of Nations or the outcome of fighting against the Bolsheviks on the Russian Archangel Front.

This mattered not at all to Alcock and Brown seated side-by-side in their open cockpit engrossed in their specific duties. Alcock was committed to the controls, with both his feet fully occupied and the heavy machine never letting him have more than one hand free at any time, while Brown was sending wireless messages. From an early stage he found his signals were not being sent out – but his time was still fully occupied in checking all the indicators, including the engine revs, the radiator's temperature, oil pressure and petrol consumption. Pumping petrol by hand into the forward tanks as their fuel was consumed was yet another of his major responsibilities.

In the event the weather proved much worse than their expert had forecast: although occasionally clear, for much of the time they flew through 'lowering, unscalable clouds, fog, rain, sleet and snow at higher altitudes'.[9] With the sun rarely in sight, Brown relied for the most part on dead reckoning. When he was able to use his sextant to take their direction, he had to kneel up in his seat and twist around to sight the sun. Afterwards he told reporters in Ireland that on taking his first sun sight he had a queer but definite premonition of their safe arrival.[10] After two hours a potential disaster occurred when an exhaust pipe from an engine split away leaving the engine unsilenced if still running smoothly, although the noise was now deafening and it made speech impossible.

For the first part of their journey they flew through unbroken cloud but at a quarter past midnight it cleared and Brown's sextant measurements told him they were nearly halfway across. After eleven hours, however, they had a terrifying experience when the plane flew into the centre of a storm and, out of control, spiralled down from 4,000ft to some 60ft before they could start to regain height and reset their course. The adverse weather was not yet over, for above 8,000ft they entered another storm when ice threatened the engines' air intakes and masked the fuel intake gauge that indicated the correct supply of petrol to the engines. Brown, gammy leg notwithstanding, had to hoist himself up in his seat and kneel on the edge of the fuselage in the freezing 100mph airstream to clear the gauge.[11] He had to do this a further half a dozen times.

By 8 a.m. on the morning of Sunday, 15 June, Brown knew they must be close to Ireland and fifteen minutes later within the expanse of open water they began to make out two small islands off the Irish coast.

At 8.25 they flew over them and then along a deep sea bay to reach the town of Clifton in Connemara, where they faced the decision whether to continue (they had enough petrol to get to Brooklands) or land. The deciding factor was the rival

Arthur Whitten Brown (left) and John Alcock outside the Clifton Wireless Station shortly after their successful Atlantic crossing on 15 June 1919. (Royal Aeronautical Society/ National Aerospace Library)

Handley Page aircraft which might well have left Newfoundland at roughly the same time and could conceivably have overtaken them during the night. As Northcliffe's prize was for the first who landed anywhere in the British Isles they decided to fly no further.

Alcock looked for a possible landing area and saw what seemed to be a wide expanse of green grass near the Marconi radio station. It turned out to be Derrygimla bog and on landing its surface gave way to bring their nose digging into the soft ground and their tail pointing skywards. The time was 8.40 GMT and – bog or not – they had successfully flown non-stop across the Atlantic, covering 1,890 miles in fifteen hours, fifty-seven minutes at an average speed of 118mph.

The King, the President of the United States and the Prime Minister all sent their congratulations and on 21 June both fliers were knighted at Windsor Castle.

On 22 June the *Daily Mail* held a lunch at the Savoy Hotel where they were presented with Lord Northcliffe's cheque by Winston Churchill, Secretary of State for War and Air who said:

> Think of the broad Atlantic, that terrible waste of destructive waters, tossing in tumult in repeated and almost ceaseless storms and shrouded with an unbroken canopy of mist. Across this waste and through the obscurity, two human beings, hurtling through the air, piercing the clouds and darkness, finding their unswerving path in spite of every difficulty, to their exact objective across those hundreds of miles, arriving almost on schedule time and at every moment in this voyage liable to destruction from a drop of water in the carburettor, or a spill of oil on their plugs … They are the real victors.[12]

As Churchill well understood, crossing the Atlantic proved an unrepeatable experience for both fliers, whose later days were dogged by tragedy. Alcock paid the price for his daring when, just five months later on 18 December 1919, he was taking a Vickers Viking aircraft in bad weather to an aeronautical exhibition in Paris when it crashed near Rouen and he was killed. Following this, Brown never flew again, although he married and had a son who was tragically killed flying over Arnhem in the Second World War. Brown himself died four years later from an overdose of sleeping pills prescribed for him after he had suffered a nervous breakdown.

Alcock and Brown's achievement in their converted Vimy bomber can be better appreciated when, despite a number of attempts by other European states, it would be eight years before the Atlantic was crossed non-stop again, this time by the remarkable and self-reliant American Charles Lindbergh in a solo flight from New York to Paris in his aircraft *Spirit of St Louis*.

Three weeks after Alcock and Brown's epic flight the British scored another success when they again crossed the Atlantic, this time in the Royal Naval airship R34 piloted by the RAF officer Major G.H. Scott. The airship, an early copy of the German Zeppelin L33 captured in 1916, set off from its base at East Fortune in Scotland on 2 July and crossed the Newfoundland coast, completing its journey of 108 hours, twelve minutes to Long Island on 6 July. On its east to west journey it battled against headwinds and rough weather with engines that were neither very powerful nor reliable. Conditions were easier on the return journey when the more favourable winds enabled the crossing from New York to be completed in seventy-five hours and three minutes, before it reached its appointed base at Pulham in Norfolk.

The double crossing of the R34 owed much to the piloting skills of Major G.H. Scott, who pronounced it severely underpowered – although it was in fact the flimsiness of the airships' coverings and their unmanageability that would make them unable to compete with heavier than air machines.

———————•◆•———————

Prior to Alcock and Brown's success, ideas had already been circulating about travelling by air from Britain to Australia where, although none of the individual legs were half as far as the Atlantic, the 14,000-mile journey was vital before the possibilities of commercial navigation to the Far East could be considered.

The Britain–Australia Air Race

In 1918 Brigadier Borton had carried out preliminary work surveying an air route from Britain to Calcutta and in 1919 he extended possible landing points to Bandung in the Dutch East Indies (from where there remained a further 1,760 miles to Darwin). The idea of a prize for a Britain–Australia air race had already been conceived by the Australian Prime Minister Billy Hughes when on Christmas Day 1918 he had visited wounded Australian soldiers who raised the prospect of returning to Australia by air.

On behalf of the Australian Government, Hughes accordingly offered a prize of £10,000 for flying to Australia (the equivalent amount offered by Lord Northcliffe for crossing the Atlantic), although he specified that it should only be open to Australian nationals in aircraft constructed in the British Empire, and that it should be completed within thirty days before midnight of 31 December 1920. In response the Royal Aero Club laid down the detailed routes for the competition, Shell agreed to distribute supplies of petrol along them, and Wakefield Ltd provided the oil.

The race attracted seven contestants, including the gallant Frenchman, Etienne Poulet, who as a non-Australian, could not win the prize. This did not stop him setting off on 14 October 1919 in his Caudron light aircraft in an attempt to be the first to make the flight and he almost succeeded, for he only gave up after reaching Moulmein in Burma some 100 miles beyond Rangoon.

In the case of the six 'genuine' contestants, as Hughes intended, the race demonstrated the quality of Australian flying personnel. However, the efficiency of the aircraft supplied by British manufacturers proved distinctly variable and without regular and skilled maintenance to both engines and airframes their chances of success were small.

The first attempt took place on 21 October 1919 when Captain George Matthews of the Australian Flying Corps with Sergeant D. Kay as his mechanic set off from Hounslow Heath in their Sopwith Wallaby biplane. Despite repeated delays and other major problems they too had the end of the race in sight when on 17 April 1920 they crashed at Bali, where Kay sustained broken ribs and the Wallaby was damaged beyond repair.

They were followed on 12 November 1919 by a crew led by Captain Ross Smith in a Vickers Vimy aircraft that took off from Hounslow, the details of whose journey are given later in this chapter.

The very next day a single-engined Alliance Endeavour built by the relatively unknown Alliance Aeroplane Company of Acton left Hounslow. It was piloted by Lieutenant Roger M. Douglas, who had been awarded a Military Cross at Polygon Wood in November 1917 before transferring to the Australian Flying Corps in 1918. As navigator he had Lieutenant Leslie Ross, who had joined the Australian Flying Corps in 1916. At Surbiton, 6 miles from Hounslow, the aircraft emerged from clouds at about 1,000ft, went into a spin and crashed. Ross was killed outright and Douglas died soon afterwards of his injuries.

A fourth attempt came on 21 November 1919 when a Blackburn twin-engined bomber sporting a pouch (unsurprisingly named the Kangaroo) left Hounslow. It had two pilots, Lieutenant Valdemar Rendle, who had been in the Royal Flying Corps from 1917, and Lieutenant David Reginald Williams of the Australian Flying Corps. Its navigator was Captain George Wilkins, who had been commissioned into the Australian Flying Corps and who had been awarded the Military Cross and Bar for acts of heroism under enemy fire. Their mechanic, Lieutenant Gainsey St Clair Potts, who also held a commission in the Australian Flying Corps, completed the crew.

After encountering repeated bad weather when crossing Europe they suffered severe engine problems and crashed at Crete's Suda Bay, miraculously escaping injury, after which they returned to London and ended their attempt.

On 4 December a fifth team in a Martinsyde A1 biplane set off from Hounslow piloted by the remarkable Captain Cedric Howell, who at 40 was the oldest crew member in the race. He had served as a sniper in France before transferring in

1917 to the RAF, where he distinguished himself in Italy piloting Sopwith Camels, and was awarded the DFC and DSO and credited with destroying thirty-two aircraft. He was accompanied by George Henry Fraser, who in 1917 was with the Australian Flying Corps as a mechanic before completing a course in navigation at Andover.

Like the Kangaroo, the Martinsyde experienced atrocious weather conditions over northern Europe and after five days, when they were leaving Taranto bound for Athens, their plane fell into the sea at Corfu about a quarter of a mile off-shore and both men were killed. Howell's body was subsequently taken back to Australia to be buried with full military honours.

On 8 January 1920 the final contestants entered the race. They were Lieutenant Raymond Parer of the Australian Flying Corps who, while on loan to the Royal Flying Corps, was with the Despatch Pool for whom he flew all types of aircraft to France and was recommended for the Air Force Cross. He was partnered by John McIntosh, who had transferred from the infantry to the RAF at the end of the war and had made only one ascent. Although Parer and McIntosh set off in their much-used DH.9 after the £10,000 prize had been won, they too completed the journey after an incident-packed flight lasting 206 days. On their arrival, they were presented with a cheque for £1,000 by the Australian Government, and a further £500 by the *Melbourne Herald*.

———•◆•———

With regard to the Vimy in which Captain Ross Smith had set off on 12 November 1919, Vickers had initially been reluctant to take on a plane for the Australia race after Alcock and Brown had successfully flown their Vimy across the Atlantic just five months before. It was only after strong pressure from Brigadier Borton that the company agreed, and Ross was able to spend a month at its works learning about the plane before taking delivery.

A wartime ace with eleven certain victories, he was the most highly decorated of the contestants, having been awarded the Military Cross and Bar and the Distinguished Flying Cross and two bars. He was also by far the most experienced over the course of the proposed journey, having acted as personal pilot to T.E. Lawrence and having flown Brigadier Borton in a Handley Page after the war while making the survey of the No. 1 air route from Cairo–Calcutta, before accompanying him in exploring the sea route from Calcutta to Australia.

For co-pilot and navigator, Ross chose his brother, Keith MacPherson Smith, another air enthusiast who had paid his own passage to England to join the RAF, for whom he became an instructor at Gosport's School of Special Flying. To complete his crew Ross recruited Sergeants Jim Bennett and Wally Shiers, earlier considered

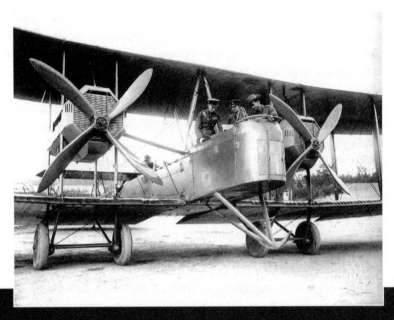

The crew inspecting their Vickers Vimy for the England to Australia flight. In the front from the left: Captain Ross Smith, Lieutenant Keith Smith and Sergeant W.H. (Wally) Shiers. In the rear cockpit is J.M. (Jim) Bennett. (Royal Aeronautical Society/National Aerospace Library)

the most able mechanics in the Australian Flying Corps's No. 1 Squadron and who had already worked on the Handley Page aircraft used by Ross and Brigadier Borton when they flew from Cairo to Calcutta.

Ross not only had a plane proven for long-distance flying but a hand-picked team to support him during a protracted journey where he would be required to make no fewer than fifty-five landings following flights varying from 20 to 730 miles.

Ross's enthusiasm for the aircraft upon which the ultimate success of the expedition depended was clear enough. He wrote: 'The aeroplane is the nearest thing to animate life that man has created. In the air a machine ceases indeed to be a mere piece of mechanism; it becomes animate and is capable not only of primary guidance and control but actually of expressing a pilot's temperament.'[13]

Whatever the plane's qualities, it had to be kept in peak condition during a marathon journey of almost 18,000km lasting twenty-eight days and involving 135 hours, fifty-five minutes' flying time. Ross attempted to achieve this by allocating specific duties to all the crew. On landing, the pilot would immediately make the administrative and social arrangements for the present and next stage. The navigator was responsible for fuel supplies and both pilot and navigator would join in the process of refuelling – a laborious and exhausting procedure requiring manhandling tons of fuel held in separate cans and passing it through a special silk filter. Following the refuelling the navigator and pilot also laboured every night in memorising the landscapes they would see and must recognise.[14]

The mechanics concentrated on the engines, which were their prime concern, usually requiring immediate work together with any other necessary repairs: so determined was Ross to carry as many spares as possible that when the weight seemed excessive he reduced the crew's personal equipment to the clothes they wore, plus shaving gear and toothbrush,[15] with everything else following by sea.

He also tried to establish a regular routine. He favoured an early start usually around 3 a.m., which meant a maximum of four to five hours' sleep whatever the climatic conditions or the welcome offered them. The sense of tiredness that, if anything, increased during the twenty-eight-day race, was made tolerable by the unvarying routine of each man's duties.[16]

Ross and his crew took off from Hounslow's snow-covered field at 8 a.m. on 12 November 1919 in weather declared unfit for flying, which led them to experience problems similar to those of other competitors over northern Europe.

As Ross related, on the first leg for Marseilles they experienced thick cloud interspersed by sunshine and extreme cold. In their open cabin:

> Goggles were useless owing to the ice and we suffered much agony through being compelled to keep a look-out with unprotected eyes, straining into the 90 mile an hour snow blast … About 1pm I suggested to my brother that we should have some sandwiches for lunch. On taking them from the cupboard we discovered they were frozen hard. Fortunately we carried a thermos of hot coffee and the 'pièces de resistance' were a few sticks of chocolate which were part of our emergency rations. I have never felt so cold and miserable in my whole life.[17]

He added: 'The only really cheerful objects of the whole outfit were our two engines. They roared away and sang a deep-throated song filled with contentment and gladness.'[18] However, when they landed at Marseilles the crew quickly forgot their earlier cold.

The next leg was to Pisa, where the plane became bogged down and demanded all the crew's adaptability and methods to make it airborne. On take-off Bennett held the tail down until the machine was moving, then made a running jump for the rear cockpit, where Shiers was holding a guy rope tied around Bennett's waist so that, as the plane left the ground, he could pull him headfirst into the cockpit. From Pisa they set out for Rome, where heavy headwinds reduced their air speed to an average 50mph.

After Rome it was on to Taranto and then Suda Bay in Crete, where they were greeted by an RAF officer and the engineers were given extra time to overhaul the engines for the coming overseas flight. At Suda Bay they had a telegram from Prime Minister Hughes, who was clearly having second thoughts about an aeroplane covering such a journey: 'Do your best, but do nothing foolhardy. If you cannot make Australia within 30 days, never mind. Good luck.'[19]

The weather was warming up, although on the journey from Cairo to Damascus they met with torrential rain, which in their open cabins, made them most uncomfortable. Ross, however, continued to be full of praise for their Rolls-Royce engines that hummed away rhythmically to the next objective Baghdad, where they encountered a simoom (a hot and dry gale) following which they had to dig their plane out of the sand.

On 24 November it was on to Basra, to Karachi the next day, and then Delhi and Calcutta on the 28th. These flights were relatively trouble-free but long in an aeroplane that travelled at no more than 100mph. By the time they reached Delhi they had covered 5,790 miles from London in thirteen days, and Calcutta marked the end of their journey across India. Singapore lay before them and then 2,310 miles further on was Darwin, their first landfall in Australia. On 29 November they overtook the Frenchman Poulet, thus cancelling out his six-week start and after Rangoon they left him even further behind.

After Calcutta they no longer had the benefit of using RAF bases with their trained personnel and were compelled to land on racecourses or very small airfields. They made ten take-offs between Calcutta and Darwin, six of which would prove extremely dangerous with, for instance, their Vimy only just clearing the boundary fence when they left Rangoon. Crossing the mountain ranges of Thailand, they encountered massive cloud banks, which with their instruments limited to a compass, airspeed indicator and inclinometer, forced them to take the Vimy up to its maximum height of 11,000ft to overfly them. At Don Muang airport in Thailand the engines were at last beginning to show signs of their long journey, and the two mechanics had to spend all night regrinding two valves in the starboard one.

From now on the rudimentary landing strips proved particularly dangerous. When Ross decided to land at Singora, halfway down the Malay peninsula, he found the airstrip studded with tree stumps 18in high, which he somehow avoided although his tail skid was shattered. Bennett fixed this by using a lathe turned by unskilled workers and after the stumps were cleared they set off for Singapore.

The next crisis arose when landing at Surabaya in Eastern Java. There the crust of the reclaimed surface gave way and the aircraft had to be pushed, pulled and tugged on to mats placed on drier ground. By the end of the day all efforts to get ready for take-off failed. Finally, late at night Keith Smith asked whether they could lay a double path of mats along the whole 300 yards needed for take-off. At dawn truckloads of mats arrived and some 200 Indonesians were engaged in sorting, laying and lacing them together.

At 11.55 a.m. on 8 December 1919 the plane finally succeeded in taking off and its landings at Bima and at Alamboea on the island of Timor were uneventful. From here it was 470 miles to Darwin, where at 3.40 p.m. after a seven-hour trans-ocean journey, they brought their Vimy down at Fanny Bay, twenty-seven days, twenty hours after leaving Hounslow.

At Darwin the brothers were told they had been awarded knighthoods and their engineers bars to their Air Force medals. From there they flew the Vimy 2,396 miles to Melbourne, where Prime Minister Hughes handed over the cheque for £10,000 which Ross decided to divide equally between the four crew members. At the subsequent celebrations the Prime Minister declared with no undue modesty that: 'This latest and greatest development of the possibilities of aerial navigation has not only been concerned and organised by Australians, but has also been consummated by Australians.'[20]

Like other such pioneers, not all would enjoy their celebrity for long – Ross Smith, for instance, was preparing for a round-the-world flight for which Vickers constructed the Vickers Viking amphibian. When testing it at Brooklands on 13 April 1922 it crashed, killing him and his faithful mechanic Bennett, who had left a thriving motor business in Melbourne to re-join his chief.

The others survived longer. Keith Smith became a director of Qantas Airways until his death in 1955, and Wally Shiers lived on for another eleven years until 1968, when he died suddenly at the age of 79.

———————◆·———————

The increased distances covered by aerial journeys during the immediate post-war years owed much to the determination of such men, whose skills had been developed during the war and who for the most part used wartime equipment. As such they were the undoubted trailblazers, although commercial flights along the routes were still some years away. In the case of the Atlantic, it would be twenty years before it became recognised as one of the great highways of Western civilisation, comparable to the Mediterranean some 2,000 years before. As for the journey made by the Smith brothers to Australia, a partway route was opened from Britain to India in 1929 and the first regular once a week passenger service to Australia commenced in April 1935, although it was not used by an appreciable number of passengers until after the Second World War – 'and not until the earlier heroes and deaths had been replaced by images of safety, reliability, pleasure and comfort'.[21]

PART 2

NEW PERSPECTIVES
1926–33

ALAN COBHAM: BRINGING AVIATION TO THE PEOPLE OF BRITAIN

In post-war Britain road and rail communications were so good that, despite the wartime developments in military aviation, there seemed little need for civil flying.

The early small airlines carried passengers to Europe rather than within Britain and although in 1919 ex-service pilots succeeded in crossing the vast and inhospitable Atlantic Ocean and even flying to Australia, they did so in aircraft that were not designed for civilian purposes. The situation was not likely to change quickly for, with the large numbers of wartime aircraft cheaply available and the virtual standstill of the British aircraft industry because of the lack of orders, the design and production of more advanced civilian aircraft promised to be a relatively slow process.

As pioneer airman Alan Cobham remarked forty years later, 'In the early '20s as far as I can remember there was little worthwhile development in new types of aircraft.'[1] Cobham believed that such aircraft were limited to Armstrong Whitworth's three-engined Argosy of 1926, de Havilland's DH.66 Hercules of the same year and Handley Page's H.P.42 Hannibal Class in 1930. Apart from such progress, the British skies were remarkably free of aircraft – the RAF's annual pageant at Hendon being the notable exception – for Hugh Trenchard, its Chief of the Air Staff, had deliberately sent most of its active squadrons overseas.

Following the establishment of Imperial Airways in 1924 with its regular flights from London to the Continent and then on to Cairo, powered flights within Britain were largely restricted to flying in and out of Croydon, the company's home airport. Exceptionally, the small aircraft company of de Havilland's, which since its establishment in 1920 had decided to build civil aeroplanes for charter flights, offered a much restricted aerial taxi service to the likes of newspaper photographers and reporters or those who had missed their boat train to Cherbourg.

Geoffrey de Havilland attempted to augment this by designing other small aircraft that were relatively low powered and had one or two seats aimed at the wealthier middle classes and early air enthusiasts. A very significant development came in 1925 with his DH.60 Moth, a small biplane of plywood construction with a 60–80hp four-cylinder Cirrus engine (achieved by cutting Renault's wartime engine in half).

The Moth, which was marketed at just £599, encouraged the formation of flying clubs across Britain and the Empire, one of the earliest being The London

A Tiger Moth light aircraft. (Author's collection)

Aeroplane Club at de Havilland's headquarters at Stag Lane, Hatfield. When the British Government granted selected clubs small annual subsidies, their members were able to fly for as little as £1 an hour.

Important as this movement was, despite the widespread development of gliding clubs in Germany and of light aviation in France for both sporting and commercial purposes, in Britain flying was still thought of primarily as a sport attracting a minuscule number of people.

The expansion of flying in Britain was due in the first instance to improved engine technology. Wartime engines requiring frequent and extensive maintenance were succeeded by new models such as de Havilland's 100hp Gypsy, Bristol's Jupiter and Siddeley's Jaguar.[2] Their improved reliability enabled solo pilots to attempt long-distance flights that brought widespread publicity, with Londoner Alan Cobham, assuming the role of self-appointed protagonist for British aviation. An instance of this came about in May 1925 when Cobham flew a prototype Moth from Croydon to Zurich for lunch (a distance of some 500 miles), returning home again in the afternoon with a total flying time of thirteen hours, fifty-one minutes, at an average speed of 70mph.[3]

Through the 1920s and early '30s Cobham's many initiatives acted as a most powerful spur to British civil aviation, especially when during the 1920s he enjoyed the powerful support of Sefton Brancker, who in 1922 had become Director of Civil Aviation.

In common with other early notables in the industry, Cobham did not come from a prosperous background. He was born in 1894 in Camberwell, London, and despite attending Wilsons Grammar School he became a pupil farmhand, with no prospects of owning his own farm, before joining the city lingerie firm of Hicks and Smith. There he did well until, like so many others of his generation, the outbreak of the First World War changed his life. After enlisting as quickly as he could, his knowledge of horses enabled him to become an NCO veterinary assistant before, while on leave from France in 1917, he revived an earlier enthusiasm for aviation, which he decided 'was a growth area within which a man would be able to prove himself and do great things'.[4]

With the help of a Mr Grose, a family neighbour and civil servant at the War Office, Cobham was accepted as a cadet at the Royal Flying Corps Depot at Hastings, where he showed a natural aptitude. Within four months of qualifying as a pilot, in May 1918 he obtained a commission and was made a flying instructor. On demobilisation in February 1919 Cobham decided to continue in civil aviation despite the widespread dismissal of test pilots and others following the cancellation of their wartime contracts.

Sir Alan John Cobham. (Royal Aeronautical Society/National Aerospace Library)

After making extensive and unsuccessful enquiries to possible employers in London and the Home Counties, he met the brothers Fred and Jack Holmes. Fred was a good fitter and mechanic while Jack was a former wartime pilot. In May 1919 the three united to found the Berkshire Aviation Company, offering flights to civilians. Much of its £900 capital was borrowed and most went into its single Avro 504K aeroplane bought from Frederick Handley Page's Aircraft Disposal Company. Alan Cobham was appointed pilot with Fred Holmes its maintenance engineer and Jack responsible for administration.

After converting their Avro into a three-seater they offered joyrides in both England and Scotland throughout 1919, although their main problem was to find suitable landing fields and permission to use them. Much of the plane's maintenance had to be done at night for while it was 'off the road' it no longer earned money. When Cobham crashed it, the precarious nature of their enterprise became fully apparent, for without an immediate replacement they were bound to go out of business. Cobham immediately bought another plane on the strength of their anticipated insurance pay-out, registered it and within forty-eight hours had restarted the business. They also enjoyed a stroke of luck when Fred was able to restore the damaged plane and make it their 'spare'.

Cobham revelled in the excitement and uncertainty. At one stage they met the famous comedian Will Fyffe, who suggested they went to Scotland at Christmas as it was the only time of year when the Scots could be persuaded to part with their money. It was on the journey north that Cobham was fortunate enough to meet his future wife, Gladys, who was starring in a revue at Middlesbrough.

In a speculative attempt to expand the business they engaged several pilots and mechanics to work the seaside resorts, only to find their backers had walked away. Like the other two, Cobham lost his money and after a number of false starts had just £3 to his name when he was taken on as a pilot in the aerial photography department of Holt Thomas's Aircraft Manufacturing Company (Airco). Cobham found flying aerial photographers in all weathers both exciting and demanding work at which he excelled, and when Airco was forced into liquidation it sold its photography department to de Havilland's Aero Films – on the condition it kept Cobham on as pilot.

Working for de Havilland, Cobham perfected his map reading and flying skills and, while acting as a taxi pilot, became very familiar with Britain's cities and countryside. Having built up his departmental team to ten he boasted he was ready to fly anywhere, anytime. As well as his personal commissions for de Havilland's he acted as a general chauffeur for a wealthy American Lucien Sharpe, whom he flew on a 5,000-mile tour of Europe and subsequently across much of North Africa and the Middle East. Cobham reckoned he acquired two things from his duties with Sharpe: the ability to bring an aircraft down safely whatever the country or climate, and (probably more important still) a desire to see 'the large world that lay beyond the limits of Europe and the Mediterranean lands and conquer it for civil aviation'.[5]

The determination to develop civil aviation was to remain central to Cobham's ambitions and when he learned that Sir Sefton Brancker was due to go by liner to India to investigate docking facilities for airships, Cobham argued that he should go by air – with Cobham as pilot. The pair took off from de Havilland's Stag Lane on 20 November 1924 in a DH.50G, serial number G-EBFO, taking with them Cobham's mechanic Arthur Elliott and a Romanian general who for some unstated reason Brancker decided to bring with him.

The journey was extended to Rangoon and because of their aircraft's limitations in overflying the mountainous territory they experienced many terrifying and dangerous moments. Early in the journey Cobham had to land in Germany's Black Forest region on a steep hillside in 3ft of snow. Nevertheless, by the end of it he felt sure he had persuaded Brancker that a liner would always be slower and less adaptable.

Their flight created a sensation and convinced Cobham that his own massive confidence in air travel was starting to get across: 'I wanted people to stop thinking of flying as a stunt and start thinking of it as a normal means of transport.'[6]

In spite of his unfortunate experience with the Berkshire Aviation Company, Cobham still wanted an airline of his own for which he could develop world air routes. Initially he wanted to explore Africa, which he believed had the greatest potential, and planned a flight to Cape Town and back that required the positioning of oil and petrol supplies together with aeroplane spares, at places such as Cairo, Khartoum, Kisumu and Johannesburg. To finance his expedition he decided to write a book entitled *My Flight to the Cape and Back* and, more ambitious still, to film the whole flight, which meant carrying a Gaumont cameraman in addition to his regular mechanic Arthur Elliott. In the event his faith in the film succeeded in earning him a remarkable £8,000.

Cobham flew to Cape Town and back in nine days and had he not been held back by tropical rains he was certain he could have done it in six. Reflecting on the journey he wrote: 'I made a nice profit ... I had never been so popular in my life ... it wasn't me, it was what I stood for – civil aviation that is – I stood for closer links between the scattered peoples of the British Empire and also for an end to the isolation of those who lived in small and remote places.'[7]

Cobham also believed his flight had challenged the ocean liner for, although unbeatable 'as regards elegance, space and comfort', it lacked the speed that most travellers wanted. But, as he well knew, such flights still 'needed to be asserted, developed, pressed forward'[8] and – through flying skills such as his – to end in a safe return. To his surprise, after returning to de Havilland at Stag Lane on 15 March 1926, Cobham found he was required to go to Buckingham Palace to give King George V a full account of the flight.

On 30 June he took off again for Australia on a journey of some 11,000 miles. It was to become the most celebrated of Cobham's long-distance flights, during which he planned to fly through the heart of the monsoon in both India and Burma. His faithful DH.50 was converted into a seaplane by adding metal floats supplied by Short Brothers, and when he had completed the journey he planned to deliver a petition to the House of Commons on behalf of civil aviation, which he would bill as a flight from Rochester to London via Australia.

Apart from arranging for petrol and oil supplies along the route, such a protracted journey necessitated a chain of suitable landing places on lakes, rivers, harbours and estuaries all with mooring facilities. On reaching Australia he planned to pick up an undercarriage at Darwin for the flight across the country and back before refitting the floats for the journey home. The floats' extra weight meant he could no longer take a photographer, although his engineer Elliott remained a vital passenger.

After taking off from Stag Lane the flight across France was uneventful, but for the first time on such trips Cobham reported that he felt depressed – something alien to him – which he attributed to 'being possibly homesick and suffering from both mental and physical exhaustion'.[9] Although his journey followed a well-tried routine, this condition stayed with him.

After Basra he met with dust storms and he was flying low to keep ground features in view when at some 40ft altitude he heard a violent explosion coming from the passenger cabin, and a note passed from Elliott explained that the petrol pipe leading from the reserve tank had burst: he had been hit in the arm very badly and was 'bleeding a pot of blood'.[10] Cobham was faced with the agonising decision about whether to land and try to treat Elliott himself (which would be very hazardous because Elliott would be unable to help anchor the plane) or fly on to Basra where there was sure to be medical assistance. He chose the latter and within an hour he landed on mud flats where, with help from natives, he removed Elliott from the plane and laid him on the ground. After his wounds were temporarily plugged with cotton wool, two launches arrived with medical staff and the injuries further cleaned up before he was taken to hospital. His earlier presentiment of danger made Cobham determined to find out what had actually happened. His plane was towed to the Royal Air Force's inland dock and it was found that a bullet must have hit it, smashing the petrol pipe before passing through Elliott's arm and left lung until burying itself under his right armpit. Upon discovering this, the RAF planned to fly Cobham back the next morning to where it happened.

That night he visited Elliott in hospital to assure him he would not resume the journey until he got better but after returning to his quarters he went to bed only to be woken by the news that Elliott had had a sudden relapse and died at 11.15 that night. Determined to investigate the cause, Cobham joined an RAF flight and identified the Arab encampment most likely to have been involved.

Further investigations identified the Arab who had fired at the plane and he was arrested, but after much enquiry it was decided that as a hunter he could have been taking aim when the plane flew across him, and that he unintentionally pulled the trigger. It was concluded that Elliott's death was accidental and the man was set free.

Meanwhile, the RAF buried Elliott with full military honours and Cobham received calls from such notables as Sir 'Sam' Hoare, Sir Sefton Brancker, Sir Charles Wakefield and Sir John Siddeley (together with his wife Gladys) urging him to continue his journey while the RAF offered to lend him a first-class engineer in Sergeant A.H. (Arthur) Ward, another Londoner who had volunteered to go with him.

On 14 July Cobham and Ward took off from Basra and flew on across India to Calcutta, then via Singapore and Timor to Darwin without major incident. From there they flew 'in the most uneventful manner across the outback and back' before retracing their footsteps to touch down on the Thames at Westminster precisely on schedule. From Westminster the 32-year-old Cobham was taken to Buckingham Palace, where he was knighted by the King.

Cobham wrote a book about the flight and also described it in his later memoirs. In the former he stated that:

> Anybody else, I felt, could have done the same thing. Well perhaps not anybody. To complete such a journey successfully, one needed to be a fair pilot at least, with a good knowledge of simple navigation and a thorough understanding of one's machine. One also needed care and judgement, especially when it was a question of deciding whether to go ahead or turn back. Apart from these lone qualifications it all depended upon very careful planning at every stage and upon reasonable prudence in matters of food and drink. And there was always the mysterious and unpredictable factor of luck.[11]

Whether Cobham genuinely valued his skills so modestly or not, in essence he hoped that those who cheered and celebrated his journey to Australia were, in fact, celebrating the idea of air transport as such. Notwithstanding that the early heroic days might have been over, without a pilot and organiser of Cobham's calibre such journeys were still far from becoming routine.

In 1927 Cobham severed his connections with de Havilland and set up his own company, Alan Cobham Ltd (which in the next year became Cobham/Blackburn Ltd), to offer services as aviation consultants, aerodrome experts and air route surveyors. His main ambition was to fly across Africa, and in preparation he made another long-distance flight in a large Singapore Mk 1 flying boat lent to him by the Air Minister Sir 'Sam' Hoare. Despite experiencing major difficulties in Malta his flight round Africa would prove a great success, and in 1931 Cobham went on to survey a route along the Nile to the Belgian Congo in a triple-engined Short Valetta twin float seaplane.

Such flights proved far easier, however, than getting support to establish his airline against entrenched interests. Lord Birkenhead, for instance, who was Secretary of State for India at the time, showed little interest in speeding up transport between himself and the home country, and Lord Inchcape, chairman of P&O, saw such advances purely in terms of their damaging effects to his company.

Cobham in DH.51 G-EBIM. (Royal Aeronautical Society/National Aerospace Library)

Cobham was also in competition against Imperial Airways, whose management believed that as the official carrier *it* had the sole right to operate an overseas air service across both Africa and India. To help achieve this, its strategy was to buy up any troublesome competitors, including Cobham/Blackburn Air Lines, and as a result Imperial gained the right to use the routes Cobham had pioneered. With Sefton Brancker keeping a watchful eye on things, Cobham received £24,750 in cash and 25,000 £1 ordinary shares in Imperial Airways as compensation.

With the chance of having his own airline over, from 1929 and into the early 1930s Cobham sought other ways to raise the profile of air travel in Britain, notably through the establishment of municipal aerodromes and initiating a National Aviation Day Campaign that he would ultimately consider his greatest single contribution to civil aviation.

Cobham hoped his Municipal Aerodrome Campaign would not only help to establish them across Britain but extend his activities as an aviation consultant. To achieve this he undertook a most punishing programme where over twenty-one weeks between May and October 1929 he visited 110 towns and cities in his de Havilland DH.61 aircraft, which he had purchased for £3,250 before equipping it with a powerful Armstrong Siddeley Jaguar engine and naming it *The Youth of Britain*. His routine reflected the urgency he felt for the project: following an early start, by 11 a.m. he would meet up with mayors and town clerks and take them into the air to view their towns, including possible aerodrome sites, some of which would become well-known centres of aviation.

The flights for the civil officers would be followed by others for children (which explained his naming the plane *The Youth of Britain*), and 10,000 children in all enjoyed the experience of flight. After these flights he would take lunch with the mayors and their town clerks, during which he again emphasised the need to establish municipal airports. Finally, from 2.30 until 9 p.m. it would be the turn of the public to be given seven-minute flights, with a total of fifty quite usual during this time.

The campaign was rounded off with a massive party sponsored by Lord Wakefield that commenced with a cocktail party, followed by dinner at the Savoy attended by some 300 mayors and town clerks.

Following this Cobham sold his DH.61 to Imperial Airways for £3,000, which seemed good business considering the 40,000 passengers carried and its 5,000 landings, although to his disgust it was straightway crashed by Imperial's chief test pilot – and Cobham's bête noire – Charles Wolley-Dod.

Afterwards Cobham reconnoitred the most suitable sites for airports in his open-top car with Gladys driving while he stood up, map in hand, surveying the countryside. During such work he said he thought continuously about the:

> sad fact that the general public simply were not air-minded at all. Most people had never seen an aircraft except as a distant speck in the sky. Aviation, civil or military, meant nothing to them, and so long as this remained the case, there would be little parliamentary support for its development by public authority.[12]

To change things for the better he decided to establish National Aviation Day in selected towns, where he would take aviation directly to their inhabitants by demonstrating the capabilities of aircraft and offering them joyrides. If such initiatives succeeded he hoped they might become annual fixtures.

This involved much preparation. As well as small acrobatic machines, he needed a simple robust aircraft to carry ten people for each joyride and on 17 April 1931 he joined with the young designers A.H. Tiltman and Nevil Shute Norway in setting up Airspeed Ltd to build these Ferry aircraft, the first of which joined him within a year and the second two months later.

Next he set out to establish his headquarters and assemble an executive team including skilled ground engineers. He recruited H.C. Johnson as his chief test pilot and acquired Ford Aerodrome near Littlehaven in Sussex as the team's home base.

During 1932 Cobham planned to take his Aviation Day to no fewer than 110 places, and because most were without established aerodromes, suitable fields had to be found. With such a demanding timetable, the distance between them could be no more than 60 miles; any further and the cumbersome lorries carrying all manner of equipment would not arrive there soon enough to erect tents and boundary fences and reassemble their motley aircraft fleet.

In 1932 the country was still recovering from a period of serious economic depression and hardship, and Cobham recognised that his name and presence had an electrifying effect on localities starved of such mass entertainment. The crowds he attracted made it imperative that his team exercise strict discipline, especially flight discipline: Cobham observed that his staff lived like a regiment on overseas service, and in military fashion they were divided into three classes. First were those with their own transport and cooks who prepared the field and worked to their own timetable; second were the engineers who, after servicing the aeroplanes early in the morning, had breakfast and took off with the pilots for the coming day's show, leaving their tents and baggage to be brought up by truck; and finally there were the pilots who slept in local hotels so that they were thoroughly rested. Cobham himself usually slept on-site in a caravan he shared with his chief test pilot.

Cobham was a showman in the tradition of Grahame-White's pre-war displays at Hendon, and his show was great value for the 1s 6d gate money. It began with an impressive parade or flypast of all the different aircraft including the giant Handley Page HP.35 Clive airliner, the Ferrys, the Moths, Avros and even an Autogyro, all of them being put through their paces. This was followed by the aerial display, an afternoon of aerobatics, inverted flying, racing around pylons, wing walking, 'crazy' flying, mock bombing, parachute jumps, picking up a handkerchief from the grass

Cobham's autogyro. (Author's collection)

with a spike at a plane's wing tip, and other exploits of every description. After the show, for a further 5s male or female spectators could experience their first flight.

Cobham's first season stretched from 12 April–16 October 1932, followed by a winter tour of South Africa 'to keep his core team fully occupied'. In 1932 and 1935 he put on two tours operating simultaneously. During these four years, between 3 and 4 million people came to see 1,250 displays, with 990,000 of them taken on joyrides. Under such conditions there were inevitable accidents but remarkably few given the improvised conditions. Cobham loved them; he was sure the early 1930s were a romantic period for people caught up by the wonder of aviation, and who for 5s or 10s were able to experience it for themselves.

Looking back to those years Cobham wrote that:

> Aviation has not ceased to be fun but it has ceased to be as simple as it then was, as cheap, as freely available to the young and the poor and if I can claim to have done something useful with my life, this is chiefly because I did so much to bring so many people into contact with it, while its heroic age still lasted.[13]

When Cobham's aerial circuses were at their height, some attempts to establish commercial air transport within Britain were at last justifying his missionary work.[14] Along with the single aircraft operators, Edward Hillman, for instance, started his first air service on 1 April 1932 at Maylands in Essex and Captain Ted Fresson's inaugural flight of his Highland Airways took place a year later, both of whose activities are described in Chapter 12.

———————•◆•———————

During the late 1920s and '30s another startling development occurred when lone British aviators who benefitted from the increasingly reliable aero engines and sturdier airframes began to make long-distance journeys along Cobham's routes and elsewhere, and to attempt ever more ambitious flights.

Among those from Britain and the Commonwealth was the Australian Bert Hinkler, a brilliant pilot and mechanic who serviced his own aircraft. He had flown in Britain with the RNAS and RAF during the war and from 7–22 February 1928 he became the first to fly solo from England to Australia in a small Avro Avian, using a torch, compass and a page from an atlas to guide him, while during 1931 in a Puss Moth he went on to become the first to fly solo over the Southern Atlantic Ocean.

Women were equally intrepid and two notable female aviators, Mary Lady Heath and the Honourable Mary Bailey, came to prominence during the mid 1920s onwards, both of them of Irish descent.

Mary Lady Heath, who was born in Knockaderry, County Limerick, had both high ambitions and ferocious energy. Prior to the First World War she was one of the

Bert Hinkler. (Royal Aeronautical Society/ National Aerospace Library)

first women to be awarded a first-class degree at the Royal College of Science in Dublin, and during the war she acted as a motorcycle dispatch rider. At its conclusion she helped to found the Women's Amateur Athletic Association and became Britain's first woman javelin champion. Turning to aviation, she was the first woman to hold a commercial flying licence and the first pilot, male or female, to fly a small open cockpit aircraft from Cape Town to London, where on arrival she made nothing of the discomfort experienced.

Following the death of her husband, Major William Lynn, early in 1927, by October of the same year she had married Sir James Heath, a wealthy ironmaster some forty years her senior, who helped finance her flying expeditions until, in 1929, she was seriously injured in an air crash and never fully recovered her health. However, after divorcing Heath she married the English airman G.A.R. Williams and set up her own flying school at Kildonan near Dublin, where she helped train the generation of pilots that went on to establish the country's national airline, Aer Lingus. Indomitable to the end, she died in 1939 as the result of falling down the steps of a London tram. Her husband subsequently scattered her ashes from an aircraft over Surrey.

The Honorable Mary Bailey, the daughter of Derrick Warner 5th Baron Rossmore, gained her pilot's licence in 1927. She was the first woman to fly across the Irish Sea and, between 9 March and 30 March 1928, she went on to make an 8,000-mile solo flight from Croydon to Cape Town in a DH Cirrus Moth. Her 18,000-mile return journey combined the longest solo flight and also the longest flight accomplished by a woman so far.[15]

Bailey was recognised as the world's outstanding aviatrix when awarded the prestigious Harmon Trophy for the years 1927–28 and in 1930 she was made a Dame Commander of the British Empire before joining the Women's Auxiliary Air Force during the Second World War. She was married to Sir Abe Bailey, by whom she had five children.

In 1934 another female aviator, Jean Batten, flew solo from England to Australia in a Gypsy Moth aircraft in a world record time and two years later she set another world record with a solo flight from England to her native New Zealand of 14,224 miles.

Whatever their achievements, the best-known woman pilot between the wars was Amy Johnson, who was born at Kingston upon Hull in Yorkshire's East Riding. In 1930 she achieved worldwide recognition when she became the first woman to fly solo over the 11,000-mile journey from England to Australia in a small secondhand DH Gypsy Moth that she named *Jason*. For this she was awarded a CBE and on her return to London more than 1 million people gathered to greet her. Of her flight, the London weekly *Spectator* wrote: 'old gentlemen in London clubs might cease to drivel about our decadence if they saw how young England yearns for the air, where we must renew the greatness we won through centuries of seafaring'.[16]

In one of her many attempts to gain financial backing for her Australian flight, Johnson had written directly to Sir Sefton Brancker arguing that 'if as a woman, she could be seen succeeding in flying alone to such a distant

Amy Johnson. (Author's collection)

point of the Empire it must encourage the public to have confidence in mass air travel'.[17] Brancker acknowledged the strength of her argument and put her in contact with the philanthropic oil magnate Lord Wakefield, who gave her his powerful assistance. During the 1930s Johnson made many other long-distance attempts, including a solo record-breaking flight to the Cape and back during November–December 1932 in a DH Puss Moth. On a number of these Jack Humphreys and her husband Jim Mollison acted as her co-pilots and she was rarely out of the news due to her aim of encircling the globe and because of her high-profile separation and divorce from Mollison in 1938.

After the outbreak of the Second World War Johnson continued to make the headlines. In 1940 she joined the Air Transport Auxiliary (ATA) that transported Royal Air Force Aircraft around the country, until on 5 January, while flying a two-engined Airspeed Oxford from Blackpool to RAF Kidlington near Oxford, she went off course in poor weather conditions. It was likely that her aircraft ran out of fuel for it crashed into the Thames Estuary during freezing weather and heavy seas. When her parachute (apparently along with another) was seen entering the water by the crew of HMS *Haslemere*, a balloon barrage vessel captained by Lieutenant Commander Walter Fletcher, he entered the water in a vain rescue attempt. In the adverse conditions he not only failed to find Amy Johnson's body but also died from hypothermia and shock, and was subsequently awarded a posthumous Albert Medal. Although she was never found, 'two bags containing Amy's clothing and personal possessions together with the Christmas presents from her sister's family were recovered from the sea'.[18]

More than half a century later the mystery was given another twist when in 1999 Tom Mitchell, a wartime member of an aircraft

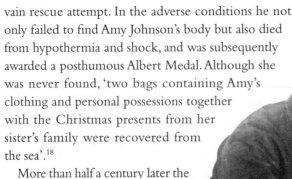

A trained mechanic, Johnson was quite prepared to get her hands dirty. (Author's collection)

battery in the Thames Estuary, gave an unsubstantiated report that Johnson had been shot down after giving a wrong recognition signal, about which their officers had sworn them to silence.

As well as the remarkable women pilots, two other men are worthy of mention with Bert Hinkler as the most famous flyers between the wars, namely Jim Mollison (Johnson's husband) and Francis Chichester (who would subsequently have a second distinguished career as a solo round-the-world sailor).

Mollison was considered by many as the greatest long-distance solo flyer of the 1930s when he set many records, including the first non-stop solo flight across the Atlantic from east to west, a distance of 2,650 miles. Prior to this he was in India with the RAF, where he flew decrepit, near obsolete aircraft and acquired a taste for alcohol. Although he was to gain a deserved reputation as a playboy, Mollison was undoubtedly a highly skilled pilot who took to record breaking to make his name. In July–August 1931 he set a magnificent record by flying from Australia to Britain in eight days, nineteen hours, and in March 1932 another for flying from England to South Africa in four days, seventeen hours.

His marriage to Johnson, to whom he proposed after knowing her for just eight hours, brought problems for both of them. They were never free from the attentions of the press and their joint flights enjoyed mixed fortunes: their intended flight across the world ended in a crash at Bridgeport Connecticut, while in October 1934 they had to retire from the MacRobertson Air Race after using non-aviation fuel.

In the case of Francis Chichester there seemed little in his early life that equipped him for a career in aviation. His extremely short sight affected his sporting ability at Marlborough College, where he had been sent by his clergyman father. Something of a loner at school, he was determined to leave at 16, whereupon his father sent him for employment as a farmhand. After reputedly using his farmer's horses for racing he was shipped by steerage to New Zealand. Strong, self-reliant and practical, he took different jobs in coal mines, gold diggings and sawmills, during which time he saved £400. On moving to the country's North Island he tried his hand at sales before entering business with another young man, Geoffrey Goodwin, and together among their other ventures, they imported commercial aeroplanes.

After six generally successful years, during which time he learned to fly, Chichester decided to return to the UK and improve his flying skills at Brooklands 'towards his long-held ambition of making a tour of Europe followed by a solo flight to Australia by Gypsy Moth'.[19]

With his fierce independence and broad experience, Chichester proved extremely well suited to solo flying. After a series of hair-raising adventures, on 26 January 1930 he arrived to a rapturous welcome at Sydney after a twenty-three-day journey[20] from London, the next pilot after Bert Hinkler to complete the journey.

Chichester was a talented author and in 1931 he published a book called *Solo to Sydney* to help finance his next projected flight,[21] which Christopher Beaumont writing in the magazine *Airways* called: 'One of the extraordinarily few classics of aviation literature, full of the art that conceals art.'[22]

Chichester's next objective was to fly solo across the 1,450-mile Tasman Sea from New Zealand to Australia, a journey that required the most accurate navigation to land on Norfolk and Lord Howe Islands, two small but vital stepping stones along the journey. It was due to his abundant resourcefulness that he succeeded, for at Lord Howe Island he had to virtually rebuild his plane. He was the first to be awarded the Johnson Memorial Trophy 'for the best feat of air navigation in the British Empire' which was presented to him by the Prince of Wales, later Edward VIII.[23]

Like Johnson, Chichester's greatest ambition was to circumnavigate the world, and in the autumn of 1931 he set off in his Gypsy Moth. However, during the journey he crashed at Katsuura in Japan after hitting telephone wires and suffered thirteen broken bones and other wounds, bringing an end to his aerial career. In his book *Solo to Sydney* Chichester graphically described his reactions as a solo flyer:

> that feeling of cutting out big distances in an apparatus controlled and directed by yourself, along with the attempt by you, a solitary soul from among two thousand millions, to do something that no other of the 1,999,999,999 has done tickles

Francis Charles Chichester is welcomed by Chief Civic Commissioner Garlick after his successful flight from England to Australia. (Royal Aeronautical Society/National Aerospace Library)

your vanity, your sense of power, your sense of romance, your love of excitement, as nothing else in the world can do.[24]

Notwithstanding Chichester's conclusions, before the rise of movie stars, the exploits of such lone flyers caught the imagination of people from across the world, who followed their aerial progress through radio communiqués or special newspaper editions.

Whatever these incredible, if essentially self-serving, achievements, Cobham's contributions were surely greater. He was no less ambitious as a pilot and his Aviation Days, including their opportunities for spectators' flight, led to far more concrete results. All the 4 million who attended his air circuses could smell the hot engine oil, be deafened by aero engines running at full throttle and be thrilled by the swooping planes accompanied by their intermittent walls of sound. A good proportion were able to go up themselves and the living proof of Cobham's success with the million or so that flew on his confidence-building trips around the airfields came when 75 per cent of the RAF's new recruits at the beginning of the Second World War acknowledged they had participated in them. Through such achievements Cobham's reputation as Britain's supreme air publicist during the interwar period is surely unassailable. Affirmation of this came following his death some half a century after his first long-distance journey when, with airliners criss-crossing the world, *Flight* magazine referred to him as 'an enthusiast, salesman and visionary all rolled into one'.[25]

BRITISH CIVIL AVIATION: AIRSHIPS, THE DOOMED CRUSADE

The idea of using airships to carry civilian passengers was given encouragement by the relatively slow expansion of Imperial Airways aircraft fleet. Although as Britain's national carrier it was responsible for both European services and those across the Empire, it first looked to Europe. However, in the face of severe competition from Continental airlines with their far greater subsidies, it felt compelled to restrict such services.[1]

From 1924–29, for instance, Imperial Airways ran just three European routes: London to Le Touquet, London to Cologne and London to Zurich via Paris and Basle.[2] It was not even the chief provider on these, for in one week of September 1925 Imperial carried 183 passengers on its London–Paris service while the French Air Union carried 432,[3] and British travellers to other European destinations were obliged to go by other carriers.

Although from 1929 onwards the company extended its services from Cologne to Budapest with another route to Prague, this still left the vast majority of the Continent unaccounted for.

This situation was well known to Sir 'Sam' Hoare, the Secretary of State for Air, whose inaugural flight to India in one of Imperial's new de Havilland aeroplanes was an attempt to demonstrate the safety and reliability of its air routes across the Empire. Following this he professed his belief that Imperial Airways' mission was from then on to be Imperial not European.[4]

Hoare combined his belief in the Empire's air routes with an enthusiasm for airships that he believed were particularly suitable for travelling long distances and capable of carrying far more passengers than Imperial's aeroplanes.

In reality the earlier British experiences with airships had been distinctly mixed, with air commentator Peter Allen concluding that 'the history of British airships is not distinguished, a story of too little and too late, of rashness and timidity, of interference and indifference, of parsimony and extravagance, of quality and achievement and of bungling and ignorance'.[5] From the time of their emergence before the First World War there were serious difficulties. Although in 1907 the country's first airship, proudly named *Nulli Secundus*, showed promise, the same could not be said for its successor, *Nulli Secundus II*, which was soon broken up. The disappointing pattern continued when in 1911 HM Naval Airship No. 1 collapsed while emerging from its shed and instead the Navy developed a fleet of relatively small, non-rigid airships, dubbed 'blimps', to patrol British coastal waters.[6]

Enthusiasm for the rigids recovered after the Battle of Jutland (31 May 1916) when the British admirals wrongly concluded that the escape of the German High Seas Fleet had been due to their Zeppelins giving warning of the trap set by the Grand Fleet. Fortuitously at this time, one of the latest German Zeppelins, L33, was forced down and captured intact and the War Office decided to incorporate its technical advances into a new class of craft, with three ships R33, R34 and R35 to be replicas of the German design and for R36 and R38 to be completed later.[7] After numerous delays, with higher priorities given to both aeroplanes and tanks, none of the R33 class were delivered before the end of the war. Even so, authority was given for the construction of another class of rigid airship, the R80, to be built at Vickers Ltd by the outstanding young designer Barnes Wallis, ably assisted by Hartley Pratt. While much smaller than the R33 class she had a fully streamlined form and superior components, but her first flight was delayed until July 1920 and then, with no further military interest, the last took place on 20 September 1921, following which she was dismantled.

At the end of the First World War it was decided that airships, like aeroplanes, should come under the control of the Air Ministry, which meant they would be flown by RAF officers. One can imagine the dismay of those appointed to airships when they learned on 14 and 15 June 1919 that two ex-RAF officers, Captain John Alcock and Lieutenant Arthur Whitten-Brown in the employ of Vickers Ltd, had captured the Blue Riband of the air by making the first non-stop crossing of the Atlantic in an aeroplane, a converted Vimy bomber, that covered the 1,680-nautical mile journey in fifteen hours, fifty-seven minutes at an average speed of 105–6 knots.

The airship flyers responded a week later when the R34 under the command of Major George Herbert Scott successfully crossed over from Scotland to Long Island in 108 hours and, unlike the Vimy which after flying from Newfoundland to Ireland ended up in an Irish bog, made the return journey in a flight lasting seventy-five hours, during which she carried up to twenty passengers but sustained some damage after running through a storm.

In spite of the R34's success and seeming superiority, airships could never compete in price with aeroplanes designed as bombers. The R34, for instance, cost an amazing £350,000 compared with Blenheim and Whitley bombers produced in the mid 1930s for an average cost of £8,435 and £22,450 respectively. Airships were also more fragile, a fact underlined on 25 January 1921 when, after sustaining serious damage on a training flight, the R34 was broken up. An even more serious event occurred later in the year when the R38, reckoned to be one of the world's largest and most advanced ships, broke her back during a test flight and fell into the Humber, killing some of the best British and American airship personnel.[8]

The loss of the R38, followed by that of the American airship USS *Shenandoah* and the French *Dixmude*, led to the belief in Britain that the age of the rigid airship – originally intended to give the Royal Navy a means of long-range air reconnaissance[9] – was over.

This would surely have been the case had not these great ships attracted their influential supporters, including the Secretary of State for Air.

From early 1922 a number of attempts were made to revive interest in airships, including one by Major Scott (the ex-skipper of the R34) who contacted the Royal Navy to point out their advantages in voyaging across the main Empire trade routes. Scott met with little positive response from Roger Keyes, Assistant Chief of the Naval Staff, who, with the Navy's concern for its sea vessels, brusquely informed him that 'it is out of the question to commit ourselves to providing a subsidy for civil airships for commercial purposes at present'.[10]

At this point a more formidable individual entered the discussions in the person of Sir Charles Dennistoun Burney, son of Admiral Sir Cecil Burney. Burney was a former naval commander who had benefitted financially from his invention of a paravane device that deflected mines placed in the path of merchant ships. As an entrepreneur and strong Empire supporter Burney sought to establish better Imperial communications by proposing an airship company backed by £4 million capital, towards which Vickers and Shell would be expected to contribute £100,000 with the remainder in the form of debenture shares guaranteed by the Government for a ten-year period.

Burney suggested that his company should be given the right to lease existing airships and the Air Ministry stations at Cardington and Pulham for a peppercorn rent. His aim – which enjoyed the enthusiastic support of Hoare – was to establish a bi-weekly air service to and from India with an additional weekly flight to Australia, using five massive airships holding 3.5 million cu.ft of hydrogen gas to be built by a subsidiary of Vickers. In anticipation of success Burney had already consulted leading Zeppelin expert Hugo Eckener about the scheme's feasibility and recruited a team of outstanding British talents, including Barnes Wallis, P.L. Teed, Wallis's assistant at Vickers-Armstrong, aerodynamicist J.E. Temple and H.B. Pratt, Wallis's one-time chief at Saunders-Roe. Although Hoare favoured an extra airship the Air Ministry and the Navy agreed to the proposed scheme.

The Navy was won over by the chance of having such airships available in wartime and similarly the RAF by their belief that airships would give them a double-string capability for their imperial communications. Upon this the Government agreed that Hoare should negotiate with Burney about the building and operation of the new airships. Things went so well that a week after registering his company Burney entered into a draft agreement with the Treasury, and during May 1923 travelled with Barnes Wallis to the Zeppelin works to negotiate a draft treaty of support and co-operation.

Such plans suffered unexpected opposition following the General Election of December 1923 that brought in the first Labour Government under Ramsay MacDonald, who appointed his close friend Brigadier Christopher Thomson as Secretary of State for Air. Although the Labour administration was short-lived, Thomson greatly influenced Britain's final phase of airship construction in which Barnes Wallis emerged as its outstanding designer.

Like Burney, Thomson came from a service family with his father a major general in the Royal Engineers. In 1894, after attending the Royal Military Academy at Woolwich, Christopher followed him by becoming a Royal Engineer officer. After serving in the Anglo–Boer War he spent much of the years 1912–17 in the Balkans where he was a member of General Allenby's staff in Palestine but after attending the Peace Conference in Paris during 1919 he resigned his commission to enter politics.

Although Thomson was a forceful and accomplished speaker with a wide circle of friends across the political divide, as a socialist candidate he was unsuccessful in both the 1919 and 1923 elections. Following Labour's 1923 election success he was made a baron and significantly chose the title of Lord Thomson of Cardington from the Air Ministry's airship station there.

Whatever his enthusiasm for airships, as air historian Robin Higham observed, 'he had no training for this position and was thus a military man holding a service department, rarely a wise arrangement'.[11]

Notwithstanding his credentials, Thomson mounted an immediate and energetic attack on the Burney airship proposals because they lacked Government control and he put forward an alternative plan for the Government to build a single huge airship capable of holding 5 million cu.ft of hydrogen gas to carry out a regular

Lord Thomson, Secretary of State for Air.
(National Portrait Gallery)

travel service to India (for which mooring facilities would be needed in Egypt and India). Following the R38 disaster, Thomson was convinced that safety should be all-important and he announced that he expected the Government's building programme to be slower than that proposed under the Burney Scheme. However, in the event construction would be most seriously affected by economic difficulties including the General Strike of 1926 and others in 1927–28.

Expenditure for the airship was set at £1.4 million over a four-year programme compared with the £4.8 million involved with the Burney proposals, although these would have involved less public money due to the bulk of the capital coming through debenture shares placed on the open market. As a concession Thomson offered Burney's Airship Guarantee Company the chance to build a second private airship up to a maximum cost of £350,000, with an option to buy it back at a reduced price of £150,000 if it was made available for a service to India.[12]

The Government ship was given the serial number R101 and the 'private' one R100. This provoked a number of questions in the Commons about why the Government ship should have a later number than the commercial one. Major Scott, who was due to be made responsible for the R101's flying performance, infuriated Barnes Wallis – who would design the private ship – by telling him it was because the R100 would be the last of an established line while R101 would be exciting, with new ideas.[13] Scott's argument seemed reasonable enough when the Government ship, together with its research programme, was scheduled to cost more than four times that of the commercial one.

In exaggerated terms Thomson told the House of Lords of his firm beliefs in airships and stressed how valuable it was to have two great ones built within three years from which 'multitudes would be flying worldwide at the end of ten years'. Not all his listeners were won over, including a critical Duke of Atholl, who pointed out that by creating two separate organisations Thomson had subdivided the relatively small number of experts in airships.

In the event both ships took a full five years to build: work commenced in mid 1924 but it was not until 12 October 1929 that R101 was finally brought out of her shed, with R100 not emerging until 16 December.

There were legitimate reasons for the prolonged construction period, the chief being that they were twice the size of anything previously built. At 707ft long the R100 was slightly smaller than the R101 because it had to fit into the existing airship shed at Howden. Even so, it was only 50ft shorter than the great passenger liner *Mauretania*. In such a situation the designers had to return to first principles in calculating their structures, dimensions and weights, while before any construction could begin their great sheds had to be prepared; the private one at the former airship station at Howden, East Yorkshire, needed some renovation and adaptation while the Government one at Cardington, Bedfordshire, required major heightening and a mooring mast to be constructed adjacent to it.

The MacDonald Government lasted just nine months but when the new Conservative Prime Minister Stanley Baldwin reappointed Hoare as his Air Secretary he chose to continue with Thomson's centrally controlled and less flexible scheme in the belief that it was 'better to proceed rather than once again throwing development into the melting pot'.[14] There were practical reasons for such a decision since the two design teams had already assembled. In the event the teams were soon to take different approaches, in the course of which the current small number of experts became apparent.

In the case of the Government team, the post of Director of Airship Development went to Squadron Leader (later Wing Commander) Reginald Colmore, a good administrator and devotee of airships who was not overly ambitious and whose promotion, like other serving officers, depended on the annual gradings given by his superiors, the most senior of whom was the Secretary of State for Air. The chief designer, or in service jargon, 'assistant director of airship development technical', was lieutenant Colonel Vincent Richmond, whose earlier expertise as a physicist was restricted to the use of dope for strengthening airship covers – predictably earning him the sobriquet 'Dopey' – and who while familiar enough with the theory of aircraft construction enjoyed no 'hands on' experience in airship design.

Richmond was, however, receptive to innovative ideas and he owed much to Squadron Leader Michael Rope, whom the enthusiastic Peter Masefield believed to be 'a design engineer of genius'.[15] Despite the quality of his mind and his undoubted technical ability, the deeply religious Rope lost the chance to meet his colleagues socially when he decided to move his family away from the heavy drinking culture at Cardington. Although he was responsible for much innovation with the R101 there were suspicions that Rope sometimes moved away from conventional design practices for intellectual rather than practical reasons. While hardly impartial, Barnes Wallis, the leader of the private team, was unimpressed by Rope's gasbags suspended from independent wire nets that in bad weather could 'slosh' from side to side due to their heavy wiring, which occupied a large amount of internal space. Rope was also responsible for designing automatic valves for the gas bags that, when the R101 rolled more than 3 degrees, opened and vented gas.

Responsibility for the R101's engine development was given to Wing Commander Cave-Browne-Cave who, due to his rank and seniority, had earlier been a strong contender for Colmore's position as project director. The engines for the Government ship had to be diesel-powered (and British) because they were considered safer but Cave-Browne-Cave accepted ones that were twice the estimated weight, thus causing his ship to be lacking in lift. And although chief designer Richmond personally favoured petrol he felt he could not override Cave-Browne-Cave's decision.

The last of the 'big three' supporting the Government's chief designer was the unquestionably daring and experienced airship pilot Major Scott, who had already

The Government airship, the R101. (Author's collection)

established his reputation by flying the Atlantic in the R34 and who as Assistant Director Airship Development was responsible for the ship's flying performance. By this time, however, Scott's natural conviviality had moved into a drinking culture whereby he attempted to survive the duller periods of the protracted five-year construction cycle.

In such an environment where notions of duty and rank were so prevalent, the director's authority – and to a lesser extent that of the chief designer – was liable to be challenged from above in a way unthinkable in the private venture team under Barnes Wallis. This would prove particularly important when towards the end of the construction programme the Conservatives were defeated and in June 1929 a second Labour Government assumed office, with Lord Thomson again taking over from 'Sam' Hoare.

During his term, both airship teams encountered difficulties and he had already faced questions in the House of Commons about achieving speedier results, especially with the impressive progress being made in Germany in building the *Graf Zeppelin*. Even so, Hoare's natural caution would have made him unlikely to ignore expert advice on safety measures by attempting to speed up construction, although by June 1929 the R101's maiden flight to India was already overdue.

From this point the accession of Thomson as Air Minister brought increased urgency from a strong, enthusiastic, if not overbearing, individual who, come what may, was determined to set off for India by the end of September 1930 and return to take part in the opening of Parliament later in the autumn.

In the case of the R100's smaller team, despite suffering from similar delays, things were undoubtedly far easier for its chief designer.

Their far tighter budget made many of the innovations adopted at Cardington unaffordable and although Wallis had the benefit of prior experience with the R80 he had a reputation for never seeking novelty for its own sake but opting for handsome and practical solutions. Wallis's record was already proven: his R80 had shown its superiority over the earlier Zeppelins in achieving an air resistance of only 3 per cent (when using a flat plate the same diameter as the airship), as opposed to the 16 per cent of the Zahm-designed craft.[16] Airship historian Douglas Robinson rated Wallis's R80 extremely highly, believing that with it we at last 'see a home grown ship equal to the Germans' best, created by a designer sure of himself and producing a rigid airship which reflected credit both on himself and on his country'.[17]

Understandably, Wallis's well-founded design skills proved of immense value when building the R100. Although ultimately subject to Burney as head of the Airship Guarantee Company and Sir Robert McLean the formidable managing director of Vickers, at Howden, Wallis was the unquestionable boss, with nothing executed without his knowledge and approval. He selected Nevil Shute Norway for the crucial

Barnes Wallis, airship and aeroplane designer. (National Portrait Gallery)

role of chief calculator to check the stress and load factors vital for such a huge airship, with Shute acknowledging the three eminent men who most assisted him: Professor Bairstow, the authority on aerodynamics, Professor Pippard on structures, and the most practical and useful of all, J.E. Temple, who had earlier worked with Wallis as chief calculator for the R80.

Even so, Shute had no doubt about his own responsibility: 'My job was to get together a staff of calculators to do the work on R100 translating the theories of the consultants into forces and stresses in each member of the ship and so providing the draughtsmen with the sizes for each girder and each wire.'[18]

Much has subsequently been made about Shute's withering attacks on Government meddling during the building of its R101 and his talents as a novelist rather than a calculator, but Wallis, who always demanded a great deal, thought highly of Shute's mathematical abilities.

Due to monetary shortages not experienced by the R101 team and his essentially pragmatic approach, Wallis kept to the well-tried techniques used for the advanced Zeppelins and his earlier airship the R80.

The R100's main frame consisted of a series of transverse rings latticed together in a geodetic construction combining lightness with strength, which Wallis would later adopt in his aircraft. Like the Zeppelins, he employed duralumin (a strong

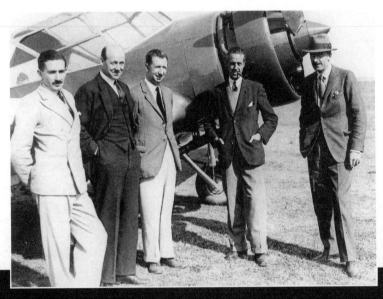

Nevil Shute Norway, (centre) airship calculator and author. (Royal Aeronautical Society/National Aerospace Library)

The private airship, the R100. (Author's collection)

but light form of aluminum), although after the R100's completion he believed metallurgical advances would have enabled a ship of similar design to weigh 15 per cent less. Although its super streamlined shape owed much to his earlier R80, the R100 had only sixteen sides, fewer than previous airships and, unlike the R101, its framework contained fourteen massive gasbags hanging from a single axial girder running along the ship with a capacity of 5 million cu.ft of hydrogen gas. Despite Government pressure to use diesel engines, Wallis decided to power his airship with six reconditioned Rolls-Royce Condor petrol engines and he also retained manual flight control systems.

The immense size of the R100 was evident from the amount of the components used, including 58,200ft (11 miles) of tubing, 5 million rivets and 400,000 bracing pieces, although these were made from only nine basic and fifty different parts. The ship's cover took 225,000 sq.ft of material with a further 502,200 sq.ft for the gas bags.[19] The outcome of Wallis's design skills and the work of his team was that the R100 succeeded in performing up to its design expectations.

Although during its speed trials on 18 January 1930 peculiar wrinkles developed in its outer cover, they disappeared when its speed was reduced to 70mph. From this Nevil Shute came to the alarming conclusion that its outer cover had degraded during the prolonged construction time and was barely strong enough for its purpose, although replacing it at such a late stage was considered impractical. R100 went on to complete successfully her endurance trails over the three days of 27–29 January 1930 in standard winter weather, following which the ship was taken into the shed at Cardington for checking and minor repairs. Towards the end of March during another trial a new problem occurred when the tail fairing collapsed, but this was quickly dealt with.

Six months later, on 29 July, all was put to the test when the R100 left its mast at Cardington bound for Canada carrying forty-four people, 2,000lb of food, 500 gallons of drinking water and 10,440 gallons of fuel for the 3,242-mile journey. On its arrival it had 1,500 gallons of fuel left.

After what proved to be a relatively straightforward journey on entering the St Lawrence estuary, the R100 encountered a violent storm and sustained damage to the coverings on both her port and starboard fins, which were repaired on board by a fifteen-man team.

The return journey was uneventful except for some water entering the hull and mechanical trouble being experienced in one of the engines. At a time when a full double crossing was beyond the ability of aeroplanes, the R100 had proved the soundness of its construction, even though its superstructure was heavier than the *Graf Zeppelin*. Its calculator, Nevil Shute, concerned as he was about its outer cover, continued to believe that travel by airship would always be a gamble.

Such beliefs would prove accurate with the 'Government ship' some 720ft in length and 130ft in its beam, which was highly experimental and more complex, although her workmanship was rather better than that of the R100. It was also ultra-streamlined and its remarkable thirty-sided hull reduced air resistance to a mere 2 per cent when tested with a flat plate of the same diameter as the airship – a magnificent achievement. But however streamlined, adequate power was still essential and here things were much less successful. Despite having seven 650hp diesel engines expected to exceed the required 70mph they not only weighed a massive 3,000lb each but also produced less power than expected. This was serious enough but additional weight came through the installation of complex balancing rudders and servo motors to operate the controls.

Michael Rope also installed a number of revolutionary features: its mainframe, for instance, consisted of huge rings of steel and duralumin without diametrical wiring, while its gasbags were contained within a complex and relatively heavy netting system. The bags' automatic valves opened when the ship pitched, the frequency and extent of which had been underestimated. The result was that in a way unknown to Wallis's airship the R101's early performance tests were marred by excessive weight and a series of technical failures, during which it was found that the ship's disposable lift (required for the carrying of passengers, fuel and water, etc.) was only 35 tons compared with the smaller R100's 54 tons.[20]

This problem was exacerbated when during the airworthiness tests resonance was discovered in its engine shafts, forcing them to be run at lower speeds than anticipated. (As a result their power to weight ratio was 8½ lb/hp compared with the

4½lb of the earlier Zeppelin's Maybach engines and the 2½lb of current American radial engines).

Such was the weight imbalance that on 18 December 1929, after the R101 had completed just 102 hours of her required 200 hours' flying time and had yet to undertake full speed tests, it was decided to carry out fundamental alterations to increase the disposable lift to 55 tons. This involved the removal of her servo controls, enlarging her gas bags and – most dramatically of all – inserting a new bay amidships that lengthened her to 777ft. Such late alterations were achieved through twenty-four-hour shift working.

Following this work the R101 attended the Hendon Air Show but on her return journey showed disturbing signs of instability. Even so, after just seventeen hours of test flying with the new conformation, at 6.36 p.m. on 4 October 1930 the R101 set off on her maiden flight to India. Prior to this and despite the fundamental changes made to increase her lift she had taken on board extra equipment required by Lord Thomson to entertain the expected Indian dignitaries upon the ship's arrival.

The weather was stormy and despite the length of the planned journey she behaved sluggishly from the start, with her captain, Flight Lieutenant Herbert Irwin, being forced to drop 4 tons of water ballast to help the initial climb. After circling Bedford the ship set course for London; it was now raining and windy and after slowly rising to 1,500ft she was pitching and rolling even more than before,[21] with the only too likely results for her automatic valves. Her rate of progress over southern England was further slowed by an increasing headwind and mechanical trouble with one of her engines.

She crossed the English coast at Hastings and by mid-Channel was already showing signs of becoming dangerously heavy. Mr Cook, the engineer in charge of the port midship engine, said afterwards that he could distinctly see the waves of the sea being lashed up and considered the R101 to be extremely low over the water, noticing that several times she got lower and then climbed again. Despite the worsening conditions, the ship's crew continued with their appointed tasks and at about 1 a.m. she passed Paix aerodrome between Abbeville and Beauvais, where a French observer M. Maillet said he had the impression that she was struggling very hard against the wind.[22]

Things could hardly continue this way and when at 2 a.m. the ship's watch changed she went into a long and rather steep dive in which the escaped gas inside the envelope rushed upwards to the raised stern. Under the lift of the gas the stern rose against the elevators,[23] down went the nose once more and she hit the ground, immediately bursting into flames. The passengers asleep in their cabins had no chance of escape and things were little better for the crew, whether at their stations or not. Eight men survived out of fifty-four, one of whom was later to die in hospital, either thrown out by the rush of water when the ballast tanks burst or through rents in the airship's fabric.

Among those who died in the crash were Lord Thomson; Sefton Brancker, Director of Civil Aviation; Wing Commander Colmore, Director of Airship Development; and Lieutenant Colonel Richmond, the Assistant Director (Flying Officer).

The disaster not only raised serious questions about the R101's abysmal performance on the day but about the continuing viability of airships as a means of travel. A three-man enquiry that was to report to the new Air Minister, Lord Amulree, had Sir John Simon, lawyer and statesman, as its chairman with pioneer aviator John Moore Brabazon and Professor C.E. Inglis of Cambridge University as members. In the event its findings proved remarkably uncritical, concluding that:

> the accident was caused by the loss of a quantity of gas but how the vessel began to lose gas can never be definitely ascertained … but it seems very probable that it was connected with a specific misfortune such as the ripping of the fore part of the envelope … the explanation that the disaster was caused by a substantial loss of gas in very bumpy weather holds the field … and is the unanimous view of all three members of the Council of Inquiry.[24]

In their defence, with so few surviving witnesses, the Board of Enquiry could never be sure what had actually happened, although it acknowledged that 'the R101 would not have started for India on the evening of 4 October if it had not been that reasons of public policy were considered as making it highly desirable for her to do so if she could', [25] with the Secretary of State urging 'that a start should be made to take him to India and return him for the Imperial Conference'.[26]

However hard the board attempted to be impartial, Lord Thomson's conduct was bound to attract criticism, not only for the signal part he played in the R101's departure time, but also because of his paramount influence over Government policy towards airships. This policy brought about the replacement of Burney's commercial Airship Guarantee Company and its six airships by one Government ship (with permission for a private one to be built by another design team) at a cost of more than £2 million, at a time of collapsing trade, rising unemployment and a growing lobby for aeroplanes.

There was no doubt about Thomson's own high regard for airships, which he spelt out in his book, *Air Facts and Fancies*, where he declared unambiguously that 'lighter air machines are indispensable for the final conquest of air'[27] where airliners would fly 'regularly across continents and oceans with excursion airships and air yachts cruising around our coasts forming part of the regular apparatus of civilization'.[28] He went further, forecasting that in twenty years' time 'great airships (would circle) the globe transporting passengers at prodigious speed and in luxurious safety'.[29]

Ironically, Thomson's near messianic faith in the airship would, if anything, have been buoyed by the successful voyage of the R100 to Canada (which he greeted on its return to Cardington), and he could never have realised the full seriousness of the problems besetting the R101, nor for that matter his personal influence.

What made the tragedy worse was that Thomson's optimism was not shared by the R101's crew, who were more knowledgeable about the ship's problems. The ship's first officer, for instance, had no doubts about its shortcomings. Noel Grabowsky-Atherstone kept a log in which he recorded his personal, often critical, reactions to the preparations for flying to India.

Towards the end of September he wrote: 'I suppose it will be another flap and panic like getting the ship ready for Hendon and I suppose the flying staff will again be called upon to save the faces of the "heads" by taking over the ship in a semi-ready and nearly totally un-airworthy state.'[30]

Despite such remarks, how far Thomson can be held responsible for the lack of proper trials following major alterations to the ship is far more difficult to assess, although the fate of his nationalisation policy and future political advancement undoubtedly rested on R101's journey to India. Whatever the extent of his knowledge about R101's technical difficulties, he rashly increased its lift problems by ordering aboard silver cutlery, glassware, fine porcelain, crates of champagne and an Axminster carpet to cover the floor of the airship's lounge and a 600ft corridor when the lounge alone was the size of an average tennis court. The crew must have been aware of the seriousness of such a decision for they had already been ordered to leave their parachutes behind at Cardington in order to save weight.'[31]

Following the accident, reactions were mixed. On the one hand, Nevil Shute was highly critical, describing the R101 as the plaything of a politician whose belief in the healthy efficiency of a state-run enterprise blinded him to the ship's shortcomings and who embarked on an experimental ship that had never been flown at full power.[32]

In contrast Sir Peter Masefield, a notable supporter of the R101, passed over the design faults and placed blame for the crash squarely on Flying Officer Steff, the R101 control room officer who instead of calling for full power, which along with releasing ballast would have enabled R101 to gain height, in a snap judgement fatally ordered a shutdown of power.[33] Whatever the cost of Steff's decision, Masefield could not deny the serious difficulties that occurred prior to it, nor for that matter dispute that the developmental curve of the aeroplane had been rising above that of the airship.[34]

On Thomson's death Ramsay MacDonald appointed Lord Amulree, a Scottish lawyer, as the new Secretary of State for Air (who like Thomson had no knowledge of aerial matters) and decided that expenditure on airships would be restricted to just £140,000 a year. However, the economic crisis in the latter part of August 1931 caused the Prime Minister to reduce this to a nominal £20,000 a year, and to recommend the successful R100 be sold as scrap without engines and gasbags, and her remains torn apart and run over by a steamroller. The charred remains of the R101 at Beauvais were also broken up and brought back to be made into pots and pans. This marked the end of airships as far as British Aviation was concerned, including as it did the abandonment of a heady project for a R102 of 8.9 million cu.ft with a disposable lift of 226 tons.[35]

———————•◆•———————

By this time Barnes Wallis – the British designer whose airships compared with any in the world, with his successful R100 and his R80 having achieved performance in 'speed, and endurance with ships twice the size'[36] – had moved on to design aeroplanes, and Britain's final airship programme together with its leviathan craft quickly faded into history.

Two quite different Secretaries of State for Air were responsible for its implementation: the determined single-minded but technically ignorant Christopher Thomson, and the ambitious but far more cautious and establishmentwise 'Sam' Hoare. Thomson paid for his ignorance and impatience with his own life and those of many who accompanied him on the R101's inaugural flight while Hoare – who afterwards much regretted letting Thomson's nationalised scheme go forward – was haunted by the fate of those who had taken part in the journey. Although Hoare went on to have a long political career, further questions about his judgement returned with a vengeance during 1936 when as Foreign Secretary he joined the French Prime Minister Pierre Laval to acquiesce in Mussolini's occupation of Abyssinia. This brought about his resignation and resulted in his considerable political achievements to be deliberately unremarked by the House of Lords after his death.

Whatever Thomson's and Hoare's love affair with airships and the hold such great craft had over others in Britain at the time, the vast expenditure on them would surely have been better directed towards investment in more advanced passenger aeroplanes and the development of the country's air routes in both Europe and across the Empire.

BRITAIN AND THE SCHNEIDER TROPHY

The owner of *The Times* and the *Daily Mail*, Alfred Harmsworth, Lord Northcliffe, prided himself on knowing the British psyche as always ready for a challenge, and prior to the First World War he offered massive cash prizes of up to £10,000 for a succession of high-profile air races. He hoped these would not only serve to make the country more air conscious but also encourage the competing constructors to make significant technological advances. His Blue Riband race was a non-stop flight across the Atlantic that had to wait until 1919 before the triumph of Alcock and Brown in their converted Vickers Vimy bomber.

Even so, his races never achieved the international success of those instituted by French aircraft enthusiast Jacques Schneider, although Schneider had nothing like Northcliffe's financial resources and was to die in relative obscurity in much reduced circumstances. Unlike Northcliffe's great prizes, as well as a lavish trophy of silver and

The Schneider Trophy.
(Author's collection)

gold, Schneider's monetary prize of just 25,000 francs (£1,000) went to the winners of the first three competitions only. The races were also more specialist, being limited to seaplanes or what at the time were called hydroaeroplanes. Schneider's races were scheduled to be annual but were in fact only held twelve times between 1913 and 1931. They were normally held over a triangular course with laps of 280km, although later, with higher speeds, these were extended to 350km. The races were staged as time trials with aircraft setting off individually at pre-agreed intervals, usually fifteen minutes apart.

Schneider's intention was to encourage technical advances in aviation and the contests were meant to be held between different nations' aero clubs that could enter teams up to a maximum of three aeroplanes each. The Aero Club of France was to host the inaugural event but following this the winning country was expected to take on such responsibilities. Any club that won the contest three times in five years would take permanent possession of the trophy,[1] representing speed conquering the elements of both sea and air.[2] The races proved very popular and in Britain they attracted crowds of spectators numbering 200,000, with up to 500,000 watching the final one in 1931. The competition attracted teams from France, Italy and the United States as well as Britain and, as Jacques Schneider hoped, it gave a strong incentive to aviation development, especially in the case of engines and the aerodynamics of airframes at a time of utmost financial stringency. With traditional British xenophobia, the British Air Minister, 'Sam' Hoare, considered the trophy 'a very ugly statuette of a symbolic figure in bronze',[3] although the editor of *Flight* magazine acknowledged that 'the importance of the spur which a fixed definite date of such a contest provides cannot easily be overrated'.[4]

The latter's conviction was fully justified by the remarkable advances achieved during the competition's eighteen-year life. By 1931 the competing planes were flying seventy-five times faster than in 1913, and in 1931 the British Rolls-Royce engine produced about fifteen times more power than the widely used Gnome of 1913. Such increased speeds needed streamlined airframes capable of standing up to the vastly increased torque involved[5] where pilots worked under conditions that previously had been considered beyond the limits that men could sustain. In the event, Britain would win the contest five times, more than any other country, and apart from the victory in 1914 of Sopwith's brilliant little Tabloid (a tractor biplane with a 100hp Gnome engine), the four post-war successes were won by the Supermarine Company. Napier Lion engines were used for the victories in 1922 and 1927, to be succeeded in the final and fastest races by the engines of Rolls-Royce.

Like so many achievements in British aviation, its successes in the Schneider Trophy were due to outstanding individuals – two men and one woman playing prominent parts.

Henry Royce (1863–1933) warrants pride of place for his momentous work with aero engines. A Londoner, his early life was one of severe struggle and privation. His father suffered from Hodgkin's disease and after entering a London poorhouse died there before Henry's 9th birthday. At just 4 years of age Henry was made to go bird scaring for money, and this habitually undemonstrative man described one evening, when he was so cold and hungry, how he found it better to join the dog in his outside kennel than stay indoors.[6]

Following his father's death, Henry sold newspapers for W.H. Smith and delivered telegrams in Mayfair after just one year of schooling. At 14 things improved when an aunt agreed to pay £20 a year for him to become an apprentice at the Great Western Railway Company's works in Peterborough. In his spare time he sold more papers and attended evening classes in English and mathematics (probably funded by his newspaper activities). He also learned much about machines and machining from Mr Yarrow, his landlord, who as a craftsman with the Northern Railway had installed a lathe and other tools in his garden shed.

After three years of his apprenticeship his aunt's support ceased and Henry was forced to find work, eventually being taken on as a toolmaker and paid 11s for a fifty-four hour week. After acquiring some knowledge of electricity he installed street lighting in Liverpool until his employers went into liquidation, by which time he had painstakingly saved £20 to join with his friend Earnest Claremont (who contributed £50) to form F.H. Royce and Co., Electrical Engineers. The company set up at Cooke Street in Manchester, where it made electric lamps, and Henry also designed a drum-wound armature for a dynamo.

He worked ferociously, rarely stopping to eat or sleep, and predictably the business progressed before, in 1893, it gained additional strength when the partners somewhat calculatingly

Henry Royce, outstanding engine designer. (Royal Aeronautical Society/National Aerospace Library)

married the two daughters of a licensed victualler and printer, thus bringing in further capital of £1,500. The firm began to design electrically driven gantry cranes and such was its progress that Royce was able to employ a leading architect to build him a family house in the picturebook town of Knutsford, Cheshire. At this time he bought a De Dion quadricycle to save time in travelling from his home to work, and also developed an enthusiasm for gardening, using a patent floodlight to help him plant fruit trees late at night.

By 1902 his long-sustained overwork brought about a collapse, upon which his doctors advised him to visit South Africa. On his return he replaced his quadricycle with a car, a 10hp two-cylinder French Decauville, but predictably it was not long before Royce became dissatisfied with its performance and made a number of improvements, at which his fellow directors gave him permission to build three 'Royce petrol motor cars' to extend the scope of the company's products.

Royce took the Decauville to pieces and had every part drawn before improving and reassembling it with particular help from a gifted toolmaker, Arthur Wormald. The new components proved so accurately constructed and Royce had them so thoroughly tested that for its day the car distinguished itself for both reliability and quietness in running. His fellow director, Henry Edmunds, sent details of the car, complete with photographs, to his friend, pioneer balloonist, racing driver and automobile agent, the Hon Charles Rolls, and arranged a lunchtime meeting for the three of them at the Midland Hotel, Manchester. Afterwards Rolls tried out Royce's car and he was so impressed that he agreed to sell all the cars Royce could make, providing they were called Rolls-Royces. Rolls wrote enthusiastically about their meeting:

> I was fortunate enough to make the acquaintance of Mr Royce, and in him found the man I had been looking for, for years ... in addition to carrying out the general ideas and designs that came from my side, that is from my other colleague, Mr Claude Johnson, and myself, his extraordinary genius has enabled him to effect clever improvements in general and in detail which have been possessed in no other make of car.[7]

Rolls quickly realised that Henry Royce never stopped learning and testing his motor car parts until they approached the limits of their endurance, while on his part from 1904–06 Rolls advertised Royce's cars through a series of reliability tests, trials and races. Rolls-Royce Cars Ltd was registered on 15 March 1906 with a capital of £60,000 and in the following year the site for a new factory was chosen at Derby. There Royce designed the layout for its primary product, his six-cylinder Silver Ghost where, in June 1907, after taking part in the Scottish Reliability trials of more than 15,000 miles, its only problem had been caused by a vibrating petrol cap – which was rectified in thirty seconds. The Silver Ghost remained in production until 1925 and was undeniably the best car in the world, with Royce specifying that 'if any new

Memorial to Charles Rolls. (Author's collection)

feature was intended for it, it should be subjected to 10,000 miles of intensive road test before adoption'.[8]

By 1908 Charles Rolls had become an aeroplane enthusiast and he was keen for the company to manufacture the Wrights' aeroplanes and for Royce to adapt a motor car engine for use in an aeroplane. But like so many others at this time, Royce could see little future in aviation and he refused. The company's car output had risen from six to more than 300 chassis by 1910–11 and he told Rolls that 'if I make an aero engine all my best men will concentrate on the new toy – and cars are our concern'.[9]

After Rolls's fatal air crash in July 1910 at the Bournemouth Aviation Meeting, it was not until the advent of the First World War that Royce was again asked to design an aero engine. By now his earlier punishing work schedules had caught up with him and since 1908 he had experienced serious health problems. Following an operation in 1911, Rolls's great friend and co-director Claude Johnson, aware that he remained the firm's greatest asset, came to the remarkable decision that he should live in the small village of Canadel at the most southerly point of the French Riviera, with adjacent premises for a drawing office complete with skilled draftsmen. A villa named

'La Mimosa' was built to Royce's specifications and this most unusual separation between Royce's design blueprints and production facilities at Derby would continue throughout his life. Remarkably it succeeded and he continued both to initiate and to control the firm's main design projects, including those for aero engines.[10]

In 1911 Royce and his devoted nurse, Ethel Aubin, discovered West Wittering on the English south coast. Royce's wife, Minnie (who had a horror of illness and pregnancy) and their adopted daughter Violet lived separately and in 1921 Royce would buy them a house at Bexhill. At West Wittering Royce and Ethel found a property called Elmstead, which became their summer house, from where after the war he would go to the south of France during the winter and early spring.

In 1914, at the outbreak of war, the Rolls-Royce Company was asked to make the Renault aero engine and the Royal Aircraft Factory's air-cooled RAF1a, but almost inevitably Royce found shortcomings in both and decided to design one himself. Commander Wilfred Briggs of the RNAS liaised with him concerning service requirements and by 11 September 1914 drawings of a provisional engine had been made. This became known as the Eagle, which was first tested in February 1915; it soon produced 225hp, which was increased to 360hp by the end of the war when most other engines produced little over 100hp.[11] Some 6,100 engines were ordered in all and the Eagle took Alcock and Brown on the first west–east crossing of the Atlantic in 1919. A smaller engine, the Falcon, was eventually produced and an even smaller engine, the Hawk, was designed for airship propulsion. Although they had 50 per cent more parts than other comparable engines, all three became noted for reliability.[12]

In 1918, Royce's powerful Condor engine appeared, giving 650hp at 1,900rpm, but after the war the Air Ministry favoured Hispano-Suiza and American Curtiss D12 engines, although they wanted them made by Rolls-Royce. While the company and its chief designer had gained a deservedly high reputation for its wartime aero engines, and continued to produce superlative cars, its aero engine production figures slipped to third place behind cheaper ones produced by Bristol and Napier.

In spite of adverse market conditions for aero constructors during the 1920s, Royce and his staff at West Wittering would never compromise on quality. Powerfully assisted by A.J. Rowledge and E.W. Hives at Derby, they pressed forward with sophisticated new aero engines embodying their latest technical knowledge. In July 1925 they produced an engine called the F10, subsequently renamed the Kestrel, that at its first attempt produced 490hp, soon followed by more powerful supercharged versions. In 1927 they developed the larger and more powerful Buzzard engine giving up to 825hp, the first prototype of which was built in July 1928. This was fortuitous since during the year discussions took place with both Supermarine and the Gloster Aircraft Company about the use of a Rolls-Royce engine for the 1929 Schneider Trophy race, to replace the ageing Napier Lion.

Rolls-Royce's senior directors were far from unanimous about such a limited and specialist contract. Not so the leading aircraft designers at Derby – A.J. Rowledge, E.W. Hives and A.C. Lovesey – who were strongly in favour, and on a bright October morning they went to see Royce at West Wittering. He proved enthusiastic and amid the sand dunes Royce used his walking stick to sketch out a rough outline of a racing engine. During this session 'each man was asked his opinion in turn, the sand raked over and adjustments made. All agreed the key to the engine was simplicity,'[13] and they decided that the projected engine size should be a modified Kestrel with twelve cylinders, against the eighteen in the Italian Isotta-Fraschini and the twenty-four of the American Packard. The secret of the new engine's increased power would lie in supercharging.

Time was to prove remarkably short, for it was not until late February that the Air Ministry's support was finally guaranteed for a race scheduled for later in the year. Royce expected to produce an engine of around 1,500hp but by August it had far exceeded this, running for one hour, twenty minutes at 1,850hp. The race was held at Calshot Water and from a haystack on his small farm Royce was able to watch his new engine power the British entrant to a decisive win. In the following June he was made a baronet, choosing the title of Sir Henry Royce of Seaton in Rutlandshire.

Due to both the RAF's and the Government's reluctance to support the next race in 1931, Royce and his team had just nine months to develop the 'R' engine, which produced an amazing 2,530hp at a specific weight of just 64lb/hp. This duly performed in the race and later in the year the Supermarine S.6b piloted by Flight Lieutenant Stainforth fitted with a sprint version of the 'R' engine put the world air speed record up to 407.5mph.[14]

The engines Royce and his team produced for the 1929 and 1931 Schneider races represented the climax of his life's work, although his thinking did not stop there. With E.W. Hives he had already seen the need for a fighter plane 'that would provide Britain with high quality air defences'[15] and his Schneider engines became the basis for a twelve-cylinder engine of about 1,000hp, first called the PV (private venture) 12, that evolved into the legendary Merlin, the first version of which ran in October 1933.

Royce died at home in 1933 and his obituarists struggled to capture the essentials of such a modest and retiring man. Aerial commentator Ivan Evernden unflatteringly believed he was essentially a mechanic, commenting, 'he was suspicious of academic learning and regarded it as just another tool in the toolbox to be used only as a last resort'.[16] However, Royce's fellow director Sydney Veale had no doubt that the secret of his achievements lay in his universally high aims. His life was dominated by the demon of perfection, never knowing peace of mind until he was satisfied that a thing could not be improved upon. He hated mediocrity. For Royce, only the best was good enough[17] and from 1929 producing engines to win Schneider Trophy races challenged him to the limit.

———— • ◆ • ————

However good Royce's engines, the British successes in the post-war Trophy races would have been impossible without airframes, developed by the pre-eminent aeroplane designer of his time, R.J. Mitchell. Born in 1895, Reginald Mitchell was the eldest son of Herbert and his wife Elizabeth, who with their five children lived in Stoke-on-Trent. Herbert was managing director and sole owner of a printing works at Normacot that put the family in a comfortable financial position, although not much expense was spent on Reg's education and like so many other major figures in aviation at this time he was obliged to seek self-help. At 16, after finishing school, where he had already shown a keen interest in designing, making and flying model aeroplanes, his father enrolled him as an apprentice at the locomotive engineering firm of Kerr, Stuart and Co. of Stoke. During his five-year term there he took evening classes in engineering drawing, higher mathematics and mechanics, where he excelled in mathematics.

Although on the outbreak of war Mitchell volunteered for the forces he was rejected because of his engineering skills, but in 1917 at 22 years of age he applied for a post as personal assistant to Hubert Scott-Paine, managing director of the small aviation company of Supermarine at Woolston, Southampton. He succeeded and it was there that all his subsequent work as an aircraft designer took place. The factory, which came under Government control during the war, made seaplanes and flying boats and in his design work at this time Mitchell's son, Gordon, believed he soon showed an 'intuitive understanding of aerodynamic problems' over those 'whose formal training in aerodynamics had gone much further than his own'.[18] In 1918 he was made assistant works manager when the firm's design team still numbered six draughtsmen and a secretary, but following the departure of the chief designer in the next year, Mitchell succeeded him.

After Supermarine regained its independence its owner, Scott-Paine, wanted to build a plane to compete in the first Schneider Trophy race after the war. With both time and money short, it was decided to use the Supermarine Sea Baby that had been built during the war to Air Ministry specifications. It was given a 450hp Napier Lion engine and renamed Sea Lion I, but it hit an obstacle and sank before Mitchell's work on modifying the original design could become evident. The race, held off Bournemouth, was marred by fog and although the Italians came in first it was found that they had completed a shorter course than intended. The result was therefore disallowed, but it was agreed that the next race should be held in Italy.

Although Scott-Paine's ambitions for the Schneider contests did not slacken, neither Supermarine nor any other British manufacturer entered the 1920 and 1921 races for they could not afford to send their planes to Venice and have some of their workforce stay there for weeks at a time. The Italians won the trophy on both occasions, while at Supermarine much attention was paid to the development of long-distance flying boats.

Scott-Paine decided to enter the 1922 contest but, lacking official support, money was short and Mitchell therefore had to modify the company's entry of three years before. While this again used a 450hp Napier Lion engine, Mitchell attempted to gain what advantage he could from 'cleaning up' the fuselage. The plane was produced in strict secrecy and during its trials, including one when the engine cut out over a mass of moored shipping, it reached creditable speeds of up to 163mph. Following this it was shipped over to Naples to compete against teams of Italian and French aircraft that had received substantial government assistance.

The day before the race all the French flying boats retired with engine trouble, leaving the single Supermarine entry to face three Italian contenders. During the race Mitchell's plane, piloted by the company's chief test pilot, Henri Biard, set a relatively low lap speed of 147.5mph, although it exceeded the fastest Italian aeroplane by just 2.5mph. This proved an outstanding success for Supermarine and its dated aircraft and Mitchell, still only 27, set out to strengthen his design teams to meet the increased orders expected. He was enthusiastically supported by Commander James Bird who, after becoming a director in 1919, took over the company from Scott-Paine in 1925. Bird well knew that the high demands Mitchell habitually asked of his fellow employees were only possible because of his own fierce application and readiness to take on any task, following which he became 'one of the boys' outside working hours when he took part in their sporting activities.[19]

After Supermarine's victory, the 1923 Trophy race was due to be held at Cowes, where curiosity was aroused by a new and powerful challenge from the Americans with their three seaplanes (two Curtiss CR-3s and a Wright NW-2) sponsored by the American Navy and flown by specially trained service pilots, Lieutenants Rittenhouse, Irvine, Gorton and Weald. Although the Italians failed to appear, the French entered three flying boats and the English challenge again relied on two private entries, the Blackburn Pellet (built on a small budget and not assembled at Southampton until 26 September) and Supermarine's Sea Lion III. Owing to the limited time in which to build a contender, Scott-Paine borrowed back Sea Lion II from the Air Ministry and gave Mitchell the task of increasing its speed by at least 10 knots. Despite such limited scope, Mitchell reduced the wingspan, produced more streamlined floats and 'neatened' the plane's nose section, while Napier played its part with an extra 50hp of engine power.

On the day of the race only Sea Lion III and one French aircraft went to the starting line against two American Curtiss CR-3s, but it quickly became obvious that the Americans were faster; Biard in the revamped Sea Lion III could only come a well-beaten third, more than 20mph behind the Americans. At Supermarine they were badly shaken by the result, seeing their designs 'as clearly out of date and with their parsimonious Government they doubted whether it would ever return to Britain, for the Americans had changed the game, moving the trophy into an inter-air service contest with the competing countries' 'best machines pitted against each other and Governments footing the bill'.[20]

Mitchell's bold riposte was to discard the flying boat for a new British seaplane, while Supermarine underlined its confidence in him by extending his post of chief engineer for a further ten years. Although he was fully involved in designs for a number of other planes, including a land plane, the Americans sportingly agreed to postpone the next Schneider race until 1925 when Mitchell could compete again. His constructive genius became apparent with the building of a revolutionary monoplane with cantilever wings requiring no external struts nor wire strengtheners. Such developments were expensive but fortunately the Air Ministry's Technical Branch agreed to allocations from their experimental funds because air racing provided an unrivalled proving ground 'in which development would be forced along in the white heat of competition'.[21] Such beliefs were not shared by Sir Hugh Trenchard, the RAF's redoubtable Chief of the Air Staff, who continued to have strong misgivings about such races and even more about Air Force personnel spending their time flying in them. In such circumstances the technical board made their acceptance conditional upon the planes being loaned to the makers, flown by the makers' pilots and maintained by their crews when actually racing.

For the 1925 Schneider contest, Supermarine's entrant, the S.4, was a monoplane, still very largely of wooden construction and covered with a plywood skin although it was said to have set a new standard for 'clean and elegant aerodynamic lines, in its design round a twelve-cylinder, 700hp Napier Lion engine'.[22] By August 1925 it was ready, having been built in just five months, and on 13 September Mitchell's advances in design became apparent when Henri Biard used it to set up a new world air speed record of 226.75mph, although its racing performance around a set track was yet unproven.

In mid September the Supermarine team left for America in the SS *Minnewaska* along with two Gloster III racing biplanes and their pilots. Supermarine's high hopes ended suddenly when during its test flights at Baltimore the plane crashed into the sea, although its pilot was picked up after almost an hour in the icy water. Various reasons were put forward for the crash including a stall, aileron flutter and, most disturbing of all, because it was thought the cantilever wings had exceeded the bounds of aerodynamic and structural knowledge at the time.

The race was won by the American pilot Lieutenant Jimmy Doolittle flying a Curtiss racer at an average speed of 232.57mph, with one of the Glosters coming second at 199.1mph. Afterwards Doolittle set up a new world air speed record of 245.71mph in a machine that more than anything else represented a fighter prototype on floats.

Italian dictator Benito Mussolini, whose enthusiastic support brought about his country's success in the Schneider Trophy. (Author's collection)

However serious the setback, Mitchell still believed he was on the right lines with his new monoplane conformation, but with the 1926 Schneider contest due to take place in Virginia and with Supermarine having insufficient time to design a new machine there was no British entry, although Air Vice-Marshal Sir Geoffrey Salmond, the air member for supply and research on the Air Council, went against his CAS in hoping that Britain might be able to produce a winner by 1927.

The Americans aimed for a third victory and outright ownership of the trophy but their aircraft had reached the end of their development cycles, and the country was fast losing interest in speed races in favour of developing long-distance air transport.

It was different in Italy where Benito Mussolini had come to power. He *commanded* his aerial constructors to win the trophy, giving them virtual carte blanche as far as money was concerned. In response they produced a beautiful monoplane on floats, the Macchi M.39 (an amalgam of Mitchell's S.4 and the American Curtiss) powered by a Fiat V12 liquid-cooled engine producing 800hp. In the hands of

The ultra-streamlined Supermarine S.5. (Author's collection)

Major de Bernardi it succeeded in winning at a speed of 246.5mph, 15mph faster than the American Lieutenant Frank Schilt, who came second.

Supermarine returned to the contest for the 1927 race, where Mitchell kept faith with his designs so far. His plans centred on a seaplane that he numbered S.5 after carrying out a series of wind tunnel and tank tests on his earlier S.4 at the Royal Aircraft Establishment and the National Physical Laboratory. Without such assistance the cost would have been beyond the resources of Supermarine. However, the company still lacked the support required for organising its entry or trained service pilots (like the Americans) to fly its planes, but Trenchard remained blind to the merits of a contest that he believed was 'merely producing freak machines'.[23]

It was May 1927 before the Air Ministry relented and agreed to take on the organisation of the British entries, and Trenchard finally gave his consent for the formation of an RAF High Speed Flight to pilot British aircraft in the race (other British entries included three Folland-designed Gloster biplane aircraft and a Roy Fedden-designed Short–Bristow seaplane with an air-cooled engine).

For this competition Mitchell gave his low-wing S.5 an all-metal fuselage from which the pilot enjoyed better visibility. However, its wings were still made of wood with spars and plywood skins, and he kept the 900hp Napier Lion engine, despite the possibility of a new Rolls-Royce engine with greater capability. In July 1927 Flight Lieutenant S.N. Webster flew it at more than 275mph and reported 'very nice, no snags'.

Following the withdrawal of the Americans and French, the British had only the Italians for opponents. In what proved an eventful race, there were only two finishers: Flight Lieutenant Webster who, in Mitchell's S.5, reached an average speed of 281.66mph (a new air speed record for both sea and land planes) and the other S.5, piloted by Flight Lieutenant Worsley, who came second. Afterwards Webster played tribute to both Mitchell's skills and his personal qualities, referring to him as 'an ideal man to know, kind, steady, duty-minded with no conceit. He was a good mixer and got on well with his workpeople and the RAF pilots'.[24]

During the following year Supermarine was taken over by Vickers but as Mitchell was the firm's greatest asset it was made conditional on him signing an agreement to stay at Supermarine until the end of 1933. For its part Vickers agreed to keep his design team together.

In 1928 it was decided to hold the Schneider contest every two years instead of one, which meant the next race – to be held in Britain – would not be until 1929. This proved invaluable for Mitchell, giving him more time to design a new aeroplane in which he decided to install a Rolls-Royce engine, thus finally uniting the work of the two leading designers in British aviation. The benefits soon became evident when Rolls-Royce gave Mitchell the assurance that the engine would produce at least 1,500hp, and be capable of development up to 1,900hp with little or no increase in its frontal area. For this new design Mitchell decided that both the wings and fuselage would be of duralumin with the radiators made of a light alloy rather than copper.

The Supermarine S.6 with its more powerful Rolls-Royce 'R' engine. (Author's collection)

The elegant Italian Macchi M.52. (Author's collection)

Despite the British success in 1927, Trenchard again proved reluctant to form a new RAF High Speed Flight, not giving his permission until February 1929, although the opposition slackened with the withdrawal of the French team following the death of their best pilot in a crash and with the single American entry failing to turn up, although the Italians arrived at Cowes before the end of August. Mitchell quickly established good relationships with the service pilots, although his S.6 experienced difficulties during the trials, including an inability to get into the air that he quickly solved by transferring more of the fuel to its starboard float. The problems continued up to the eve of the race. S.6 serial number N248 sprung a leak in one of its floats, which was successfully sealed, but on the night preceding the race a far more serious problem came to light: while the plugs for N247 were being replaced it was realised that an urgent engine change was required. Fortunately, a party of Rolls-Royce mechanics had come from Derby to watch the race. They were roused from their beds by the police and after working through the night succeeded in having the plane ready by early the next morning.

Flying Officer 'Dick' Waghorn won the race in N247 at the sensational average speed of 328.63mph, with the older Italian Macchi M.52R coming second at 284.3mph (more than 40mph slower). Mitchell's older S.5 piloted by Flight Lieutenant Greig was just behind with a speed of 282.1mph and shortly afterward Squadron Leader Orlebar (Head of the Racing Flight) set up a new world speed record of 357.7mph.

Mitchell's beautiful new plane powered by its magnificent Rolls-Royce engine had utterly outclassed the Italians and just one more victory was needed to give

Britain the trophy outright. Unbelievably, Mitchell's chances of competing in 1931 seemed poor, for with the serious economic depression worldwide, the Government seemed unlikely to support the building of two new aircraft, while Trenchard's RAF co-operation was again unsure when he repeated that he could see no value in the Schneider Trophy and even persuaded himself that the whole thing was bad for morale.

In January 1931 the situation became even worse when the Labour Government's Chancellor of the Exchequer, Philip Snowden, said he wanted to end 'the race's pernicious rivalry between nations' and announced that the machines and pilots of the High Speed Flight would not be loaned to defend the trophy, nor would the services of the Navy or the Air Force be available to help with its running.'[25] Snowden made his decision despite a stream of newspaper articles and petitions in its favour, including one from the Society of Aircraft Manufacturers, which predictably maintained that the 'British victories in the last two Schneider Contests have given the British techniques, both in aircraft and engines, a prestige in the eyes of foreign buyers. A loss of the Trophy will mean a loss in export trade'.[26] In support of his chancellor, Ramsay MacDonald ruled that the machines and men could only be loaned out if £100,000 was made available from private funds, something that seemed most unlikely during the prevailing financial convulsions. The situation was finally saved by the colourful, if unlikely, figure of Lady Fanny Lucy Houston, whose life up to that point had followed bewildering twists of fortune.

Born in 1857, the ninth child of a woollen warehouseman and draper who lived in St Paul's Churchyard, the striking-looking Lucy became a chorus girl known as 'Poppy'. At 16 she attracted the attention of Fred Gratton, a millionaire brewer who left his wife to set up home with her in Paris, where she learned

Lady Fanny Houston. (National Portrait Gallery)

society manners by mingling with archdukes and princes and even the future English king, Edward VII. On Gratton's death she was left with an income of £6,000 a year that enabled her to take a house in Portland Place. Her social respectability was further enhanced when she married the bankrupt knight, Sir Theodore Brinkman, whom she eventually divorced in 1895 after a long separation. In 1901 she married again, this time to the 9th 'red-nosed' Lord Byron and, as his wife, attended the coronation of George V.

From now onwards Lucy exhibited a keen interest in politics, becoming an active suffragette who at one time bought 615 parrots (in red, white and blue cages) and tried to teach them to shout 'votes for women'.[27] During the First World War, after setting up a rest home for nurses who had served at the front, she was made a Dame Commander of the British Empire.

Byron died in 1917 and in 1922, while she was a guest on Sir Thomas Lipton's yacht, Lucy met the reputedly 'hard, ruthless, unpleasant bachelor'[28] Sir Robert Houston, a wealthy shipping magnate and Member of Parliament for West Toxteth, who two years later became her final husband. Lucy had no difficulty holding her end up with him for, on being shown his will in which he left her £1 million, she tore it up 'declaring that if that was all she was worth, she wanted nothing'. At this 'the will was redrawn and when Lord Houston died in 1926 he left her not only six million

LEFT TO RIGHT.
M & CO.   F/LT. E. J. L. HOPE, A.F.C., THE LATE LT. G. L. BRINTON, R.N.,   "FLIGHT" COPYRIGHT PHOTO
FLT LTS. F. W. LONG & G. H. STAINFORTH: SQDN LDR. A. H. ORLEBAR, A.F.C.,
F/LT. J. N. BOOTHMAN, F/O. L. S. SNAITH, F/LT. W. F. DRY.

Squadron Leader Orlebar and the members of the RAF Special High Speed Flight for the 1931 Schneider Trophy Race. (Author's collection).

pounds'[29] but his yacht *Liberty*. The Houstons lived on Jersey as tax exiles and after his death she personally gave a cheque for £1.6 million to the then Chancellor of the Exchequer, Winston Churchill, to cover her husband's death duties and enable her to re-enter British public life.

As a self-assumed champion of the British state, she publically berated the Prussians, the Russian Bolsheviks and the Labour Governments of Ramsay MacDonald, and in 1931 offered the £100,000 required for the Schneider Trophy that year in order to see Britain supreme everywhere.[30] MacDonald had little option but to pass on her contribution to the Royal Aero Club and the new head of the RAF, Sir John Salmond, saying: 'On balance I'm bound to come to the view that Britain ought to take part in the race.'[31]

Mitchell was thus able to go ahead and prepare for a contest just seven months away. With the race so close, rather than going for a different aircraft he contented himself with changes to the S.6 design. In essence this meant accommodating a more powerful Rolls-Royce engine, which after ear-shattering and prolonged tests at Derby produced a remarkable 2,500hp. Mitchell constructed two new S.6B seaplanes with serial numbers S1595 and S1596, and modified the S.6As to take the latest engines, while a new RAF High Speed Flight, again under Squadron Leader A.H. Orlebar, was formed. On 21 July the first S.6B arrived at Calshot and was taken out by Squadron Leader Orlebar, following which Mitchell quickly solved major problems with regard to its lift and stability – although a tragedy occurred when the High Speed Flight's Lieutenant 'Jerry' Brinton of the Fleet Air Arm was killed taking off in a modified S.6A.

On 3 September the future of the race was again brought into doubt when both France and Italy put in a formal request for postponement to carry out further work on their planes, only to have them refused by the British Royal Aero Club. As a result Britain remained the only competitor, although plans for the race went ahead with Flight Lieutenant J.W. Boothman being selected to go and win the trophy, while Flight Lieutenant Stainforth was scheduled to set a new world air speed record.

On 13 September 1931 Flight Lieutenant Boothman completed the seven laps of the course at an average speed of 340.08mph, although to avoid overheating he did not open his throttle fully. Later he capped his day by setting a new world air speed record of 379.05mph. With this third victory Britain won the Schneider Trophy outright – upon which the Air Ministry immediately set about dismantling the High Speed Flight and returning Calshot to its normal flying boat duties, in spite of both Supermarine and Rolls-Royce wanting to exceed the magic 400mph. Following a personal appeal by Sir Henry Royce, Flight Lieutenant Stainforth in S1595 finally achieved an average speed of 407.5mph using an engine that produced 2,350hp. Following this success, while speaking at an official dinner the following month, the Mayor of Southampton declared that at 36 years of age Mitchell was 'one of the most brilliant aircraft designers in the world'.[32] In his reply Mitchell not only revealed his continuing ambitions but also what he believed were the unique contributions of the Schneider Trophy by reminding his audience that 'we have now reached the stage … that we may digest and utilise the mass knowledge and experience that we have now gained'.[33]

During early 1932 on BBC radio Mitchell again talked about the special impetus from the Schneider Trophy: in such a case 'it is not good enough to follow conventional methods of design. It is essential to break new ground and to invent and involve new methods and new ideas'.[34] The same beliefs were felt at Rolls-Royce, for after the 1931 contest A.F. Sidgreaves, the company's managing director, issued the following statement about the trophy's importance for his company:

> From the development point of view the Schneider Trophy contest is almost an economy because it saves so much time in arriving at certain technical improvements. It is not too much to say that research for the Schneider Trophy contest over the past two years is what our aero-engine department would otherwise have taken six to ten years to learn … for the last few years Britain's supremacy in the manufacture of aircraft is generally recognised, and is due to the experience and knowledge gained in contests such as that for the Schneider Trophy.[35]

As Sidgreaves well realised, following Mitchell's earlier achievements in the competition and the coming together of Royce's and Mitchell's companies for the 1929 and 1931 Schneider competitions, Britain obtained that spurt in engine technology and airframe development that would subsequently give it the interceptors needed against massed German air assaults and help return the RAF to a more credible aerial strategy:

Winners in the Races for the Schneider Trophy 1913–31

Year	Pilot	Country	Aircraft	Engine	Speed	Location	Distance
1913	Maurice Prevost	France	Deperdussin	160hp Gnome	45.75mph	Monaco	280 km over water
1914	Howard Pixton	GB	Sopwith Tabloid	100hp Gnome	86.78mph	Monaco	280 km over water
1919	Sgt Guido Jannello	Italy	Savoia	250hp Isotta-Fraschini		Bourne-mouth	Disqualified race void
1920	Lt Luigi Bologna	Italy	Savoia S.12	550hp Ansaldo	107.22mph	Venice	371.17km
1921	Giovanni de Briganti	Italy	Macchi M.7	250hp Isotta-Fraschini	117.00mph	Venice	393.6km

1922	Henri Biard	GB	Supermarine Sea Lion II	450hp Napier Lion	145.7mph	Naples	370.5km
1923	Lt David Rittenhouse	USA	Curtiss CR-3	465hp Curtiss D-12	177.38mph	Cowes	344.69 km
1925	Lt James H. Doolittle	USA	Curtiss R3C-2	600hp Curtiss V 1400	232.57mph	Baltimore	350km
1926	Major Mario de Bernardi	Italy	Macchi M.39	882hp Fiat AS2	246.5mph	Hampton Roads	350km
1927	Flt Lt S.N. Webster	GB	Supermarine S.5	900hp Napier Lion VIIA	281.65mph	Venice	350km
1929	Fg Officer H.W. Wagnorn	GB	Supermarine S.6	1,900hp Rolls-Royce R	328.63mph	Calshot	350km
1931	Flt Lt J.N. Boothman	GB	Supermarine S.6B	2,350hp Rolls-Royce R	340.08mph	Calshot	350km

Lady Fanny Houston's massive contribution of £10,000 for the 1931 Schneider contest was replicated two years later by a similar contribution – with the guarantee of a further £5,000 – for the Houston Mount Everest Expedition of 3 April 1933, which succeeded in sending two single-engined aircraft to look down on and photograph the top of Mount Everest.

GENEVA TALKS: BOMBERS UNDER THREAT

With the end of Hugh Trenchard's long reign as the RAF's Chief of the Air Staff, change was only to be expected. What could never have been anticipated was that, after his skilled and undoubtedly successful defence of his service, in less than three years there would be a mortal threat not only to its offensive capability but to its very existence.

In the face of such a challenge the ability of the RAF's Secretary of State for Air and its Chief of the Air Staff were of obvious importance. After Trenchard's near decade in office, there was a general understanding that his successor's term of office should not exceed three years. Yet whatever Sir John Salmond's length of office he was bound to have enjoyed Trenchard's approval, since his prior achievements were such that he had to be the prime candidate. Salmond's biographer, John Laffin, believed him to be an outstanding figure, both great and enduring, whose stature was no less than that of Trenchard and whose ideas were always ahead of his time.[1]

Yet even Laffin acknowledged that Salmond was something of a contradiction – quietly voluble, restrainedly spectacular, a perfect gentleman who knew, however, how to be ruthless.[2] Beneath Laffin's literary flourishes one gathers that, however capable and unquestionably committed, he did not see Salmond as a natural publicist, nor someone like

Sir John Salmond. (National Portrait Gallery)

Trenchard with the endurance to fire off endless memoranda or excel in forthright exchanges with dissenting politicians or the heads of the other two services. This was unfortunate for from the time of his arrival he had to debate with politicians seeking a formula for disarmament who grossly overestimated the effects of the RAF's bombing capability, leading RAF air historian Henry Probert to believe that in the circumstances he could have been expected to do little more than mark time.[3]

As sons of a general, both John and his brother, Geoffrey, took the Sandhurst entrance examination, which John passed at his second attempt.

Gazetted as a second lieutenant into the King's Own Royal Lancaster Regiment, he went to South Africa during the Anglo–Boer War and was then seconded to the Nigerian West African Frontier Force, thereby satisfying his desire for adventure where he reputedly 'learned much about leadership, fellowship, administration and politics.'[4] He also developed an enthusiasm for aviation and on returning to the UK as a captain his chosen subject for the young officers' annual essay competition was 'The use of airships and aeroplanes in war'. In his submission he maintained that 'aircraft would play an increasingly important role in warfare through reconnaissance and that bombing would become a standard operation'.[5]

From now on, aviation was his passion and after passing his flying test in 1912 he was attached to the Royal Flying Corps, attending its Central Flying School at Larkhill. There he quickly proved to be a capable pilot and skilled instructor, and in December 1913 he set a British altitude record of 13,140ft.

At the outbreak of war, Salmond was made commander of 3 Squadron in France, whose crucial role was to discover information about German troop movements, before he went back to England to command the RFC training wing at Farnborough. On returning to France, he commanded the RFC's 2 wing in the rank of Lieutenant Colonel. There he showed himself personally fearless, becoming involved in the development of air fighting tactics before being promoted in 1916 to Brigadier-General to reorganise pilot training in Britain.

Under his energetic direction the number of flying schools increased from forty-seven to seventy-eight, and after he had personally undertaken the course at Gosport, the advanced methods of his instructor, Colonel Smith-Barry, were adopted throughout the RAF.[6]

In October 1917 Salmond's career accelerated further when, aged just 36, he was promoted to Major General and appointed to the Army Council, the youngest to be so chosen, although as a dashing commander he apparently became most 'frustrated with the political intrigues endemic in London and yearned to return to the Front'.[7] In January 1918 he got his wish when succeeding Trenchard as commander of the RFC (and then the RAF) in France. He had sixty-three squadrons at his disposal during the time of the great German offensive and the Allied counter-offensive, in which the RAF played a major part despite suffering high casualties in the process.

It was entirely fitting that Salmond should command the RAF contingent[8] at the post-war Victory Parade and then be made Air Officer Commanding Mesopotamia, which was undergoing an insurgency at that time. Trenchard believed it could be policed by the RAF at far less cost than the Army, and Salmond justified Trenchard's faith with judicious bombing of the opposing tribesmen followed by the rapid movement of troops by air to restore order to the endangered areas.

On his return to Britain he commanded the operational Air Force, but with money extremely short, the great majority of his planes including his bombers were of First World War vintage, despite Trenchard's current doctrine that 'since there was no way of fully defending one's country against air attack, the main weight of the Air Force must be committed to strategic bombing of the enemy's main centres of military preparations'.[9]

Although Salmond had held all the most important subordinate posts[10] before becoming CAS in 1930, none of them could prepare him for disputing with senior politicians about the RAF's continuing place in national security. Such circumstances required skills beyond those of military command, and needed the full support of his Secretary of State for Air, and in this, Salmond was unlucky, for during his term as CAS this post suffered a high turnover.

His first chief was Lord Christopher Thomson, who became Secretary of State for Air on 8 June 1929 after having acted in the same capacity during Ramsay MacDonald's short-lived Labour Government of 1924. Thomson was an ex-soldier and, although a keen supporter of international government through the League of Nations, he believed the RAF was needed to 'defend us and our shores against attacks by continental Air Forces'.[11] However, Thomson's particular passion was for airships rather than aeroplanes, and any opportunity to develop a close working relationship between them was cut short by his death in the airship R101 at Beauvais in France on 5 October 1930. Thomson was succeeded by Lord Amulree, a veteran Scottish lawyer and industrial arbiter with no particular knowledge of air matters, who was catapulted into the post on Thomson's death.

Amulree's term of office was undistinguished and lasted just one year, during which time his most important tasks were setting up a public enquiry into the loss of the R101 and the introduction of the Air Estimates for 1931–32 on 17 March 1931. These showed a net total of £18,100,000, not much above a third of the Royal Navy's, although they included a small increase over the previous year to help bring the RAF's Home Defence Squadrons up to forty-two – still ten below the figure proposed by 'Sam' Hoare when he was Secretary of State eight years earlier. Only two-thirds of these belonged to the regular Air Force, with the others working on a non-regular basis or belonging to the Auxiliary Air Force.

In view of the country's current economic difficulties, despite the RAF's small size and low cost compared with the other two services, Salmond faced repeated demands for cutbacks during Amulree's term of office. In the spring of 1931 an independent committee under a leading actuary, Sir George May, was committed to achieving practicable and legitimate reductions by not only recommending the end of expenditure on airships, but also looking at other departments of the Air Ministry.[12]

The pressure was so strong that Salmond, who still valued the support of his old chief, Trenchard, wrote to him on 4 May 1931 telling him that he had had a whole morning with the committee 'and the first question I was asked by the Chairman was to justify the existence of the Air Force as a separate service. I talked for an hour and a half describing our commands and operations and the enormous amount of money we have saved the Government …'[13] Trenchard might well have concluded that little seemed to have changed since his own time as CAS, although in his case he would never have sought the approval of a predecessor.

In October 1931, on the election of a national Government, Amulree was replaced by the Marquess of Londonderry who, at this time, also acquired a seat in the Cabinet. In just over a year Salmond acquired his third political chief who, in addition to his aerial duties, would be required to deputise for the British Prime Minister, Ramsay MacDonald, at the coming International Disarmament Conference beginning in Geneva on 2 February 1932. This effectively served to divide his loyalties, although Londonderry soon raised concerns about the implications of the discussions for the RAF.

Before the conference convened he had specifically warned against what he viewed as irresponsible disarmament proposals, believing it was time to face realities and recognise what was happening elsewhere, notably the Japanese invasion of Manchuria, its bombing of Chinese towns and the fighting taking place between the two countries in disregard of the League's Covenant. In his book *Wings of Destiny*, where he subsequently justified his own conduct at the conference, Londonderry recalled how he went 'to Geneva with an open mind determined to maintain a common-sense attitude in regard to the general question of disarmament and particularly in relation to the Air Forces'.[14] Whatever his writings, no Secretary of State for Air could approve disarmament proposals that effectively neutralised the RAF, especially as he discovered that France and Italy (and subsequently Germany) looked on the talks at the conference as largely academic and certain to be barren of a result.

Whatever Londonderry's stance, most of the Cabinet were decidedly not open-minded, with Stanley Baldwin genuinely believing that if Britain stopped rearming, other nations would follow. This was all the more alarming for the Air Secretary and his CAS because in 1932 the RAF was already in a weak bargaining position with its first-line strength having fallen behind France, the Soviet Union, the United States and Italy. Now it seemed that any attempts to increase its squadrons towards the long anticipated figure of fifty-five were about to cease for two years. The Air Estimates for 1932–33 made things no better, for when they were introduced in Parliament they showed a further reduction of £700,000 on the previous year, when as Londonderry observed in his book, 'with the exception of ourselves, no Power, small or great, had any intention of reducing its armed forces'.[15]

For all that, the conference's discussions went beyond reductions to consider the actual cessation of bombing, a decision requiring the partial disbandment of national air forces, including that of Britain.

It was against such an unfavourable background that Salmond, as head of the RAF, and Londonderry, his recently appointed Secretary of State for Air – who periodically had to deputise for the Prime Minister – strove to maintain the independence and efficiency of their service.

Londonderry possessed a strong platform for political advancement, coming as he did from a leading family with a long history of public service, whose forebears included the famous politician and second Marquess, Lord Castlereagh, to whom Londonderry aspired. After Eton he went to the Royal Military Academy Sandhurst and was commissioned into the Royal Horse Guards. With his military credentials secure, at his father's urging, in 1897 he entered politics and was elected as Conservative MP for Maidstone, a seat he held from 1906 to 1915 until he succeeded his father as 7th Marquess. During the First World War he acted as ADC to Lieutenant General Sir William Pulteney, following which he was made second in command of his regiment and was twice mentioned in despatches.

Following the war, Londonderry's first acquaintance with aviation came in 1920–21 when he was made Finance Minister to the Air Ministry, and after a period as Commissioner of Works during 1931 he was appointed Secretary of State for Air in Ramsay MacDonald's National Parliament. Although a genuine air enthusiast, Londonderry's position was not favoured by the general belief

Anthony Eden, Under-Secretary for Foreign Affairs and until 1930 a strong believer in disarmament. (Author's collection)

that he owed the appointment (together with his place in the Cabinet) to the close friendship of the Prime Minister with Londonderry's wife, Edith, the set joke being that the ex-crofter MacDonald changed his tune from the 'Red Flag' to the 'Londonderry Air'!

He aggravated this opinion for, instead of being grateful, the haughty Londonderry believed he had already missed his best chances to gain high responsibility (a prevailing belief of his) and that his talents had not yet been properly used.[16]

In any event, the pacifist feeling within the British Cabinet at the Disarmament Conference made it highly unlikely that either Salmond or Londonderry would achieve their personal ambitions, in Salmond's case to emerge from the shade of his great predecessor and in Londonderry's to show others that he was undoubtedly qualified for the highest offices of state – with the RAF only too likely to lose out as a result. To their credit both quickly spoke in favour of its continuing independence.

In June 1932 Salmond pointed out that while the RAF was only the fifth largest air force in the world it had a massive responsibility to defend London, which was 'to a unique degree the heart, arsenal and treasury of the Empire and just fifteen minutes flying time from the coast'.[17] To keep parity with France he maintained that either the RAF should be built up or the French should be pared down, although the imbalance between the two countries was made even worse by Britain's inferior position in civil aviation, where France had eight times as many civil airliners. As a result he rightly concluded that further disarmament or even further restrictions on the RAF would be a fatal mistake.

Londonderry struck a similar warning note with his patronising observation that it was time for the Cabinet to come back to earth and recognise reality. He referred once more to Japanese aggression in complete disregard of the League Covenant and justly observed that: 'When a Great Power has made up its mind on a certain course of action which will involve it in accusations of a breach of the Covenant and of the Kellogg Pact, it is certain that it will not be deterred from its course of action by such a minor matter as a theoretical breach of the Convention.'[18]

This was contrary to the majority views of British politicians at the conference, who sought a written agreement whatever its effect on the Air Force's viability. After the Disarmament Conference formally opened on 2 February 1932 Stanley Baldwin, an ex-Prime Minister and President of the Council, urged the British Government to begin discussions concerning what he described as a prohibition of bombing. Baldwin enjoyed the powerful support of other senior Cabinet members including Sir John Simon (Foreign Secretary), Sir Philip Cunliffe-Lister (Secretary of State for the Colonies), J.H. Thomas (Secretary of State for Dominion Affairs), Sir Maurice Sankey (Secretary of the Cabinet), Anthony Eden (Parliamentary Under-Secretary to the Foreign Office, who was representing the Foreign Office in Simon's absence), and the Army and Navy officials. In opposition, Londonderry and Salmond could depend on the lone support of Sir 'Sam' Hoare, former Secretary of State for Air.

The situation became even more serious for the RAF when on 7 July 1932 Anthony Eden – who was even more committed to limiting air armaments than his superior, John Simon – delivered a white paper calling for the prohibition of all bombing, save within limits to be laid down as precisely as possible by an international convention. This also called for a prohibition against aerial attacks on the population, together with weight limits on military and naval aircraft and a reduction in their numbers.[19] In such circumstances Trenchard's doctrine of deterrence – against which serious queries were already being raised – would have become completely unworkable.

The next week Eden's superior, Simon, went even further by proposing an unconditional ban on bombing.

In response, Salmond said he believed Eden's paper represented a dangerous and irresponsible step, for 'if a country is fighting for its survival it is inconceivable that any threatened nation would observe an agreement that has nothing in logic or common sense to recommend it'.[20]

At the same time Londonderry pointed out that British security was absolutely dependent on bombing aircraft – because air defences could not be assured by fighters alone and empty promises were insufficient to ensure security and *merely gave an illusion of security*. He revealed his exasperation in a letter to his wife: 'It is really like a man sitting on the bough of a tree, sawing it off and being surprised that he has fallen on the ground. However I am quite in a minority here in this pacifist and sentimentalist atmosphere, and I feel most out of place discussing these fatuous doctrines every day.'[21]

Even so, Londonderry's response went no further than telling the Cabinet it was advisable that an attempt be made to guide the debate at Geneva into the realm of practical politics. In contrast, Salmond's frustration with Eden's proposals led him to take the remarkable step of going to the French delegate at Geneva (whose country was quite recently considered as Britain's likely enemy) and asking him to oppose the British Government's proposals.

Sir Geoffrey Salmond, who succeeded his brother as Chief of the Air Staff before his early death. (Mapson Collection, Library of Congress)

Although the Prime Minister learned of his disloyalty he appreciated Salmond's fierce dedication to his service and decided to look the other way. Salmond however did not receive the peerage that was his due on retirement.[22]

Fortunately for the RAF, in spite of the limited effects of Londonderry's and Salmond's efforts, there was general disagreement at Geneva over how the participating nations' civil aeroplanes should be used, especially as Germany was so strong in this respect. And although Germany returned to the conference table in January 1933, Hitler's appointment as German Chancellor inevitably stiffened his country's attitude against disarmament measures.

Amazingly this did not prevent Baldwin from making a final and desperate attempt in March 1933 when he told his Cabinet that he saw two great dangers to the country's safety, aerial bombing and German rearmament – especially in the air – *and so he was willing to trade the RAF to remove both of his fears.*[23]

In spite of the heady – and unrealistic – ideas circulating within the British Cabinet, by 1933 the structure laid down at Geneva was unravelling and when in October Germany withdrew from both the conference and the League of Nations all hopes of disarmament ended, and the meeting adjourned permanently in June 1934.

The RAF had been saved at the last minute by external events. Although a CAS with a greater appetite for staff negotiations and a more highly regarded Secretary of State for Air might have put the RAF's case to greater effect, neither office holder at this time would have been likely to prevail against the senior members of the Government.

At Geneva both Salmond and London-derry could justly feel they were under siege. Salmond was par-ticularly unfortunate in having taken over from Trenchard, who had seemingly directed the RAF's affairs for so long – and was commenting

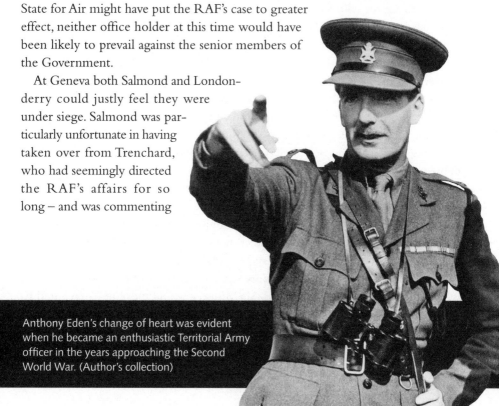

Anthony Eden's change of heart was evident when he became an enthusiastic Territorial Army officer in the years approaching the Second World War. (Author's collection)

critically on his performance – when it was Trenchard's over-emphasis on the destructive power and devastating psychological impact of bombing that had driven the British Cabinet to seek other solutions. Salmond knew that despite Trenchard's high hopes, the initial attempts of his independent bombing force during the First World War had been distinctly disappointing and the dire predictions concerning bombing by the Italian air theorist Giulio Douhet and the American flyer Colonel 'Billy' Mitchell were also largely unproven. This had not prevented British politicians from accepting the most pessimistic viewpoint. Air commentator Ian Philpott went so far as to believe that the last thing the British Government wanted as the negotiators went to Geneva with disarmament in mind was for their CAS to come up with new developments in air armament.[24]

Apart from the adverse political currents at Geneva, Salmond was also unfortunate that there was a severe economic depression during his tour as CAS – described by Winston Churchill as 'The Locust Years'[25] – which compelled him to continue using equipment that was increasingly out of date and affected his service's recruitment and morale. It was therefore even more cruel that when impending German rearmament appeared to offer his brother Geoffrey – who was due to replace him as CAS – the chance for a Salmond to achieve the desperately needed modernisation measures, Geoffrey's sudden illness and rapid death caused the post of CAS to pass to Air Chief Marshal Ellington, who had never been considered his equal.

John Salmond was devastated by his brother's death and the subsequent career of someone who was happiest when leading his flyers on wartime operations proved less than outstanding. He had, for instance, refused the position of chairman at Imperial Airways because he had no stomach for the political struggles that were bound to go with it. During the Second World War, after being made Director General of Flying Control and Air Sea Rescue, ill health forced his retirement in 1943, although he continued to show his allegiance to the RAF by attending every major function including the dinner to celebrate its fortieth anniversary and the one ten years later immediately before his own death.

Londonderry also paid a high price for his opposition to most of the Cabinet at Geneva, where his superior and scornful attitude was bound to have affected his future career, although his inflated political ambitions were probably always unrealistic due to serious weaknesses in his character that went against him. These included an apparent lack of political judgement and a marked tendency to misunderstand facts. In fact, Londonderry still had two more years as Secretary of State for Air, during which political attitudes towards the Air Ministry would move in its favour. (His achievements during this time are considered in Chapter 9.)

In retrospect, late 1933 marked a low point in the fortunes of the RAF and its leaders, with Stanley Baldwin showing himself willing to sacrifice the service for the chimera of disarmament and lasting peace within the League of Nations. This all changed with Germany's withdrawal from the League and subsequent reoccupation of the Rhineland. Hitler's coming to power brought into prominence someone with a residual anger at his country's humiliation at Versailles who was determined to revive the Prussian tradition of using armed forces to gain power. This meant that bombing, whether strategic or tactical, would be sure to become a highly prized weapon of war, and in any future conflict Britain's great capital of London would represent an obvious target.

In democratic Britain, such growing dangers were not universally acknowledged, and the transformation of its small and outdated air service to one prepared for a major war would be far from straightforward. While at the end of the disarmament talks Britain's next opponent was apparent, updating the RAF still needed strong lobbying for the resources required and vital decisions to be taken about the balance and performance of new equipment, including the ratio of its future fighter and bomber fleets. Even more than in the dark days at Geneva when the whole Cabinet was opposed to renewed expansion, so much would depend on the calibre and qualities of the key individuals involved.

GATHERING WAR CLOUDS
1933–38

POST-GENEVA: THE RAF'S AGENDA FOR GROWTH

When Edward Ellington took over from John Salmond as Chief of the Air Staff on 22 May 1933 it was with a clear obligation to start redressing the earlier pernicious years of neglect, as the prospect of German rearmament changed perceptions about RAF aeroplanes from death-dealing instruments to what Hugh Trenchard had always maintained were possible deterrents to a future opponent.

This became apparent during the spring of 1934 when a powerful Defence Requirements Committee concluded that the assumption that no major war was likely for ten years was becoming gradually untenable and that *'exceedingly serious deficiencies have accumulated'*.[1] The committee confirmed that Germany was 'the ultimate potential enemy against whom "long range" defence policy must be directed'[2] and acknowledged the vital role for the RAF in national defence.

Under what was called Scheme A, a number of proposals were announced in Parliament during July 1934 that would increase the Air Force by no less than 50 per cent by adding an extra forty first-line squadrons. While such additions were undoubtedly dramatic, they started from a very low base and were expected to take place over a period of five years at a relatively moderate cost of just £2 million a year. Remarkably, despite the leisurely timescale, some doubts were voiced among the RAF's senior staff about the feasibility of achieving such increases within the present capacity of the RAF's training establishments.[3] Scheme A was, in fact, the first of no fewer than thirteen such schemes over the next four years, some of which were still-born while others were superseded in the pursuit of what seemed to be the ever-receding goal of gaining parity with German air strength.

Like the other two services, the effectiveness of the RAF's response to such recommendations would depend to a considerable extent on the ability of its most senior figures and their influence in wider Government circles. By now Lord Londonderry had been Secretary of State for Air for the better part of two years, although his incoming Chief of Air Staff proved very different from his popular, charismatic if not over-studious predecessor. While undoubtedly knowledgeable, Edward Ellington was a cautious and retiring individual who actually feared change, and had it not been for the unexpected death of Geoffrey Salmond he would never have commanded the RAF as he did.[4]

Ellington had been commissioned in 1891 into the Royal Artillery and after ten years graduated from the Army Staff College to take up an appointment at the War Office. Unlike John Salmond, although he gained his military pilot's licence in 1913 he spent most of the war as a staff officer with the Army's Royal Artillery, before joining Trenchard's staff in November 1917 to help determine the structure of the infant Royal Air Force. After the war, following a number of command appointments, in 1931 he was made a member of the Air Council before becoming Chief of the Air Staff two years later.

Remarkably, despite extensive staff and command appointments, Ellington never flew operationally, nor commanded an active squadron, wing or group. His widely used nickname of 'Uncle Ted' did not suggest a dynamic manager of men and, although by this time RAF manpower was down to a meagre 30,000 and its aircraft and other equipment had become perilously out of date, Ellington did not press for expansion and modernisation nearly as strongly as he might have done.

Air historian Henry Probert has attempted, somewhat unconvincingly, to excuse him by arguing that 'the habits of so many lean years were not easy to discard',[5] but it was in keeping with Ellington's attitude that as late as the autumn of 1936 he should tell military expert Basil Liddell Hart that there would be no war before 1942 because 'our rearmament programme will not be completed till then'. Predictably, Liddell Hart responded by remarking 'That seems to be no reason why Hitler will wait until then and it is far more likely that he will forestall us by earlier action.'[6]

This appeared to have no effect on Ellington, who during the previous year had taken the same approach when visited by Group Captain Maclean from Bomber Command, who after a visit to Geneva voiced his fears that war might break out before the end of 1938 only to be brushed aside and told 'that our own rearmament could not be complete before 1942 and the Germans were likely to take longer'.[7]

Air commentator Montgomery Hyde thought it was unfortunate that a man of such orthodox military outlook and background should have been CAS during such a critical period and Air Vice-Marshal Wilfrid Freeman, who was to play such a massive part in RAF modernisation and who had earlier served with Ellington on the Air Council, believed him 'to be the worst CAS we ever had'. Following the Second World War Freeman wrote to Trenchard about Ellington saying: 'He never, as you and Chatfield did, pulled an unofficial string. He was not only a misanthrope, but he never made the least attempt to do his job, and get to know politicians. He pretended to despise them but was, in fact, frightened of them.'[8] Trenchard (who had earlier supported Ellington) replied: 'I still think he had a great brain, but was ruined by being appallingly shy and very keen to get an important position … I agree he never understood a big job – or any job except detail, and that not too well.[9]

One can well understand the depth of Freeman's feelings, for when in 1936 he recommended establishing aircraft repair depots, Ellington blocked the proposal on the specious grounds that a modern air war would be so short and destructive that wrecked aircraft would have to be replaced by new machines. Freeman was forced to wait until Ellington retired before getting permission for such vital depots.[10] Ellington was also famously opposed to the training of fighter crews in the use of RDF or radar, since he felt that the technique, if successful, would have ended the dominance of the bomber. Fortunately, in 1937 he was overruled on this by Lord Swinton, Londonderry's successor as Air Minister.

It was not just Freeman who reacted against what he saw as Ellington's mindless conservatism. Another notable RAF officer, Air Chief Marshal Sir Philip Joubert de la Ferté, wrote that 'while he was CAS the Air Ministry policy appeared to be that which held in the RFC and RAF during 1914–18 – close support of the Army, little help to the Navy, and only a mild interest in the use of an independent air force'.[11]

It was the RAF's ill luck that at such a vital time it not only had a virtual passenger as Chief of its Air Staff but in Lord Londonderry, its Secretary of State, someone whose judgement was unquestionably suspect. The two men worked closely together until Londonderry's dismissal in June 1935, by which time air commentator Archie Jackson had concluded that Londonderry had put himself 'more or less consistently on the wrong side of the prevailing view (in Parliament)'.[12]

At Geneva Londonderry had unquestionably fought hard for his service against the majority opinion of the Cabinet, but when they changed tack and sought a rapid expansion of the RAF, both Londonderry and his CAS felt that this should not take place too quickly and not before the personnel could be adequately trained – however long they believed this might take. Fortunately their joint conviction that Germany would not be able to go to war before 1942 was vigorously contested by others, including Sir Robert Vansittart, the strongly anti-Hitler Permanent

Lord Londonderry, the most heavily criticised Air Minister between the wars. (National Portrait Gallery)

Under-Secretary at the Foreign Office,[13] and such was the strength of their views that Scheme A for RAF expansion was quite quickly superseded in favour of a larger and more rapid one (Scheme C), raising the RAF's squadrons of bombers to sixty-eight and its fighters to thirty-five.

The main agency for this was a Governmental Air Parity Sub-Committee that, as its title suggested, was dedicated to helping ensure that British air power would not be inferior to that of any country within striking distance. Some indication of its calibre was apparent when Prime Minister Stanley Baldwin chose the future Air Minister – Sir Philip Cunliffe-Lister – to be chairman. In a second report the committee challenged the Air Ministry's estimate about the number of German air pilots. These had been put at 4,000 but Cunliffe-Lister believed there were actually twice this number. By the spring of 1935 the Air Ministry's figures again came under suspicion when Londonderry became increasingly involved in a damaging controversy about the speed of German rearmament, which he much underestimated.

In the interval the Air Parity Committee made another major proposal, namely to short-circuit the hitherto traditional and protracted custom of not ordering new planes until their prototypes had been thoroughly tested. The proposed change would prove particularly important for the embryo Hurricanes and Spitfires that were so desperately needed as modern interceptors. Such acceleration enjoyed the strong backing of Air Vice-Marshal Hugh Dowding, the Air Member for Research and Development, but Ellington's advice was *not* to order them in bulk 'off the drawing board'.[14]

In the case of Londonderry, it was not just a case of dragging his feet on RAF rearmament – however serious this proved to be in 1935 – but a marked tendency to tactlessness, which did not help the RAF's cause. On 21 May he committed a spectacular gaffe in the House of Lords when in an unscripted aside he referred to the need to preserve control overseas by using bombers against dissenting groups – even on the frontier of the Middle East and India – which with the 'pacific mood in parliament' was seen as a 'highly inflammatory statement'.[15]

Predictably, the opposition seized on it to spearhead their campaign against the Government in the forthcoming General Election. On the day following his unguarded statement Londonderry suffered another major blow, when Stanley Baldwin outlined Scheme C's rearmament proposals to a packed House of Commons, where in response to a question from Churchill he made a spectacular confession about the figures (supplied to him by the Air Ministry) concerning German air strength:

> I believed I was right. Where I was wrong was in my estimate of the future. There I was completely wrong. I tell the House so, frankly, because neither I nor my advisers, from whom we get accurate information, had any idea of the exact rate at which production could be, and actually was, speeded up in Germany …[16]

The combination of Londonderry's careless remark in the Lords and Baldwin's seeming obligation to apologise to the Commons for inaccurate figures on the German Luftwaffe gave the Prime Minister the opportunity he was seeking – to demand Londonderry's resignation. Churchill subsequently referred to these statistics in *The Gathering Storm*: 'there seems no doubt that these experts and officials at the Air Ministry at the time were themselves misled and misled their chief'.[17]

Londonderry received little sympathy over his sacking. Montgomery Hyde subsequently observed that he was the 'most severely criticised of all the Air Ministers between the Wars' for although, like Salmond, he had fought hard for the RAF during the Geneva Disarmament Conference – during which time the development of radar was agreed – his chosen alignment with the stick-in-the-mud Ellington and his isolation, including his absence from the Commons, during the stormy debates on RAF expansion, gave Baldwin ample reason to dismiss him. After offering him the grace and favour post of Lord Privy Seal, in November 1935 Baldwin excluded him altogether from the Cabinet. In fact, his kinsman, Winston Churchill, had already advised him to go before he was pushed. By now a gulf had opened between them with Churchill, a natural fighter and long-term supporter of airmen since before the First World War – who harboured no doubts about Hitler's messianic plans – passionately believing they should be equipped with the best planes as soon as possible.

In spite of Londonderry's genuine enthusiasm for air matters he had difficulty comprehending the fast-moving events connected with German rearmament and Sir Maurice Dean, Under-Secretary of State to the Air Ministry at this time, concluded that he possessed neither the political stature nor the experience to handle the major issues affecting the Royal Air Force during 1935.[18] His cause was not helped in Parliament by an antique political style that apparently most resembled a Regency beau, allied with his deep resentment at what he saw as overlordship and domination by such men as Stanley Baldwin and Neville Chamberlain, neither of whom he considered his equal.

After leaving the Government, Londonderry's sorry lack of judgement became even more evident when he was unwise enough to believe that as an individual (even a notable one) he might be able to make Germany see reason. After two visits to Germany, in 1936 and 1938, during which he saw Hitler and was entertained by Goering – while Germany's rearmament was going full ahead – he spoke out in favour of an Anglo–German agreement to oppose communism. Although he acknowledged some doubts as to the extent of Germany's ambitions and its anti-Semitic policy, he was evidently far from being aware of what was actually happening, and *The Times* obituary on him after the war[19] was scathing about his diplomatic activities:

> Excellent no doubt though his intentions were in constituting himself an amateur ambassador of good will, it is not surprising that as the intentions of the Nazis became increasingly revealed he should have fallen heavily in the popular esteem.[20]

In retrospect, the contributions of Londonderry and Ellington at a time of such importance for the RAF marked a notably enfeebled time for the Air Ministry's senior leadership. Fortunately the proposals for the implementation of Scheme F, an enhanced Aircraft Expansion Scheme, would be made under a very different Secretary of State, and although Ellington had a further two years to serve he became increasingly sidelined.

It was fortunate that the energetic and capable Philip Cunliffe-Lister (later Lord Swinton) who succeeded Londonderry in June 1935 not only enjoyed the support of the Prime Minister but had two forceful assistants in Dowding, the Air Minister for Research and Development, and Cyril Newall, Staff Member for Supply and Organisation, and future Chief of the Air Staff.

As chairman of the Air Parity Sub Committee, Philip Cunliffe-Lister had already demonstrated his belief in the greater urgency required for RAF rearmament and Sir Maurice Dean, who earlier had been so critical of Londonderry's abilities, came to believe that Swinton was beyond question the greatest Secretary of State for Air between the wars.[21] The appointment of such a hard-headed Yorkshire squire with considerable political experience and a reputation for not suffering fools gladly had, however, not come a moment too soon[22] if the RAF was going to stand any chance of matching the opposing German Luftwaffe.

Unlike Londonderry, Cunliffe-Lister appeared to be lucky. His career undoubtedly benefitted from his marriage to Constance, daughter of the Revd Charles Ingram

Philip Cunliffe-Lister, Lord Swinton, who laid the foundations for the RAF's recovery. (RAF Museum, Hendon)

Boynton of Barniston, near Sowerby. Constance's grandfather was Samuel Cunliffe-Lister, first Earl Masham of Swinton. As heir to a 20,000 acre estate near Ripon, Constance's wealth enabled her to support her husband's aspirations, which he acknowledged when he changed his name in 1928 to Cunliffe-Lister. He was also fortunate in having a relatively short, if unquestionably successful, military career during the First World War. Following action on the Somme in 1916, where he was awarded an MC for gallantry, he was invalided home the next month, from which time onwards he was able to pursue his political career.

By 1920 he had become Secretary to the Board of Trade before, in 1922 at the early age of 38, he was made its President. It was a post he held in three successive administrations[23] and where he was described as an effective minister, if somewhat abrasive in style.[24] He then had four years at the Colonial Office before he succeeded Londonderry when Stanley Baldwin somewhat surprisingly agreed to him going to the House of Lords as Viscount Swinton.

The importance of Swinton's work cannot be exaggerated. Before he assumed office a revised expansion scheme (Scheme C) had been approved for the production of 3,800 new aircraft by March 1937 that did not include new monoplanes, but after his first six months Scheme F was authorised that raised the target figure of aircraft to 8,000 by 31 March 1939,[25] to be largely composed of 'reliable, high performance, all-metal monoplanes which could easily be maintained in war'.[26] Together with the increased number of aircraft, a threefold increase was scheduled for RAF personnel.

Swinton soon showed himself to be in another league from Londonderry by quickly mastering the complex details concerning aeroplane types, their changing designs and capabilities and deciding upon the contracts to be allocated to the approved firms – although he always said his predecessor had a thankless and impossible task, being unable to give the manufacturers the orders they so desperately needed.

There was no question of Swinton being overawed by his Chief of Air Staff or by members of the Air Council, for he was not only easy with his own decisions but enjoyed Baldwin's close counsel. In any case, he never believed that senior officers, nor senior civil servants, should get above themselves, including the highly ambitious Secretary to the Air Council, Sir Christopher Bullock, whom Swinton was very content to see dismissed because of a clash of personalities with Sir Eric Geddes, Chairman of Imperial Airways.

On the other hand he was determined to establish a good working relationship with the wealthy industrialist Lord Weir, who had been controller of aeronautical supplies in 1917–18 and who offered valuable advice on such vital issues as the nature of aeronautical programmes, the enormous supply demands of air warfare and the need for rapid decision-taking. Unknown to Swinton, his earlier reputation proved helpful as Weir had already promised Baldwin that if Swinton went to the Air Ministry he would give him all his help.[27] This did not prevent Swinton from making his own decisions. On one occasion Weir sent him a note recommending that the 'low-wing monoplane fighters (Hurricanes and Spitfires) now being developed should proceed, (although) they did not constitute any part of a definite programme.[28]

In response Swinton rapidly ensured they were given a definite programme and equally importantly that they would go into rapid production, rather than undertaking the traditional protracted series of tests that would have doomed the RAF to near certain defeat in 1940.

Swinton was fortunate in enjoying the exceptional assistance of Air Marshal Sir Wilfrid Freeman, who took over from Dowding as Member for Supply and Research (with Dowding becoming responsible for Fighter Command), and assumed control of production to undertake what has been described as the most urgent and gruesome responsibilities ever given to a serving officer.[29] Although Freeman's brilliance was not unknown within the RAF, Swinton rescued him from early retirement and ensured he worked directly for him.[30]

Following advice from Weir and Freeman rather than the more timid and strictly orthodox Ellington and his staff, Swinton agreed on the remodelling of aircraft production from obsolescent biplanes to stressed skin monoplane interceptors, as well as new types of four-engined bombers equipped with power-operated turrets. He also pressed forward with the development of radar where, under Sir Henry Tizard, exercises were being carried out at Biggin Hill with suitably equipped fighters receiving continuous instructions from the ground about incoming aircraft. Swinton authorised the construction of a radar chain for the defence of London and the South-East (and later along the east coast as far as the Tyne), in which Stanley Baldwin's strong support led to the whole Air Staff accepting it 'as the universally accepted practice'.[31]

Swinton's further massive contribution was his approval of Freeman's suggestions regarding so-called shadow factories. Under this scheme 'parent firms in the aircraft industry were called upon to provide complete technical data for the manufacture of their products – drawings, specifications of plant, jigs, tools, processes, test equipment, layout and so on, to educate the key men of an additional "shadow" factory ... who would be taking on a job new to them, though its personnel were highly skilled and highly experienced in a somewhat different field ...'[32]

Swinton recognised the need for a unique degree of cross-company co-operation between the parent firms and their shadow factories, especially in the case of aero engines where components made in either the parent or shadow factory had to be interchangeable. Under his authority the first shadow factory was completed in May 1937, the first shadow-produced components were delivered four months later and the first shadow-produced engine passed its tests in November of that year.

His protégé, Freeman, encouraged greater co-ordination between the engine makers, persuading Rolls-Royce and Bristol to establish a new joint company ... 'for the development of variable-pitch mechanisms for propellers ... which led to the propeller plant managed by de Havilland at Lostock ultimately (producing) more than half of all the propellers made in Britain during the Second World War'.[33]

Swinton's sweeping reforms encountered determined opposition both from within the RAF and in wider Government circles, although reservations by the Air Council were reduced by Ellington's retirement on 1 September 1937 and Swinton's appointment of the more like-minded Air Chief Marshal Sir Cyril Newall (whose achievements together with those of Swinton's own successor are considered in Chapter 14).

Swinton met an unexpected challenge to his autonomy when in February 1936 the Prime Minister appointed Sir Thomas Inskip as a defence co-ordinator to help resolve inter-service disputes over Britain's defence strategy. As a little-considered lawyer he was seen as a safe pair of hands, although he achieved more than anyone expected and in particular fearlessly challenged the long-held RAF strategy of counter-bombing championed by Trenchard.

The issue came to a head as a result of Swinton's demands – presented on 20 October 1937 – for the most expensive rearmament plan yet (Scheme J) involving major increases to Bomber Command together with lesser ones for Fighter Command. Inskip demanded cuts to the proposals by not increasing overseas forces and, most importantly, making drastic reductions to the anticipated size of Bomber Command. Despite Swinton's objections, the Cabinet accepted Inskip's proposals for retaining the proposed higher levels for interceptors and reducing bomber squadrons from ninety-nine to seventy-seven (Scheme J). Inskip's arguments appeared irrefutable: 'The German Air Force as I have pointed out must be designed to deliver a knock-out blow within a few weeks of the outbreak of war. The role of our Royal Air Force is not an early knock-out blow … but to prevent the Germans from knocking us out.'[34]

During the previous year Inskip had already challenged Swinton and the Air Staff over the long-contested constitutional position of the Fleet Air Arm and on 21 July 1937 he submitted a report to Neville Chamberlain, who had become Prime Minister in May, recommending that the Admiralty should have both operational and administrative control of the service, while the Admiralty's claims for the operational control of the shore-based aircraft of Coastal Command should be rejected. Inskip's report was agreed and given out to the House of Commons by Neville Chamberlain on 30 July 1937.

The degree to which Ellington had become ignored became apparent when he met Trenchard a few days before the publication of the Inskip Report on the Fleet Air Arm and told him the Air Staff were sure that their counter-case would convince the Cabinet. Trenchard's angry reply was: 'Do you never leave your office, Ellington? The thing's over. It's been decided over your head, which is well buried in the sand as usual.'[35]

Ellington handed over to Newall within a month but, far more surprisingly, Swinton himself was also replaced some seven months later.

The dismissal of Britain's greatest interwar Air Minister following three years of outstanding service brought vigorous reactions both at the time and afterwards. Lord Butler gave the address at his memorial service and in it he quoted Winston Churchill, who said of himself and Swinton, 'We were both sacked for the two best things we ever did. I was sacked for the Dardanelles ... you were sacked for the building of the Air Force that won the Battle of Britain and they couldn't undo what you had done.'[36]

This was not just Churchillian rhetoric, for he had undoubtedly been impressed by Swinton and might have had some conscience about his own role in constantly citing the unfavourable British and German strength figures that served to bring about his dismissal. Whatever the reasons, he offered Swinton high responsibility during the Second World War and afterwards.

Swinton's achievements are unquestionable. When he took over as Air Minister in 1935 the RAF was still supported by a small and outdated industrial base. To correct this required increases in funding beyond those given to the other two services together with a massive programme of modernisation and growth that, however well conducted, could never increase the number of effective aircraft quickly enough for his Parliamentary critics, including Winston Churchill and members of the Labour opposition.

In later years Swinton looked back on his term of office and the reasons for his dismissal. He freely acknowledged that the revolutionary programme of expansion and innovation, the ordering of thousands of aircraft off the drawing board, the shadow factories and the integration 'of leading scientists with the Air Staff which gave us radar could not have been achieved without the support of the Prime Minister',[37] only for this to change when Baldwin was replaced by Neville Chamberlain. With him Swinton's position nosedived and there was never the same rapport. Swinton was convinced that Chamberlain 'was not much interested in rearmament or certainly that he put a number of things ahead of it (and he) made up his mind that he must sacrifice me to get an easier time in Parliament'.[38]

However, by the end of 1937, criticism of the Air Ministry in the House of Commons had reached a high level due to the seemingly disappointing results of the massive expansionary programme – with Swinton and his advisers not willing to jeopardise their drive for quality. On 2 April 1938 Sir Warren Fisher, the Head of the Civil Service, wrote to Chamberlain about the comparative British and German air strengths known at that time, stating that German output for 1938 was 6,100 while the British was at most 2,250.[39]

Despite massively increased RAF spending, such seeming imbalance was not paralleled by the other two services. In the case of the Royal Navy, while its estimates for 1920 were £90,872,300, those for 1938 totalled £96,117,500 – a net increase

PART 3: GATHERING WAR CLOUDS 1933–38

of just £6 million. The Army's estimates were even more dramatic. From a total of £125,000,000 in 1920, by 1938 they had contracted to £85,357,000. In contrast, the minuscule RAF estimate of £22,992,230 in 1920 (that fell even lower during the 1920s and early '30s) had more than tripled to £73,501,000 in 1938.[40]

Many of the reasons for the still unfavourable totals of aircraft compared with the Luftwaffe were not easy to explain, especially since the Air Minister was stranded in the House of Lords. Swinton's initial dilemma was whether to sanction the build-up of huge reserves of aircraft that, while impressive by numbers, would not be very effective in battle, or to make a framework for vast industrial potential (through the shadow factories that could switch over from peace to war). In the event, other decisions were taken in favour of excellence, in developing the Merlin engine, and with a great bound producing Spitfire and Hurricane interceptors, with an armament of eight guns each. Despite what were undeniable delays in production, undue emphasis was paid by the House of Commons (with Churchill in the van) on numerical comparisons rather than the quality of the projected new aircraft, in the belief that the gap between British and German aircraft production not only still existed but, indeed, was rising strongly. In any case much of the secret defence equipment such as radar, which powerfully tipped the balance to the defenders, could not be discussed in open session.

During the heated debates against his critics Swinton was forced to rely on his deputy Lord Winterton (who as an Irish peer was able to sit in the Commons). Unfortunately on 12 May 1938 Winterton's performance during a pivotal debate on the air expansion programme proved abysmal. Following it he immediately resigned, leaving both Swinton and his adviser, Lord Weir, vulnerable.

The end of Swinton's own time as Air Minister was brutal. He was chairing a meeting of the Air Defence Research Committee when he received a note telling him that the Prime Minister urgently wished to see him. He told the committee to continue with their discussions, but he would never return to hear them – for when he reached Downing Street Chamberlain told him: 'I want you to go.' The Prime Minister gave no explanation beyond offering him lesser roles in the Cabinet. As Maurice Dean concluded, Swinton was the fall guy for the Prime Minister and he must have valued the words of his brilliant protégé, Sir Wilfrid Freeman, who assured him: 'If we win through in the end, it will only be because of the foundation you have laid, and all those who worked alongside you these last few years can have no other opinion'.[41]

In his subsequent memoirs Swinton acknowledged his own shortcomings and the particular difficulties created by Chamberlain:

> It may fairly be said that we did not do enough soon enough, that the financial limits laid down were too rigid, that we should have insisted on some power in peacetime to direct part of industry on to war production, a policy strenuously

opposed by the Prime Minister and the Board of Trade. On these matters I shall not attempt to excuse myself. I accepted the decisions and I bear my share of the blame.[42]

Swinton's memoirs show the immense task involved in bringing the RAF to a state of readiness after the locust years. To achieve it, the RAF's political and service leaders had not only to push through with the necessary reforms, but to argue before the Prime Minister and other senior politicians that a service that after the Great War had been seen as marginal at best was destined to take a leading part in the coming war.

Between 1933 and 1935 the RAF was not well served by Lord Londonderry as Secretary of State and Edward Ellington as his Chief of Air Staff. Whatever the outstanding achievements of Swinton and Newall, Chief of Air Staff from September 1937, together with invaluable support from Freeman and Weir, another lesser-regarded Secretary of State, Sir Kingsley Wood, had to continue with the policy of favouring the construction of fighters. Despite continuing assistance from Freeman he would need every second of the extra year gained at Munich by Neville Chamberlain's much-maligned scrap of paper to raise the RAF's force levels to meet the coming German onslaughts.

THE EMERGENCE OF MODERN INTERCEPTORS

The virtual cessation of aircraft orders during the 1920s and the restricted levels of the early 1930s brought about wage reductions, widespread dismissals and further amalgamations of the aircraft manufacturers. It was therefore remarkable that there were designers in the British aircraft industry who, along with incomparable Rolls-Royce engines, were capable of masterminding fighter planes of world-beating proportions. That the need for so-called interceptors was realised so late came about because of Hugh Trenchard's long-held belief as Chief of the Air Staff that Britain's air defence should depend on the threat of retaliatory bombing. As a result, until the early 1930s the RAF specifications for new planes were predominantly for medium bombers (that would double up as military transporters), flying boats and general purpose aircraft rather than fighters that appeared to be of little use for empire policing or for general war. As a result, during the 1920s the RAF specification for technically superior replacements (which hopefully would attract orders both in the UK and from abroad) was for limited numbers of aircraft. It therefore said much for Air Marshal Hugh Dowding, the newly appointed Air Member for Supply and Research, that in 1930, very shortly after Trenchard's retirement, he should issue a specification F7/30 for a new day and night fighter with a performance well in advance of any aircraft currently in RAF service.[1]

Dowding's imaginative requirements were for an aeroplane capable of a maximum speed of 250mph (at a time when the Bristol Bulldog had only just entered service with a top speed of 174mph) with a low landing speed and a short take-off, a steep initial climb rate, high manoeuvrability and good all-round visibility. As armament the aeroplane would have four machine guns in place of the current twin-gun system. The motive for such an ambitious specification was for it to compare with high-performance bombers (and civilian aircraft) that were thought to be under development abroad[2] and which in the event of their possible attack on Britain would have to be intercepted by fighters.

The F.7/30 requirements evoked a wide response from the aircraft industry, with submissions from Supermarine, Hawker, Gloster, Westland and Blackburn, and inspired a number of ingenious designs. Of these, Sydney Camm's at Hawker and Henry Folland's private venture build at Gloster were the most orthodox while the most bold was Reginald Mitchell's at Supermarine where – in opposition to the deeply

Reginald Joseph Mitchell. (Royal Aeronautical Society/National Aerospace Library)

entrenched prejudice within the RAF – he favoured a monoplane configuration following his entries for the Schneider Trophy races. Although the responses to Dowding's specification would in the main prove disappointing, its importance lay in the effect it had on the industry's two outstanding designers, Reginald Mitchell and Sydney Camm, who in their dissimilar attempts to surpass its performance requirements would produce two iconic interceptors for the coming war.

As the long-time chief designer and chief engineer at Supermarine (a company much strengthened by its takeover in 1928 by Vickers) 'Reg' Mitchell already enjoyed a high reputation for his flying boat designs, and in particular for his streamlined, all-metal aeroplanes that had succeeded in the final Schneider Trophy races. Although Dowding's specification came at a time of general depression when capital was in short supply, Sir Robert McLean, the dynamic chairman of Vickers, authorised Mitchell to go ahead with designing an aircraft to meet it. In the event Mitchell found that, although he had adopted the all-metal monoplane design of his Schneider racers, his new Type 224's manoeuvrability was seriously affected by its thick inverted gull wing and its short cantilever fixed undercarriage with large clumsy fairings. Most serious of all, the Air Ministry favoured using an air-cooled

Rolls-Royce engine with a fixed wooden propeller that delivered a modest 600hp compared with the 2000hp+ achieved by their engines for the final Schneider Trophy race.

Sir Robert McLean was keen that the aeroplane should be officially christened Spitfire after his feisty young daughter, Ann, but its lumbering performance proved a near disaster with its unexpectedly low speed (well below Dowding's requirements), poor manoeuvrability and the number of various problems with its air cooling system.

In fact, no other competitor could meet Dowding's demanding specifications, with the use of the Rolls-Royce Goshawk engine proving particularly restrictive. The Air Ministry ended up playing it safe by opting for the private venture plane, the Gloster Gladiator, which surpassed Mitchell's design in both air speed and rate of climb. Such was Mitchell's disappointment with his aeroplane, allied to persistent rumours about a new monoplane being built by the Heinkel Company, that during the summer of 1933 – before its formal testing – he was already working towards a radically improved alternative with a retractable undercarriage and thin straight wings. While he was engrossed in this work, disaster struck when this normally most robust and active man was taken ill: cancer was discovered and an immediate major operation was performed. He was forced to wear a colostomy bag and, worse still, his doctors acknowledged that they could not rule out a reoccurrence. However, by early 1934, Mitchell was back in full work and making no concessions whatsoever to his recent illness.

It said much for both Sir Robert McLean and Mitchell that, with the Type 224 proving such a serious disappointment, they put aside any attempt to improve it and decided to take the radical step of designing a 'real killer' fighter of their own, not restricted by Air Ministry specifications. McLean contacted his opposite number at Rolls-Royce and they jointly agreed to finance the proposed aircraft, with Rolls-Royce contributing £7,500 together with its engines. They then informed the Air Ministry that in the circumstances no technical member would be consulted nor allowed to interfere. While the RAF needed a new interceptor, Henry Folland's Gloster Gladiator biplane performed well in the role and the joint decision by Vickers and Rolls-Royce to fund a new aircraft in place of Mitchell's seriously deficient Type 224 showed their immense confidence in his design skills.

Their decision succeeded in jolting the Air Ministry into action and less than a month later, following a design conference headed by Hugh Dowding, a £10,000 contract was issued for a new 'killer fighter' in accordance with Supermarine's Type 300 proposals. The Supermarine design team immediately began a punishing programme for an aircraft with a number of revolutionary features. After discussion with his aerodynamicist Beverley Shenstone (who had probably been influenced by both the current work of the German aircraft manufacturer Heinkel and Mitchell's earlier Schneider S.4 aircraft), Mitchell decided to give its wings an elliptical shape. Like the Type 224, they continued to be of stainless steel construction, but this time Mitchell designed them to be as thin as possible (while still accommodating a retractable undercarriage), where accepted practice in aerodynamics was for straighter stouter ones.[3] He reduced the radiator to 40 per cent below what many experts considered safe, and the tail skid was also made smaller than what many believed possible. Because of its light alloy monocoque fuselage,[4] the aeroplane had an overall weight of 5,180lb, more than 1,000lb less than Camm's Hurricane its main rival, giving it a 30mph speed advantage.

Another vital change came with the replacement of the Goshawk Rolls–Royce engine by the company's twelve-cylinder PV12 (the letters PV standing for 'private venture') which eventually became known as the Merlin and was capable of producing at least 1,050hp, together with the installation of an effective ethylene-styled cooling system with a low-drag ducted radiator (developed by the Royal Aircraft Establishment at Farnborough) mounted under the starboard wing. At the suggestion of Squadron Leader Ralph Sorley, Mitchell also doubled the proposed armament of Browning machine guns in its wings to eight, making his 'killer fighter' capable of firing 1,000 rounds a minute.

By the beginning of 1936 Sir Robert McLean insisted on the new fighter being called Spitfire, despite Mitchell grumbling 'that it was bloody silly to call it by the same name as a previous failure'. This time its performance proved very different; the plane's test flight took place on 5 March 1936, two days before Hitler's reoccupation of the Rhineland, with Captain T. 'Mutt' Summers, Vickers' chief test pilot, at the controls. On landing he told his anxious onlookers what they most wanted to hear, namely that he wanted nothing touched, thereby indicating there were no major problems that needed fixing before the next flight. This did not, of course, dispense with months of tests and alterations before the 'fastest and most efficient fighter machine of the Second World War'[5] would achieve its target speed of 350mph.

The pressing need for the Spitfire to come into service was demonstrated when the German Luftwaffe held a flight competition from which two planes, the Messerschmitt Bf 109 and the Heinkel He 112, emerged successfully. The Bf 109 was given preference and would see service in Spain during April 1936.[6]

In spite of its novel features, with the Spitfire 'everything came right at the psychological moment, a rare event in aircraft and engine design'[7] and its advanced design proved so sound that it was 'capable of remarkable further development with its top speed rising from 346mph in 1939 to 460mph five years later'.[8] Mitchell's fellow designer, Alan Clifton, concluded that with the Spitfire Mitchell was 'widely considered the greatest aeroplane designer of his time when one man's brain could carry every detail of a design'.[9]

Tragically, Mitchell's cancer returned and this time no treatment was possible. During autumn 1936 the bouts of pain began to be more frequent but, unless he had a very bad day, he continued to go to work, for the contractors standing ready to build his Spitfire needed the fullest details.

Mitchell's Supermarine Spitfire Mark 1. (Digital image by Paul H. Vickers)

Mitchell's illness brought another great cost for, unbeknown to most, he was also in the process of designing a new bomber. In early 1936 the Air Staff had issued specification B.12/36 for a four-engine bomber and Mitchell's drawings for a single-spar, mid-wing monoplane protected by three gun turrets and powered by four Rolls-Royce Merlin, Bristol Hercules or Napier Dagger engines, had a projected maximum speed of 360mph. This was far in excess of the Lancaster bomber that did not come into service until 1942 and it was designed to carry a bomb load of more than 8,000lb[10] compared with the Lancaster's 7,000lb. Had the aeroplane matched Mitchell's estimates and gone into production, it was bound to have furthered his reputation, being far in advance of the later heavy bomber designs since it would reach a speed equal or superior to his prototype Spitfire and it could have outdistanced contemporary German fighters. Following a number of delays, two prototypes were built, but in September 1940 both were destroyed by German action before they could fly, although from an artist's impression the type possessed much of the Spitfire's elegance.

Mitchell never knew his bomber's fate, for in February 1937 he was forced to stop work and, despite going to Vienna for what was hoped could be a last-minute cure, he died on 11 June. By then the Spitfire was far enough advanced for Joe Smith, appointed chief designer in Mitchell's place, to complete the plane's development tests and move towards producing the 310 Spitfires already ordered by the RAF. Group Captain David Green, chairman of the Spitfire Society, would declare later that this was the ingredient that raised Mitchell to a level unattainable by the most brilliant of his contemporaries.[11]

However brilliant Mitchell's achievements, another interceptor had to be produced before the outbreak of the Second World War for the Spitfire proved far from easy to mass produce, particularly in the early stages. Percy Walker, distinguished scientist and strong supporter of the rival Hurricane, went as far as to say of the Spitfire that 'an aerodynamic masterpiece, it required little short of a miracle to turn it into a practical aeroplane'.[12]

Walker undoubtedly exaggerated its complications for during 1940, after major teething troubles, the hard-driving Minister of Aircraft Production, Max Aitkin (Lord Beaverbrook), assisted by experts from Supermarine, succeeded in producing 320 Spitfires a month in a purpose-built factory at Castle Bromwich. However, if Britain had been compelled to rely on Spitfires becoming available at the beginning of the war, the RAF would have been even more outnumbered in the Luftwaffe's early assaults, leading to almost certain defeat. That a second enhanced interceptor was produced and made available was due to another highly individual and hugely successful designer at Hawker Aviation.

Like other notable figures in aviation at this time – including Geoffrey de Havilland, Fred Sigrist and Henry Royce – Sydney Camm's background was neither

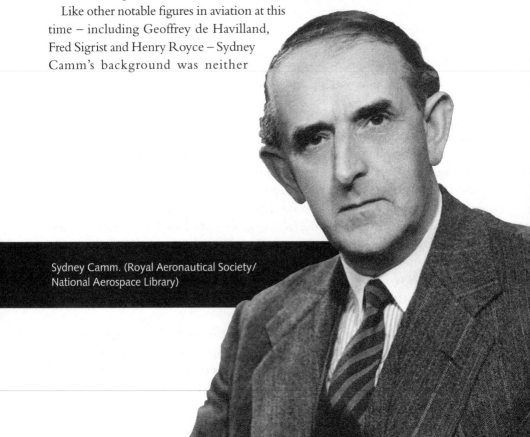

Sydney Camm. (Royal Aeronautical Society/ National Aerospace Library)

privileged nor affluent. He was the eldest of twelve children born to Frederick William Camm, a skilled carpenter, and his wife Mary, who lived in a small terraced home in Alma Road, Windsor. The Camms all attended Windsor Royal Free School that catered for children of all ages, where Sydney's aptitude for his studies earned him a foundation scholarship with all expenses paid. His family's straitened circumstances forced him to leave at 15 to become a carpentry apprentice, during which time he spent his spare time constructing model aircraft and cycling to Brooklands to watch the flying there. In 1914, as a qualified carpenter, he joined Martin & Handasyde Aircraft Company at Woking, initially on the shop floor, but such was the standard of his work that later in the First World War he was promoted to the drawing office. In 1920 the firm went into receivership. However, when George Handasyde formed his own company he took two men with him, Sydney Camm and J.D. Standbury, where the three comprised the firm's entire design team. At Handasyde, Sydney gained valuable experience when helping to draw up specifications for a series of aircraft before the company was dissolved in 1923.

By now he had shown enough to be taken on by W.G. Carter at Tommy Sopwith's Hawker Engineering Company at Kingston. There he was given drawings of the firm's old Tabloid aircraft and told to produce a modern version with half the power and half the weight.[13] His drawings for what became the Cygnet light aeroplane established him as an outstanding designer who showed 'attention to detail, design, careful weight control and [produced] a beautifully balanced design'.[14]

In 1925 W.G. Carter left to join the Gloster Aircraft Company, and Sydney took his place, thereby progressing in eleven years from shop floor woodworker to chief designer at one of Britain's leading aircraft companies, as a result of what had already been seen as a combination of 'ability, dedication, intellect and strength of character'.[15] At Kingston, Camm quickly proved a strong leader and hard task master who publically dressed his staff down, whatever their seniority, provoking Tommy Sopwith in later years to say of him: 'I cannot imagine why his men put up with him. He was a genius – but quite impossible.'[16]

As chairman of the company Sopwith did not experience Sydney's methods at first-hand and although he could undoubtedly be outrageous, Percy Walker who worked under him at Kingston emphasised the degree of affection in which he was held by his fellow designers. For, despite the public theatricals, 'deep down Percy believed he had a deep-rooted sense of justice and fair play'.[17] He was quicker than most to recruit graduates, although his 'young gentlemen' still had to prove their ability under a leader who, like his great predecessor Samuel Cody, 'was constantly searching for better ways of doing things'.[18] The pride and determination that he had instilled into his interwar team became evident in the mid 1950s, when so many of them took charge of aircraft or design organisations in Britain.

Camm's design path was different from that of his rival Mitchell, who leapt forward with revolutionary designs (which did not always come up to full expectations);

while Camm was more cautious and unwilling to go far beyond the existing states of knowledge in too many areas at once.[19] On the other hand, he was always looking towards the next project, hence the streams of aircraft following upon each other in which he routinely produced most handsome aircraft. The models followed without a break and it was to Hawker's financial advantage that more aircraft of Hawker Hart origin with their good reputation for serviceability and maintenance were built during the interwar years than any others, with 5,000 in seventy varieties not only for the RAF and the Royal Navy, but also for twenty overseas air forces.

Next came his Hawker Fury, a compact single-seat biplane fighter, a private version of which was designed to meet Dowding's F.7/30 specification powered by a Rolls-Royce Goshawk engine with a fixed undercarriage. By 1933 Camm's designs had advanced to a monoplane fighter involving a radical redesign of the Fury termed 'the Fury monoplane', which (like Mitchell's redesigned plane) would begin as a private venture. This was to have a lower cantilever wing with tapered edges, rounded tips, and a fixed undercarriage. It had an enclosed sliding cockpit, while for armament there would be four machine guns, two mounted on the sides of the fuselage and two in the wing roots.

By 10 December 1933 Camm felt able to discuss this proposed design with the Air Ministry, but by January 1934 considerable new advanced features were agreed.

Camm's rival Hurricane Mark 1. (Digital image by Paul H. Vickers)

It was decided not to proceed with the Goshawk engine but to use the Rolls-Royce PV12, and move to an engine cooler system using glycol rather than the air-cooled system favoured by the Air Ministry. The front of the aeroplane was altered to take the new engine and the undercarriage was made retractable to reduce wind resistance (although Camm insisted on it having the widest possible track). This worked right from the start without alteration and by now the aeroplane was being referred to as the 'interceptor monoplane' since it bore less and less resemblance to the Fury.

Unlike Mitchell's 'bloody paralyser' of a fighter that was supported initially by Vickers and Rolls-Royce, the Air Ministry invited Hawker to submit designs for a new specification – F.5/34. Accordingly a mock-up was completed by 10 January 1935, when one of its key attractions was its comparatively thick aerofoil wing section, well able to accommodate two sets of four Browning machine guns (which were finally approved in July 1935). By February 1935 the Air Ministry had granted a contract for Camm's new aeroplane, described as 'High Speed Monoplane K 5083', with its Rolls-Royce engine producing 1,025hp at 15,000ft giving a maximum speed of 330mph – some 80mph faster than any other aircraft in service at the time. Camm also decided to construct metal-covered wings to replace the fabric-covered ones, although they were not in place for the test flight made the next year.

The key advantage of Camm's approach was his capacity to move his designs forward by evolutionary steps: 'the whole framework of the Hurricane was in fact a straightforward development of the system which had been amply used in the Hart and Fury and their many variants.[20] Such evolving streams of aircraft enabled it to prove robust, simple to manufacture and – most importantly – easy to repair. Camm's well-tried methods were seen with the wings; these were made of such a size that they could be assembled at Kingston in jigs built into the upright girders of the old furniture depository building.[21]

On 23 October 1935, a record-beating eleven months and two days after the plane's first drawings were wired to Kingston, the prototype was delivered by road to Brooklands, where it was quickly assembled and made ready for the first flight.[22] In the process up to 2,000 drawings had been completed in Camm's austere office in Kingston. The plane's first flight took place on 6 November 1935 under Hawker's chief test pilot, Flight Lieutenant 'George' Bulman. When he returned, Sydney Camm clambered on to the wing root and looked quizzically at him sitting in the cockpit, at which Bulman turned to him saying 'another winner, I think'.[23] After ten flights totalling just eight hours, five minutes in the air, the prototype was sent to Martlesham Heath for testing, where with its Merlin engine the Hurricane reached its declared speed of 315mph at 16,000ft, making it a genuine fast interceptor.

Hawker's board showed their complete faith in the aeroplane when in March 1936, with the build-up of German forces in full swing, the directors, prior to being given an official contract, wired instructions for planning, jigging and tooling to be put in hand for 1,000 aeroplanes. With war so close, speed in production was vital and had Camm delayed by attempting to equal or surpass the airspeed of the Spitfire, the RAF would not have had any modern fighters to send to France at the outbreak of the war, and in 1940 its strength would have been too low for a successful defence of the home country.

In spite of unexpected early problems arising with the Rolls-Royce engine that necessitated a complete redesign of the cylinder head, the Hurricane (together with the Spitfire) was able to join the RAF Air Pageant at Hendon in June 1936. This was none too soon, for in the same month during the Olympic Games in Berlin the Bf 109 also made its first public appearance. The first production Hurricane flew on 13 October 1937 (with the first production Mark I Spitfire making its maiden flight on 16 May 1938). The second and subsequent Hurricane aircraft were delivered straight to 111 squadron at Northolt so that service pilots could practise flying them, while the first service Spitfire was delivered to 19 Squadron in August of the same year.

Like their two famous aircraft, Mitchell and Camm have their particular champions. Wing Commander Bob Stanford-Tuck, for one, believed the Spitfire was a true thoroughbred and that both the aircraft and its creator Mitchell would remain in aviation history forever.[24] Yet whatever Stanford-Tuck's enthusiasm, it was the more numerous Hurricanes of Sydney Camm that took the brunt of the air fighting in 1940. While the aeroplanes successfully complemented each other, their designers had more in common than is sometimes acknowledged. Both experienced a practical education after their boyhood days: Camm as a carpentry apprentice, Mitchell in engineering, and in both cases their advanced design skills were largely self-taught. Both were perfectionists who possessed a distinct aura of authority and drove their teams very hard. Camm, for instance, believed the best work was produced by small design teams under pressure. Both understood that successful fighter planes involved a near mystical union between engine and airframe, with Camm endeavouring to maximise the power-to-weight ratio while staying within safety limits and Mitchell's advanced systems giving him a distinct advantage.

Yet, although the Spitfire was quite a small aircraft, the Hurricane was only marginally larger, if almost 20 per cent heavier. Both designers produced elegant aeroplanes partly for aesthetic reasons but essentially because simple clean lines were aerodynamically virtuous; Camm with his Hawker Hart, Hurricanes and future Hunter jets, Mitchell with his Schneider S.5s and S.6s, the Spitfire and his prototype heavy bomber. If the Hurricane had not appeared at the same time as the Spitfire, it would surely have been much admired not just for its robustness and performance but also for the cleanness of its lines.

Both men were wary of intellectuals and disliked overcomplicated explanations of their aircraft. Test pilot Jeffrey Quill admired Mitchell's clarity of judgement, his practical genius where he seemed able to take the mystery out of even the most complex subject.[25] Camm never failed to point out the limitations of academic theories: 'I've only had one method: as quick as you bloody well can.'[26] In reality, however quick the work, he invariably expected them to do 'their poor best', in other words to keep to the highest standards. Whatever the demands they made of their design teams, neither forgot the dangers run by test pilots in their prototype aircraft; indeed Mitchell was always reluctant to watch them.

With such characteristics and unyielding standards it was no wonder that in both cases their test pilots should declare themselves satisfied after their first flights, and that both Hurricanes and Spitfires should subsequently prove themselves successful – as such planes must in aerial combat against formidable opponents.

BRITISH CIVIL AVIATION: SIR ERIC GEDDES AND IMPERIAL AIRWAYS

While by the mid 1930s British military aviation was taking massive strides to meet the threat from the German Luftwaffe, civil aviation – in spite of the emergence of new domestic airlines – continued its relatively staid progress until the death of Imperial Airways' dominant chairman Sir Eric Geddes in 1937.

From 1924 until the early 1930s, commercial aviation in Britain was chiefly associated with one organisation, Imperial Airways. Imperial acted as the flag carrier for developing services throughout the Empire and promoting the carriage of mail by air, while placing less emphasis on European or internal routes. However, during the early 1930s, small commercial rivals emerged that did not enjoy its favoured status.

Imperial's privileges came at a cost, for it was obliged to employ British pilots and use British aeroplanes, which it ordered from its favoured manufacturers.

The Pan American flying boat Clipper III. (Author's collection)

Imperial Airway's' Bristol Type 62 ten-seat airliner. (Author's collection)

Some were for flying boats that appeared particularly suitable for traversing an empire where in many locations airstrips were rudimentary or lacking altogether. In reality they represented a technological dead end, and Imperial's mixed fleet contrasted with the land-planes used exclusively by the German and Dutch carriers and by the Americans, before their relatively late development of the Boeing 314 'Clipper' flying boats for crossing the Pacific and Atlantic oceans.

This was not all. The specialist and conservative nature of the planes it ordered, and their relatively small numbers, served to discourage the British aircraft industry from developing methods of mass production or spearheading new engineering developments. As a result, while favoured and dominant, Imperial Airways was by no means exempt from criticisms. Although after the Second World War *The Journal of Transport History* would refer to Imperial Airway's 'sixteen years of pioneering and development – sixteen years of glorious achievement',[1] during the mid 1930s, criticisms in both the press and Parliament much increased. These included charges of nondescript management and a lack of urgency summed up as being 'slow into the air and slow in the air, and putting the interests of shareholders above those of country and empire'.[2]

Whatever the substance of such criticisms, the nature of the company's performance was largely dependent on decisions made by its senior management. At Imperial, despite the presence of a strong, austere, and long-standing managing director in George Woods Humphery and Herbert Brackley, its able but somewhat self-effacing superintendent of air staff, the most powerful voice was that of the company's chairman, Sir Eric Campbell Geddes (although much of his time was spent elsewhere).

A Scottish civil engineer with experience in railways both in the Himalayas and in Britain, Geddes flourished during the First World War when Lloyd George appointed him head of the Government's gun ammunition department. This proved a key appointment for which he subsequently received a knighthood for his forceful abilities to bring about a significant improvement in the output of shells for the Somme offensive.

Following his appointment as Director General of Railways and Transport at Douglas Haig's military headquarters in France, Geddes constructed a light railway system powered by internal combustion engines that successfully delivered shells and other supplies to the trenches. In the process his vigorous and single-minded brand of management brought him few friends at headquarters. In 1917 Geddes advanced further when he was appointed Inspector General of Communications over all theatres of war, briefly holding the ranks of major general and vice admiral simultaneously.

Lloyd George continued to favour Geddes after the war and in August 1921 he gave him massive new responsibility as chairman of a committee on national expenditure 'that sought to bring about a retrenchment in public spending' and a return to sound fiscal management after what had been seen as wartime excesses.

Sir Eric Geddes, feared chairman of Imperial Airways. (Tacoma Times, Library of Congress)

His fearless wielding of the so-called Geddes economic axe brought both terror and pain to Government departments countrywide, resulting in job losses and salary cuts. However, from 1922 he came to believe in the essential separation of political departments from private business and the latter's premier importance for the national economy.

As a self-proclaimed champion of business, in December 1922 Geddes accepted the chair of the massive Dunlop Rubber Company, where he extended its product range and paid particular attention to its production lines, installing the latest technological innovations and causing time and motion studies to be carried out.

It was such accomplishments that led to 'Sam' Hoare recommending him to be chairman of Imperial Airways with overall responsibility for commercial air services and the promoting of air mindedness in the country as a whole, a post he held, together with his continuing responsibilities at Dunlop, until his death thirteen years later. For all his ruthless drive and what he believed was unrivalled knowledge of transport, Imperial Airway's progress proved far slower than its European competitors. In fact, its early years were marked by low passenger capacity, high maintenance costs and far from over-generous subsidies, with air commentator Gordon Pirie concluding that 'shareholder value rather than Empire propagation was the Geddes benchmark.'[3] Whatever Pirie's partiality, while Imperial's European competitors were going for rapid growth fuelled by large subsidies, Geddes believed that the best solution lay in 'the steady, conservative build-up of the company'[4] until public subsidies would no longer be necessary.

Geddes's aspirations are apparent from his addresses to the company's annual general meetings over more than a decade, with the earlier ones setting the pattern. By the end of its first year of trading there could be no doubt who was in charge, for in early April 1925 *The Evening News* reported the chairman's request for the resignation of the then managing director, Lieutenant Colonel Frank Searle. As the newspaper critically observed: 'Searle's aim has always been safety first and then high efficiency, but non aeronautical members of the Board, notably the chairman, Sir Eric Geddes, are more concerned with attracting revenue and cutting down expenses to show that the business is a commercial success.'[5]

In his own defence Searle commented that the board consisted of very successful men who knew the danger of trusting the unknown but that none of them had successfully operated any new form of transport.

Geddes was characteristically unrepentant about the heavy demands on the old-fashioned aircraft the company inherited. Although his first report acknowledged a loss of £16,217 6s 3d, he assured the meeting that the original airlines had now been welded into an efficient organisation with maintenance receiving earnest attention, and declared his mantra that 'while safety would be maintained costs must be brought down'.[6]

Imperial Airways's Armstrong Whitworth Argosy, City of Glasgow. (Author's collection)

However, by the next year the losses had increased to £20,414 19s 8d. He expressed his deep regret about delays in the delivery of new planes from British manufacturers – a much-repeated theme over the years – that meant the company was unable to earn the increased revenue that the board had anticipated, with considerable traffic passing to foreign competitors. He confirmed his authority over his fellow directors by deciding they should share in the company's growing pains by taking a hefty cut in salary. In fact, it was suffering from a shortage of both aircraft and pilots, with the latter being offered parsimonious terms of service, that led to some of them going off on private ventures of their own. The regularity of its services were also much affected by persistent foggy conditions around Croydon that made it dangerous for aircraft lacking in landing aids.

In 1927 Geddes was able to declare a first ever profit of £11,000 and a rise in reliability on the European routes to 92 per cent, although expansion was still slow with the springtime passengers numbering fewer than 100 a day. However, orders were finally placed for new and more powerful three-engined aircraft in the shape of de Havilland's Hercules and Armstrong Whitworth's Atalanta, a need emphasised by the delivery of Junkers low-winged monoplanes for the German airline Lufthansa.

In the next year's report he announced an increased profit of £72,500 but felt forced to point out that with improving results the Government's subsidy was expected to be reduced from its highest level of £335,000 to £70,000 by the company's tenth year. This commitment to a deliberate rather than rapid rate of expansion meant that with fast-developing aircraft technology elsewhere, some aeroplanes would have to be retained that were obsolete and slow. He faced down his potential critics by boasting that the airline had long turned a deaf ear to croakers and sceptics[7] – although to general surprise he then announced his intention to resign, a decision he quickly reversed after strong pressure from his company colleagues.

The possibility of Geddes's resignation brought a notably spare tribute from Charles Grey, editor of *The Aeroplane*, who was well aware of his lack of popularity: 'Like all strong men he has real enemies, but has earned the esteem of people who, often against their will, recognize that he has succeeded in every task.'[8]

In 1929, ten years after the establishment of the first British airline, Geddes was able to report a profit of £60,000 (£10,000 less than the previous year) with a dividend of 7½ per cent. He announced that the airline's 100,000th passenger had been carried, during which time the company's planes had flown more than 1 million miles. In 1929 alone it had carried 35,000 fee-paying passengers and 870 tons of mail and freight.[9]

Whatever such proud statistics, the inescapable fact was that the scale of its operations compared very unfavourably with those of its competitors, for in early 1929 Imperial had nineteen aircraft in regular service compared with 240 in Germany and the USA (despite being a latecomer) with 250,[10] something Imperial's would-be critics had seemingly not yet registered.

Over the next two years all airline operations were seriously affected by a world economic blizzard, although in 1930 when his strong Francophile Air Minister Lord Thomson suggested the possible combination of its Empire routes with the French, Geddes continued to view the French airlines as rivals that should be treated as such.

In 1930 there was a profit of £60,138 but during the next year general and massive unemployment worldwide brought a 11.4 per cent contraction in Imperial's passenger traffic and a reduced profit of £27,140 – although this did not prevent Geddes from repeating his belief that the airline should become a self-supporting commercial undertaking at the earliest possible moment.[11] Apart from Short's Calcutta and Kent flying boats, Handley Page's H.P.42 aircraft were also being brought into use. These latter aircraft, referred to as the Hannibal class by the airline, weighed more than 20,000lb and were seven months overdue, with the first making its maiden flight on 14 November. They were described as stately, slow and luxurious,[12] but with their huge canvased wings and multiple struts they appeared antiquated when compared with the Junkers G.38, an all-metal cantilever monoplane flying on Lufthansa's Berlin–London route.

A Hannibal class H.P.42: heavy and slow, if with a good safety record. (Author's collection)

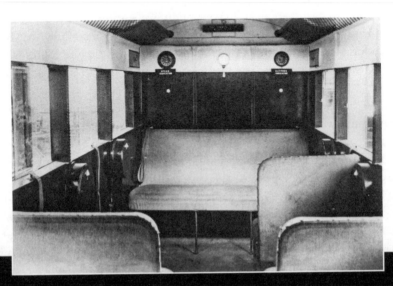

Interior of an early Imperial Airways aeroplane. (Author's collection)

Whatever the confident tone of its chairman, Imperial Airways entered the 1930s with a number of major problems. Although it emphasised its reputation for safety and reliability, its aircraft were undoubtedly slower than its European competitors, and in 1932 details about Europe's civil flying showed Imperial lagging far behind other carriers:

	Aircraft Employed	Average Payload (tons)	Pilots	Weekly Mileage
France	269	1,380	135	109,000
Germany	177	1,849	160	299,000
Italy	77	1,836	61	60,000
Great Britain	32	4,858	32	38,000

Whatever the company's meritorious achievements overseas – particularly its first carriage of mail from London to Cape Town – they involved using a motley collection of aircraft and caused the virtual stagnation of its European operations.

Early in 1932 a question was tabled in the House of Commons by Captain Harold Balfour – whose loyalty towards small airlines was well known – about what he saw as the massive subsidies being paid to Imperial on its Empire routes. This duly revealed that on the newly formed Cairo–Karachi route the subsidy for passengers was £180 with the fare just £58. This was, in fact, only to be expected

The advanced Ensign. (Author's collection)

on a newly instituted route and, under Geddes, subsidies showed a continuous decrease,[13] but this did not stop Balfour from continuing his attacks. During the 1932 Parliamentary Debates on the Air Estimates, he directed them against the airline itself, believing that Imperial's monopoly retarded British civil aviation – in spite of the number of small airline start-ups during the year, including Hillman Airways (for whom Amy Johnson flew some of its runs) and the fledgling Jersey Airways (in conjunction with Railway Air Services) for which some subsidies were provisionally agreed.[14]

Whatever justifications were made by Imperial for its aircraft, it was clear that airliners such as Boeing's 247 – an American low-winged monoplane with a crew of two, carrying up to ten passengers and a stewardess, and capable of cruising at 171mph – pointed the way forward. In fairness, Imperial was weighing up the merits of more technically advanced aircraft in the form of metal-skinned, four-engined monoplanes from Armstrong Whitworth (to be named Ensigns).

Yet, although the order for them was placed in 1934, a leisurely building programme meant that their first flights did not take place until January 1939, just before the war. Things were hardly better with the airline's sister aircraft, the de Havilland DH.91 Albatross, given the class name Frobisher by Imperial, that came into service in the autumn of 1938.

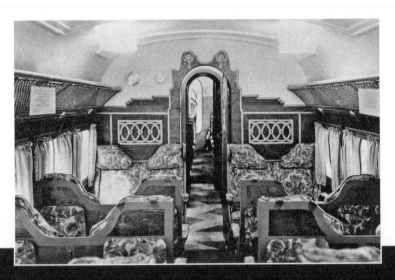

The saloon of Imperial Airways's Handley Page H.P.42 airliner. (Author's collection)

An Imperial Airways Atalanta. (Author's collection)

By 1933 Imperial's older planes were in real danger of being outclassed although the company's first stopgap, the Armstrong Whitworth Atalanta, had made its debut on the Croydon–Brussels–Cologne service during September 1932.[15]

Amazingly, instead of taking exceptional measures to obtain more aircraft, the management decided to institute a quick turnaround service at Hendon to help keep their existing aircraft working as hard as possible, a measure that represented Geddes's faith in time and motion efficiency. 'Within fifteen minutes of landing, two sturdy rostrums were placed around the aircraft, the galley restocked, the aircraft refueled ready for a final inspection and outgoing mail loaded. Within thirty minutes the aircraft was returned to the apron ready for the next flight.'[16]

However things might compare unfavourably with progress elsewhere, during the company's ninth annual general meeting Geddes appeared as confident as ever about Imperial's achievements so far. Announcing an increased profit and a recommended dividend of 5 per cent, he reported an increase in traffic of 75 per cent and a future rationalisation of air mail to the benefit of the company. He was defiant in re-emphasising its record of safety, comfort and service over sheer speed and its undoubted achievements in efficiency and cost-effectiveness – both elements close to his heart. In fact, he went even further, stating that:

From the ratio of traffic receipts to subsidy achieved, we are convinced that the taxpayer in Great Britain gets far more value for his money in civil aviation than the taxpayer in any other country in the world … we are progressing, step-by-step along the path that leads towards independence from subsidies.[17]

Such determination to work towards a wholly independent airline was at variance with other European carriers and, whatever his company's efficiency and proud profile, such a policy condemned it to a relative lack of capital – unless it decided to raise large sums on the open market.

The first signs of a belated conversion came in his concluding remarks, where he concurred with Sefton Brancker that civil aviation was a powerful means of closer international understanding rather than just a business service. 'The more rapid the means of transport, the easier and sooner we arrive at a greater knowledge and understanding between the Commonwealth of nations, the British Empire and between nations and nation.'[18]

In 1934 he went a step further when, after declaring the profit and dividend together with the increasing frequency of the company's Empire routes, he finally acknowledged that increased speed was important – if not all-important – for he still maintained that travellers would pay only a limited amount extra since in Britain the high price of fuel acted as a deterrent to high-speed travel. With his strong railway background, Geddes seemed genuinely against speed for its own sake, and critical of the fact that 'so much of the scientific development that has taken place abroad should have been concentrated on higher and higher air speed almost regardless of cost, rather than obtaining say double or treble the speed of railways at their fares and rates'.[19]

In any case, by now Imperial's chosen status was being challenged by subsidies being given for routes in Europe north of a London–Berlin line. The full significance of this became apparent during the following year when British domestic airlines including Hillman's, United and Spartan Air Lines, Highland Airways and Northern and Scottish Airways banded together to form British Airways. The new airline was due to begin operations from its home airport of Gatwick (although its runway was still grass surfaced) on 1 January 1936, aided by a small Government subsidy of £20,000 and a contract to carry air mail for the Post Office.

Most importantly, British Airways was not restricted to using British-made planes and in November 1936 ordered a small fleet of American Lockheed 10 Electras and Lockheed 14 Super Electras. It was also about to gain a strong professional reputation by equipping its aircraft with the latest navigational and weather aids as well as two-way radios, chemical de-icing and heated carburettors.[20]

Geddes's report for 1935 not only gave the regular summary of profit and dividends but also details of major projects for modernising its headquarters accommodation and its aircraft, initiatives that were likely to have been hastened by the presence of the smaller airlines.

One of Imperial's twenty-eight-strong fleet of two-decked Shorts S.23 Empire flying boats. (Author's collection)

These included plans for a new London terminus at Victoria that he declared would be a 'fitting Terminal for the greatest city in the world and for the British Empire Air services'.[21] He also made reference to the eagerly awaited Ensigns for the Empire routes with a load-carrying capacity of 3½–5 tons, together with Short S.23 Empire flying boats capable of carrying twenty-four passengers and 1½ tons of mail.

Croydon Airport was due to receive long-awaited safety devices in the form of a German Lorenz blind-landing system, the lack of which had been a near scandal and a source of much deep concern to Imperial's pilots. On the other hand, the meeting was not told about the serious unrest being experienced with the company's pilots over their conditions of employment, including delays in granting family allowances for those working overseas, which would soon result in a most damaging strike.

Sir George Beharrell, Geddes's deputy, presented the 1936 report. After announcing a record profit of £140,705, a 6 per cent dividend and a 78 per cent rise in profits from the Empire Air Mail service, he proposed the raising of the directors' fees from £6,500 to £12,000 a year and announced a coming share issue for the capital so urgently needed for further growth. Beharrell also talked enthusiastically about the purchase of the Empire flying boats[22] with their comfort and power, their two decks, smoking room, promenade saloon, 3,000hp and speed of 200mph.[23] He revealed the company's plans for increasing such orders when all the other airlines, except Pan American, were opting for land-planes.

It would not have been a Geddes report without some reference to the gratifying long service of their veteran aircraft, particularly the Hannibals, whose record he believed was second to none. However, whatever the extent of Geddes's beliefs and future plans, all were brought to an end by a sharp deterioration in his health and his sudden death on 22 July 1937.

Predictably this brought different reactions. The acerbic Charles Grey, never a strong admirer, acknowledged that while those who had worked closely with him developed an intense admiration for his abilities and his foresight, they had feared rather than loved him. Grey also concluded in his usual controversial fashion that 'the establishment of Imperial air communications by sea-going flying boats may remain for future generations a lasting monument to Eric Geddes'.[24]

In *The Times*, Sir Ralph Wedgewood called Geddes's methods 'Napoleonic but effective'[25] and understandably Sir George Beharrell gave fulsome praise. He pronounced Geddes's death an irreparable loss to the airline and stressed his belief in the great part the company 'was destined to play in the linking of the Empire and even in the closer relationship of English speaking people'[26] while not forgetting Geddes's work towards the inauguration of the new Empire Air Mail Scheme and experimental Atlantic flights.[27]

Whatever was said (or left unsaid) by the contemporary obituarists, Geddes undoubtedly played a seminal role in the development of Imperial Airways, which conformed to his commercial objectives and management style. However, air historian Robin Higham felt bound to point out he was irascible, forthright and fearsome,[28] proclivities that neither encouraged perfect harmony, nor invited full co-operation. With Geddes in the chair, no board would have dreamed of dealing directly with the staff, including the all-important pilots.

Beyond such churlishness there were his attempts at achieving fiscal soundness by working his limited numbers of aircraft to their very limits, rather than much increasing the company's capital to purchase larger numbers of modern replacements. For such reasons it is fair to say that Geddes's management pattern prevented British civil aviation from taking full advantage of the almost unlimited opportunities that beckoned in the years following the First World War. On the other hand, in its own fashion and under Geddes's strong direction, Imperial Airways never haemorrhaged money and undoubtedly played a dignified if more restricted role than it might have done in British aviation.

Following Geddes's death the airline's critics intensified their earlier attacks and its cause was not helped when, instead of appointing another high-profile figure, Geddes was succeeded in the first place by Sir George Beharrell. Despite his unquestioned gifts with figures he not only lacked Geddes's stature but demonstrated equal – or greater – shortcomings in public relations. At Imperial's general meeting for 1937 he addressed the unfinished business of the previous year by asking the company's shareholders to approve a share issue of £1 million, which he justified by telling them that over the next six years Imperial would be expected to receive £3 million from operating the Government's Empire Air Mail Scheme.

Then – in what could only be seen as unfortunate timing – he asked permission for the company's directors to receive a further £5,000 a year in addition to their recently increased £12,000 annual salary. This was bound to arouse resentment when such increases were not shared by the company's other staff who (under Geddes) had never been lavishly paid. In fact, two months before Geddes's death the company's pilots had come to feel so strongly about long-standing and unresolved issues over their pay and allowances that they formed themselves into the British Airline Pilot's Association (BALPA) through which they hoped to argue their case more effectively. The formation of BALPA was timely since the company was in the process of retraining most of its present pilots for the Empire flying boats and also recruiting additional ones. Given Geddes's attitude to staff matters it was unsurprising that BALPA should be opposed not only by Sir George Beharrell, and the company's managing director George Woods Humphery, but by his deputy Lieutenant Colonel H. Burchall and even by the pilots' official spokesman, Superintendent Major H. Brackley.

Buoyed by such unanimity among its senior staff in October 1937 the company introduced a new pay scale that, although it maintained the current pay of those pilots in employment, new ones were engaged at a much lower rate,[29] a decision that was considered both unfair and inflammatory by the pilots.

Shortly afterwards the company compounded matters by dismissing six pilots, including the Chairman and Vice-Chairman of BALPA, Lane Burslem and W. Rogers. In the case of Rogers, he had flown for the company from the time of its foundation, and previously with both the Royal Flying Corps and Handley Page Transport. Apart from the forming of BALPA, the two had further angered the company by signing a letter on its behalf suggesting that Imperial Airways's service to Budapest be suspended for the winter after an aeroplane had experienced icing that had resulted in a fall in engine power.

When BALPA asked for its association to be recognised and for an opportunity to discuss the question of the dismissed pilots, the company's response came in a solicitor's letter justifying the dismissals and denying any necessity for the pilots to belong to a union. The crisis escalated when the chairman and vice-chairman of BALPA sought the help of the Conservative MP for Stroud, Robert Perkins, an active pilot who had earlier accepted the Association's Vice Presidency and had himself complained to the House of Commons about the lack of de-icing equipment at Croydon Airport.

On 28 October 1937 Perkins duly raised the question of the pilots' wages in the House of Commons following the rise of directors' fees and before the company's aircraft were equipped to effect blind landings. Perkins ended his address on a broader and highly condemnatory note:

> Imperial Airways service in Europe is the laughing stock of the world. The pilots have tried to negotiate but the door has been slammed in their faces. We have tried to wash our dirty linen in private, but that is no longer possible and we much regret that we have to do it in public. We have no alternative but to ask *for an impartial inquiry into the whole position of pilots engaged by Imperial Airways and in fact the whole organisation.*[30]

With Lord Swinton, the Secretary of State for Air, in the House of Lords, it fell upon his Under-Secretary, Lieutenant Colonel Muirhead, to respond, and declare that the Government did not consider it necessary to conduct an inquiry.

In spite of the Government's straight bat, the company was plainly obliged to answer the public criticisms and this occurred a few days later when its Managing Director, George Woods Humphery, issued a somewhat unconvincing statement. This denied that membership of BALPA was the reason for the pilots' dismissals, while expressing his doubts whether the organisation represented Imperial's pilots. (He was misinformed for, despite the refusal of some veteran pilots, approximately 79 per cent of them had joined.) Woods Humphery went on to justify the company's lack of de-icing equipment 'because there was an absence of any reliable methods of combating ice and few airlines were fitted with receivers for a blind approach and because hardly any airports in England provided that facility'.[31] Whatever his denials about the influence of BALPA and the absence of de-icing equipment elsewhere, he finished by announcing that new pilots and radio officers had in fact been put on a more realistic pay scale.

The inadequacy of Woods Humphery's comments caused Perkins to scent blood and interpret his statement as an admission that most of his charges were justified. On 17 November he resumed the attack in the House of Commons by introducing a motion on civil aviation criticising the Air Ministry and Imperial Airways in particular, 'including its old and inadequate aircraft, its decline in cross-channel passenger traffic, the inadequacy of Croydon Airport, the long working hours and the salaries of their pilots, the company's safety record and the need for better technical support for pilots including de-icing equipment and landing aids'.

He ended with the ringing words: 'I believe that nothing short of a public enquiry will shake the Air Ministry into a sense of their responsibilities and into a realisation of the present position.'[32] Perkins succeeded in persuading the legendary John Moore-Brabazon, first holder of a pilot's licence in Britain, to second the motion, thus ensuring a positive response.

The Under-Secretary of State for Air accepted the need for a departmental enquiry. The Committee's recommendations would result in sweeping changes to British civil aviation. As for Imperial Airways, under a new and quite different chairman, it was about to lose its separate identity through a Government-sponsored amalgamation that, during his long rule, Eric Geddes could hardly have imagined, let alone countenanced.

BRITISH CIVIL AVIATION: PIONEERING AIRWAYS WITHIN BRITAIN

From its foundation, Imperial Airways aimed to develop European air routes, flying from Croydon to such cities as Paris, Brussels, Basle, Zurich and Cologne, and also to far-flung destinations within the Empire including South Africa, India, Burma and Singapore. Routes within the United Kingdom were not established until the early 1930s when fledgling companies emerged headed by inspirational, but often unorthodox, figures. These flew relatively short distances usually with only one or two planes, and the need for frequent servicing and the relatively small numbers of fee-paying passengers meant that they either ceased trading quite quickly, entered into co-operative arrangements with their rivals, or sought additional financial backing.

Their services began in 1931 when a sole operator, Michael Scott, offered flights in his Puss Moth light aeroplane between Skegness and Hunstanton. From 1931 to 1933 he was joined by fifteen other small operators, the details of whose services are given below:

	Airline	Date of Registration & Cancellation	No. of Aircraft	Scope of Operation
1	Blackpool & West Coast Air Services	Apr 1933	3	Between Blackpool, Liverpool and Isle of Man
2	British Amphibious Airlines Ltd	Feb 1932	1	Blackpool to Isle of Man
3	British Flying Boats Ltd	23 Jun–Aug 1932	1	One week operation only
4	Eastern Transport Ltd	27 Feb 1932	2	Skegness to Hunstanton, Skegness to Nottingham
5	Great Western Railway Air Service	12 Apr 1933	1	Plymouth to Teignmouth, Plymouth to Cardiff
6	Highland Airways	3 Apr 1933	1	Inverness to Wick, Kirkwall & Thurso (more aircraft later)
7	Hillman's Saloon Coaches and Airways	1 Apr 1932	4	Romford to Clacton, Romford to Paris
8	International Airlines Ltd	8 Jul 1933 (in service ten days only)	2	Croydon to Portsmouth, Southampton to Plymouth
9	Isle of Man Airlines	1932	1	Liverpool to Isle of Man

10	Jersey Airlines	9 Dec 1933	1	Portsmouth to Jersey
11	Midland and Scottish Air Ferries Ltd	10 Mar 1933	4	Renfrew to Cambletown, Islay to Renfrew Renfrew to Belfast, Liverpool to Dublin
12	Norman Edgar, Western Airways Ltd	7 Sep 1933	1	Bristol to Cardiff
13	North Sea Aerial & General Transport Ltd	11 Jul 1933	2	Humber to Grimsby
14	Portsmouth, Southern & Isle of Wight Aviation Ltd	27 Jun 1932	1	Ryde to Shoreham, Ryde to Portsmouth
15	Provincial Airways Ltd	12 Oct 1933	1	Croydon to Southampton, Croydon to Plymouth (intermittent service only)

In 1934 a major new development occurred involving the railway companies, now amalgamated into four main groups viz the London Midland and Scotland (LMS), the London North Eastern Railway (LNER), the Great Western Railway (GWR) and the Southern Railway (SR). Fearing that domestic airlines might add to the damage previously done to their traffic by luxury coaches, they obtained air transport powers through an Act of Parliament of 1929 and established a joint airline called Railway Air Services. Registered on 21 March 1934, this had a nominal capital of £50,000 and following joint discussions, Imperial Airways agreed to hold shares in the new company, supply the pilots and allow its headquarters to be in the Imperial Airways Building at Victoria.

The railways viewed their airline company primarily in defensive terms and Imperial's managing director Woods Humphery, speaking on their behalf, said that in the first instance they intended to proceed slowly and to co-operate as far as possible with existing airlines where they were well managed.[1] Understandably, the air industry was not whole-heartedly welcoming. Charles Grey feared their entry on the grounds that they 'would either try to kill air competition by cutting prices, or that with their vast financial resources they would collar existing air lines and make them so inefficient, not necessarily purposely, but possibly through congenital idiocy that the progress of air transport would be held up'.[2] Whatever their actions, the entry of such major players with large capital resources was bound to be influential.

Those most interested in aviation were Southern and Great Western. Woods Humphery suggested that Southern should consider an association with a company called Spartan Air Lines, which was setting up a service from London's Heston airport to Ryde and Cowes on the Isle of Wight, offering eight trips a day during June, July and August (with extra trips at weekends), reducing to two days a week during the winter. This was on the understanding that Spartan offered a fixed rate per mile with each party paying half the costs and receiving half the receipts.

The Honourable Clive Pearson.

As managing director of Imperial Airways, Woods Humphery had to be cautious about whom he recommended but he knew that Spartan was supported by the formidable Clive Pearson, second son of famed businessman Lord Cowdray. What Woods Humphery did not realise, however, was that Pearson would soon become the most influential figure in domestic aviation.

With Lord Cowdray's eldest son involved with the family's landed estates, Pearson was chosen to run its business empire that, under the banner of Whitehall Securities, acted as a finance and issuing house working closely with Lazard Brothers, the noted merchant bankers. It proved an inspired appointment for, although after reading Mechanical Science at Trinity College Cambridge he was awarded a Third-Class degree, Pearson stayed on for a fourth year to study book-keeping, during which time he developed a rare acumen at interpreting company balance sheets.

A gruff, serious, immensely hard-working man who eschewed publicity, he apparently made few friends but worked very happily with his wife, the former honourable Alicia Knatchbull-Hugesson, in restoring Parham Park, their rundown sixteenth century mansion in Sussex that with typical shrewdness he had bought for just £125,000.[3] Notorious for his fierce attention to detail, his daughter Lavinia recalled how for many years his three children's pocket money had been set at 5s a month. Early each month he used to take them to a bank in Pall Mall where they were solemnly asked how they would like to take their money, with the youngest usually choosing to have it in pennies and half pennies.[4] Their father required them to record every penny they spent and when he inspected their entries, if their records did not balance he would say (with tongue in cheek) 'let us just put unaccounted for – and that will make it come right'.

Pearson's interest in aviation began with the family's factory making metal propellers, whose management board included the aerial enthusiast and MP Captain Harold Balfour, a decorated pilot and authority on aerial matters who profoundly influenced him and who became Under-Secretary of State for Air in 1938. The Pearsons then acquired a small aircraft company owned by Oliver Edwin Simmonds, a senior member of the design team at Supermarine who, before he struck out on his own, had helped to produce the company's S.4 and S.5 seaplanes for the Schneider Trophy. As Balfour acknowledged later, their reason for purchasing the company was because they wanted a (relatively inexpensive) card of entry into the aeroplane construction world.[5]

Simmonds's company was in an early developmental stage. On leaving Supermarine in 1928 he began building an aeroplane in his home at Woolston near Southampton Water, apparently constructing its wings in a bedroom and its fuselage in his living room – in order to assemble the plane he had to remove multiple windows and window frames. After teething troubles it flew adequately. Subsequently with his Cruiser, Simmonds produced an aircraft capable of carrying a pilot and seven passengers. In 1930 Pearson's Whitehall Securities named the firm Spartan Aircraft Ltd.

It says much for the early difficulties experienced by domestic aviation that despite Woods Humphery's recommendation regarding a joint venture between Southern Railways and Spartan for the comparatively popular London–Isle of Wight service, it still lost money. This was certainly not due to inefficiency on Spartan's part for in the six months ending 31 October 1934 it achieved a service regularity of 99.71 per cent with no accidents nor forced landings, and during the whole of 1934 it flew a not inconsiderable 145,000 miles and carried 6,816 passengers plus 56 tons of freight.

Even so, during the year ending 31 March 1934 Spartan lost £15,523 despite receiving Southern Railway's contribution of £2,728. However popular the Isle of Wight service might be compared with others, its take-up was still well below the break-even figure and its total income (including joyrides) was just £9,748 while its outlays totalled £25,271.[6] These included sums of £4,060 for repairs and maintenance, £4,240 for depreciation of aircraft and engines, £4,008 for wages and £4,261 for overheads.

Spartan's problems demonstrated that even under favourable conditions, without subsidies from governments or other sponsoring organisations it was very difficult for a small domestic airline to survive, let alone make profits.

In the following year ending 31 March 1935 Spartan Air Lines lost a further £11,384, and by now it was relying 'entirely on loans of nearly £30,000 from Whitehall Securities, its parent company – a debt which was twice the value of the aircraft it owned.'[7]

Remarkably, in spite of such adverse conditions, two private airlines did manage to survive for some considerable time without subsidies. They were Hillman's and Highland Airways, whose founders not only succeeded in raising the initial capital but decided on the routes to be flown, selected and if necessary prepared the required airfields and – above all – ensured a safe reliable service, despite limited resources and punishing workloads.

While Edward Hillman and Edmund (Ted) Fresson of Highland Airways were widely different personalities, their common determination, business acumen (allied in Fresson's case with the highest piloting skills) and purchase of improved aircraft enabled their embryo airlines to survive against fierce odds.

Hillman came from as unpromising a background as Henry Royce, although his service during the First World War gave him the opportunity to escape his early deprivation. After leaving school at 9 he worked on a farm and then as a brush maker before, at 12, he joined the Army as a drummer boy. The outbreak of the First World War soon gave him the opportunity to show his managerial and management skills and he quickly rose to the rank of sergeant major. In 1914 he was seriously wounded during the retreat from Mons and his injuries left him with a permanent limp, resulting in him being invalided out from the Army. Undaunted, he used his gratuity to buy a taxi that he drove in London's East End before acquiring a car accessories shop in Romford, Essex.[8]

In December 1928 Hillman's extraordinary sense of ambition led him to found a coach company, for which he bought his first vehicle, a twenty-six-seater coach, on hire purchase. He drove it with his eldest son acting as a conductor and it travelled between Stratford Broadway (where he had his garage and office) and Brentwood in Essex, before he extended his service to serve the east coast towns of Clacton, Ipswich, Norwich, Southwold and Yarmouth, attempting to gain an advantage over his competitors by offering luxury coaches and short-stage fares along his routes. His fleet grew rapidly to some 300 before, in 1934 with the establishment of the London Passenger Transport Board, it was compulsorily purchased for £145,000 (£5 million in 2014).

This did not represent his total undertakings for in 1931 he met Harold 'Timber' Wood, a former RAF pilot who was managing a pub just outside Chelmsford. Hillman signed him up for a new company that he registered as Hillman's Saloon Coaches and Airways Ltd., aiming to fly those who used his coaches rather than

One of Ted Hillman's de Havilland Puss Moths. (Author's collection)

the wealthier people who flew with Imperial Airways. Fortunately for Hillman he located Maylands Farm, just north of Romford, a former joy-riding airfield that he was able to take over on 26 November 1931. The next day, his first aircraft, Puss Moth G-ABSB, capable of carrying a pilot and two passengers, was delivered by de Havilland. Hillman called it *Sonny* after his eldest son and it was quickly pressed into service as an air taxi. By December he had bought a second, followed quickly by two others.

Hillman commenced his first regular air service on 1 April 1932 between Maylands and the leading seaside resort of Clacton in Essex. The flight took thirty minutes, thus saving two-and-a-half hours over the road journey, and accordingly he set the air fares to compete with the road services, namely 12s 6d single and £1 a day return. To keep them that low he needed to keep his planes busy, flying every three hours between 0900 and dusk, filling the gaps in between with 5s flips.

At the start Hillman regarded his pilots as little better than bus drivers and he said that he did not want 'high falutin pilots' or 'toffee nosed flying hostesses'. Most were ex-servicemen, like himself, and he paid them a basic £5 a week plus flying pay that varied between 2s 6d and £1, over which he frequently quibbled.[9] He learned to fly himself to prove there was no mystique about their skills but his heavy landings were legendary, and through experience he began to realise the air pilot was in no sense just a bus driver.

Former RAF pilot John Lock, who became the company's senior pilot, recalled how Hillman told him how he wanted his passengers treated:

> See here mate passengers is passengers, treat them all the same. I don't care if it's a bricklayer or baron, they've paid their fare and they 'as their value, but don't get any special privileges from me, see? Take their tips, if they offer them, five pence or a fiver and give 'em a smile for it. If you turn it down, you will only hurt their feelings an' they won't come again![10]

Later, apart from the regular day trips and joyriding, Hillmann undertook air photography and press work: no commission was refused.

To cope with rapidly increasing demand, Hillmann ordered five larger Fox Moths capable of carrying four passengers, at a cost of £1,045, and after extending his route to Margate he claimed to take passengers anywhere for between 3d and 6d a mile.[11] Hillman never cut any corners with the servicing of his planes but he worked his pilots extremely hard: John Lock maintained that in the summer it was often midnight before they landed their last load of trippers.

In a major attempt to boost publicity, Hillmann hosted a display at Maylands on 24 September 1932 organised by William Courtenay, aviation correspondent of the *Evening Standard*.[12] This attracted a crowd of 20,000 and dignitaries, including the Lord Mayor of London and his wife, who were flown from Heston to Maylands wearing their silk hats and chains of office with an escort provided by the RAF. Lunch was provided at the White Hart Hotel in Romford, during which there were a number of speeches. When the time came for Hillmann to toast his guests he had a script commencing with the words: 'Ladies and Gentlemen – I have not had the advantages of education which you enjoy. Mine was the great university of life,' but, going with his instinct, he stopped and exclaimed: 'Oh Hell, I can't go on with that rubbish. I just wish you good 'ealth.' This apparently brought cheers and roars of laughter.[13]

Although by the year's end Hillman had lost £670 on his air travel venture, this did not stop him taking another important step, namely opening a service to Paris in direct competition with Imperial Airways. He returned to De Havilland with a request for an aircraft capable of taking twice as many passengers as the Fox Moth and ordered four Dragons for £2,800 each (plus £105 for seating), requiring them to be delivered by April 1933 in readiness for his intended service. The first aircraft was christened *Maylands* by Amy Johnson (who flew briefly for Hillman), and on 1 April 1933 the scheduled flight to Paris started. The fare, including ground transport from the city centres, was £5 10s , in comparison with Imperial's £8 10s for its Silver Wing service.

Maylands proved too small for these larger aircraft and, on 23 June 1934, Hillman moved to a new airfield at Stapleford Tawney, just 14 miles from central London.

By the year ending 30 September Hillman had carried 10,465 passengers and the company was able to report its first profit of £3,547 18s 2d, with a lucrative mail contract also in the offing.

Shortly afterwards the airline received a harsh reminder about the hazards of flight when a Dragon Rapide bound for Paris with six passengers crashed into the sea in conditions of low cloud and rain. The most likely cause was that the pilot had mistaken the horizon, and as a result the Department of Civil Aviation required all commercially licensed pilots to undergo an instrument flying test.[14]

This, however, did not prevent Hillman's continuing growth. It extended its passenger services to Castle Bromwich and later to Liverpool, before it was decided to convert the airline into a public company with a nominal capital of £150,000 made up of 600,000 shares of 5s each. Most of the public issue of 400,000 shares were soon taken up and Ted Hillman agreed to act as Deputy Chairman and Managing Director for seven years at a salary of £1,250.

With the addition of further Continental destinations, increased services and cargo and charter work already under consideration, prospects seemed excellent. All this changed when on 31 December 1934, Hillman died suddenly at the age of 45. The effect of his war service and the strains of business life, accentuated by high blood pressure, had brought on a massive heart attack.

A de Havilland DH.90 Dragonfly, sister aircraft to the Dragon Rapide, operated successfully by both Hillman's and Highland Airways. (Author's collection)

He was given a magnificent funeral at St Edward's Church in Romford with the hearse and carriages drawn by black horses and the Market Square filled with his family, staff and others from civil aviation.[15] His unique influence over the company was seen when at his death the shares dropped by almost a fifth, although in his absence the company again expanded rapidly before overreaching itself and announcing a £28,000 loss on 10 October 1935.

This opened the way for an amalgamation between Hillman's and United and Spartan Air Lines that realised Pearson's dream for a unified British airline to fly the domestic and European routes, as a counterpart to those covered by Imperial Airways across the Empire. Although a serious difficulty arose over the two sides' varying assets, with those of Hillman's totalling £45,490 against United and Spartan's £72,620, the financial power of Whitehall Securities was demonstrated when the balance of £23,673 needed for Hillman's was quickly underwritten by the wealthy Gerard d'Erlanger.

Of the founding directors for the new company, those from Whitehall Securities included Harold Balfour and Hillman's included Gerard d'Erlanger and Major McCrindle (as managing director). While Hillman was by no means the only self-made man in early British aviation, his success went well beyond normal expectations. Rugged, forthright and immensely hard working, he was feared for his moods and undoubted streak of ruthlessness. On the other hand, he was also a good judge of men and capable of swift decision-making, combining successful hands-on management with strategic insight and firm business control. He set his own stamp on civil aviation by likening his flights both in price and their no-frills nature to coach services, which like them had to be reliable and kept to strict timetables (despite varying weather conditions). By such means he established the tradition of bringing aviation to the man in the street that was later taken up by Freddie Laker and is currently developed by airlines such as Ryanair and Flybe.

———— • ◆ • ————

Like Hillman, Ernest Edmund (Ted) Fresson became a legend in his own lifetime. Born in 1891, he was brought up in Wickford, Essex, where from boyhood he took every opportunity to watch early aviation at Hendon. In 1911 he went to China as an agent for engineering goods, where he contracted typhus fever and almost died. Upon regaining his health, and with war raging in Europe, he went to Canada, where he volunteered for the Royal Flying Corps. Following his acceptance and successful pilot training he took part in convoy patrols off East Anglia.

On demobilisation Fresson married and returned to China, where his wife died of typhoid fever, leaving him with a three-month-old daughter. Although he worked round the clock to set up a small aircraft factory, when an agent from the Junkers factory arrived with a more advantageous business package, Fresson had to leave, albeit with a compensation package. Back in Britain during 1929–31 he bought a part ownership in an aerial circus. It put on displays on makeshift landing grounds all over Britain, after which it offered joyrides. Whether part owners or not, the pilots had to work incredibly hard, and on one memorable Saturday afternoon Fresson claimed to have made 114 landings and take-offs.[16]

During this time he flew a Gipsy Moth to Wick and Orkney and in late September 1931 he was approached by local businessmen to start an air ferry service between Inverness and Orkney, including the carriage of mail in each direction. This meant raising capital at a time of widespread financial difficulties but, although his attempts on Orkney proved unsuccessful, in Edinburgh he obtained the sole rights to carry *The Scotsman* newspaper from Inverness to Kirkwall. In Inverness Mr Donald of Macrae and Dick Ltd (Inverness motor engineers) agreed to help set up a company to be called Highland Airways with Fresson as its Managing Director and Donald as Chairman. An initial capital of £10,000 was agreed, with Macrae and Dick offering to provide office space and booking facilities.

Fresson's next problem was to locate a suitable site for an airfield. Acting on advice, he contacted the Inverness town clerk about turning part of the town's adjacent Longman fields into a municipal airport. This meant laying overhead telephone wires underground and finding the Longman's tenant farmers alternative grazing rights, but once these needs were met agreement was quickly given.

Things were more difficult at Kirkwall, where aircraft were seen as direct competitors to the well-established local shipping line, until a farmer offered Fresson a five-year lease – providing he filled in open ditches and levelled the ground himself. In fact, the sites (and emergency landing places) that Fresson selected and prepared at Kirkwall, Wick, Thurso, and later all over the Highlands and Islands, would be used by the RAF during the Second World War and from 1947 onwards by BEA.

A notable success for Fresson that gave some indication of the regard in which his airline had already come to be held occurred in July 1934, just a year after its foundation. He had decided upon a landing site on North Ronaldsay, the most isolated of the Orkney Islands, but when he told Mr Swanney, the island's postmaster, that the necessary construction work was beyond the capacity of his infant company, the resourceful Swanney assembled sixty men with twenty carts, who pulled down a sizable stone dyke separating the 28-acre site, before levelling the ground and clearing it of stones – all within a day. The islanders subsequently offered it to him free of charge.

The year before – on 8 May 1933 – Highland Airways Ltd had been launched on Inverness's Longman field, where Provost MacDonald's wife had named Fresson's lone Monospar *Inverness* before smashing a bottle of Highland Dew whisky against its propeller. Despite indifferent weather, Fresson took off promptly at 10 a.m. carrying a 70lb package of the *Scotsman* newspapers and three passengers: Sir Edmund Finlay of *The Scotsman*, Douglas Gabriel of Anglo–American Oil and Mr D. Smith of the White

Horse Whisky company. The journey to Wick took fifty minutes and, after a short stopover, twenty-five more to Kirkwall. The passengers conducted their business at Kirkwall before Fresson set off back at 3.53 p.m., stopping at Wick for fifteen minutes and arriving at Inverness by 5.20 p.m.

By the end of May he had carried 143 passengers and by now the weather was improving. In the event of Inverness becoming fogbound, Fresson had the foresight to select two alternative landing places, one on the high ground of Culloden Moor alongside the battlefield and another beside an elevated point before the main road from Perth descended to Inverness.

On 17 June 1933 Fresson attempted to publicise his new service in a similar way to Hillman, by holding an air pageant to celebrate the official opening of the Longman airfield. Following a well-patronised ball held at the Inverness Station Hotel, where the cost of attendance was set at 8s a head, 20,000 people watched the flying, which included aerobatics, a comedy turn with Fresson dressed as a woman, and a parachute jump. During June he carried 206 passengers, a creditable but still modest total.

The ceremony on 29 May 1934 when Captain Ted Fresson accepted responsibility for an airmail service, following which he flew from Inverness to Kirkwall with the first mail in a Dragon Rapide. (By permission of Macrae and Dick Ltd)

The fragile state of his new airline was demonstrated when in foggy conditions Fresson was forced to land in a field where there was a deep overgrown trench and his plane sustained major damage. He was not to suffer a comparable accident during the next fifteen years, but in the meanwhile he had to find another plane while his Monospar was shipped south for major repairs. He took the gamble of hiring a Fox Moth aircraft together with its pilot for a limited period before the Monospar was returned. At this time he also took delivery from de Havilland of a more powerful and larger airliner, an eight-seat Dragon Rapide, the money for which he raised by issuing £1,000 in shares, taken up by *The Scotsman*, with Macrae and Dick generously making up the balance.

With two or more aircraft, Fresson was able to take charter flights across the Highlands and began using a field at Dyce, Aberdeen, that is still the site of the city's airport.

From early 1933 Fresson had been carrying sick passengers to and from Balfour Hospital in Kirkwall, which led to the establishment of air ambulance services in the Northern Isles.

On 29 May 1934 Fresson passed another milestone when he launched the Highlands' first regular internal air mail service, for which he was given the Post Office's official pennant before flying from Inverness to Kirkwall with more than 2,000 letters. By becoming the official mail carrier Fresson added the third essential ingredient for a successful airline, the first two being passengers and newspapers. The mail contract was granted on the proviso that he gave a regular service and in the twelve months to May 1934 he achieved an incredible 97 per cent reliability. This was no flash in the pan for over the next three years, in spite of highly variable and sometimes violent northern weather, it rose to 98 per cent – a truly magnificent achievement.

In August 1934 Fresson extended his services to the Orkney Islands and on 10 August 1934 started a twice-weekly one between Kirkwall and North Ronaldsay, calling on demand at Ronsay, Westray, Sanday and Stronsay.

Fresson kept up his service during the most adverse weather conditions when boats were forced to shelter in their harbours.[17] He trained the islanders to work in teams of twelve when greeting him. The 'drill' was to allow his aircraft 'to descend almost vertically keeping the nose slightly down until it touched down and the waiting strong men were able to grab hold of the wings, struts and tailplane to prevent it lifting off again with successive gusts'.[18] Gales of 70mph were not uncommon and it was only then that the pilot could allow the tail to come down, hoping to keep the aircraft on the ground before his ground party tied it to a lorry or car while continuing to hold it by the wing tips.

By October 1934 Fresson was given a contract from the Orkney Council to fly an 'on demand' air ambulance service between the islands and between Orkney and Aberdeen, which not only saved lives but gave the more remote regions the same

Ted Fresson and Robert Donald standing beside Highland Airways's first aircraft, Monospar G-ACEW. (By permission of Macrae and Dick Ltd)

sense of security enjoyed by those on such flights from Glasgow to the Western Isles. The network of routes continued to grow when on 1 December 1934 Fresson started a mail service between Inverness and Wick, and on Friday, 5 April 1935 one from Inverness to Shetland. On 3 June 1936 came a new Aberdeen–Shetland service and on 13 May 1937 his first landing on the treacherous Fair Isle (between Orkney and Shetland) with its renowned downdraughts when approaching its sheer cliffs.

By 1935, although Fresson had proved he could keep going on his own, his continued expansion plans needed further investment and he agreed to become a subsidiary of Pearson's United Airways based in Glasgow. (In the first instance Fresson had permission to continue under his own name but when his airline came under the mantle of Scottish Airways Ltd he was reduced to becoming a director of the Inverness-based operation with a seat on the main board.)

Prior to the amalgamation, Fresson's aeroplanes (together with those of Eric Gander Gower's at Allied Airways and John Sword's Scottish Air Ferries) had already brought the advantages of air travel to the far northern communities some time before much of England and Wales. Apart from pioneering and developing the required landing grounds amid inhospitable terrain, the services required the utmost human endeavour by pilots lacking wireless aids or specific meteorological reports,

George Griffiths, chief engineer of Highland Airways, adjusting the airmail pennon for the company's second mail service from Inverness to Wick. (By permission of Macrae and Dick Ltd)

working on compass bearings while they crabbed their way through gales and fog before, on occasion, landing on airfields illuminated solely by the crossed beams of cars' headlights.

By the end of 1935 following the amalgamation of Hillman's Airways, Spartan Air Lines and the Blackpool-based United Airways, Clive Pearson completed the process by bringing in Highland, Northern and Scottish Airlines into a group he called Allied British Airways. By 29 October the title was changed to British Airways Limited, which on 11 December was converted into a public company with a funding of £250,000. This qualified for mail contracts and other subsidies without being subjected to the restrictions – such as those on purchasing aircraft – imposed earlier on Imperial Airways.

With Pearson as Chairman and the energetic and like-minded Major McCrindle as his Managing Director, British Airways sketched out future routes to Europe while there seemed a good chance of a new route to South America, which in the absence of suitable British aircraft superior planes such as the Lockheed Electra (one of which would take Neville Chamberlain to Munich) and the Junkers Ju 52 were purchased.

British Airways sorely needed a growing European market because it was far from dominant within the UK, where from 1934 onwards, apart from cross-water services such as those to the Isle of Wight, the Railway Air Services offered a trunk route. This went from London to Glasgow via Birmingham, Manchester and Belfast, which in August of 1934 received four-engined de Havilland DH.86s[19]

The railways were undoubtedly looked on with suspicion by many within the air industry for their defensive mentality if not for their direct measures against other providers. With their extensive web of travel agents, until 1936 they had proved able to deny booking facilities to British Airways and other independent airlines, who also competed against a subsidised Imperial Airways. Such suspicions were voiced by *Flight* in its issue of 21 May 1936 where it wondered whether the railway companies really wanted to help in the expansion of local airlines or 'whether they intended to stifle those companies which are in competition with them is a matter, the development of which we shall await with interest'.[20]

As late as 10 July 1939 in the House of Commons Sir Hugh Seely MP cited the railways as buying up all the internal airlines and slowly strangling them. In this regard he quoted the example of Railway Air Services from London to Glasgow where there were two services a day, the second of which had three stops after it left Victoria and therefore took six hours over the journey, roughly the same as a train[21]

While much had been achieved in a remarkably short time by British Airways and others, progress in Britain could still not be compared with the fast-expanding American airlines over their vast country or, more pertinently, with their Continental rivals. Internally the competing firms were scrapping over a market that, because of other efficient communications, remained a small one.

It was therefore essential that further attempts at rationalisation should be made during the remaining years before the war. Because of the growing criticisms being directed against it, the state-supported Imperial Airways was arguably the most obvious target for change. The nature of the attempts to expand its services and their quite unexpected effects on British aviation as a whole are considered in Chapter 15.

THE ROYAL AIRCRAFT ESTABLISHMENT: INSPIRATION AND INSPECTION

Any consideration of British aviation's interwar years and particularly those of the later 1930s is incomplete without reference to the particular contributions made by the Royal Aircraft Establishment (RAE), the traditional birthplace of British military aeronautics and arguably the oldest official aviation body in the world, whose pattern of development would directly affect its input during the period.

From the outset in 1878, when militia officer Captain James Lethbridge Templer received a grant of £150 to build an Army balloon (that made its first ascent on 23 August that year), the RAE would become known for its strong idiosyncratic characters with their own ideas about innovative progress. As a militia officer rather than a regular who was subject to the service's frequent and varied postings, he accumulated an unrivalled knowledge about the construction and use of balloons for battlefield observation. A man of some private means with an impressive physique and a waxed moustache of epic proportions, he single-handedly propelled the Army into the forefront of ballooning.

Colonel James Templer (Royal Aeronautical Society/ National Aerospace Library)

Following his unit's participation in the Army manoeuvres of 1889–90, Templer's Balloon School moved from Woolwich to Aldershot into the Royal Engineer lines.[1] There it extended its activities into constructing man-lifting kites as well as balloons and was renamed the Balloon Factory, with Templer promoted to Major. During the Anglo–Boer War (1899–1902) in South Africa, Templer's balloons came into their own by playing an important role in three major battles south of Ladysmith during December 1899 and January 1900. Subsequent plans for the kites and balloons to be supplemented by airships led to the search for a larger site needed to accommodate an airship shed. This was found at South Farnborough just 3 miles from Aldershot, on the edge of Farnborough Common.

During the opening years of the twentieth century, two other outstanding individuals emerged, Lieutenant Colonel John Capper and the celebrated American cowboy, showman and kitist Samuel Franklin Cody. After a confrontation with General Sir John French, commander of Aldershot Military District, Templer was replaced by Capper, who became both Superintendent of the Balloon Factory and Commandant of the Balloon School, where Royal Engineers' personnel were trained in aviation skills. In 1906 Capper recruited Cody as his kiting instructor, although he was given a wider brief to work on the school's airship and – most remarkable of all – to build an aeroplane.

Despite the Wright brothers' first flight in 1903, Capper planned to make Farnborough the world's leading aviation centre – although his ambitions were

Army airship sheds at Farnborough. (Author's collection)

Colonel Capper and other notable figures in early aviation attending a kite display. From the left: Mr W.H. Dines, Colonel J.E. Capper, Hon. C.S. Rolls, Mrs Bruce, German military attaché, Major Baden-Powell, Mr E.P. Frost, Colonel F.C. Trollope, Colonel J.D. Fullerton, and Mr E.S. Bruce. (Royal Aeronautical Society/National Aerospace Library)

hampered by his limited knowledge of aeronautics and the restricted financial support from the War Office. Even so, largely as a result of Cody's remarkable skills, Capper constructed the Army's first airship. The two men flew it to London, where it was irretrievably damaged.

Capper's plans for a replacement proved abortive. But on 16 October 1908 Cody succeeded in becoming the first man to fly in Britain in an aeroplane of his own making. Unforgivably Capper, who never fully appreciated Cody, failed to acknowledge his triumph and in the same month a defence sub-committee convened by Prime Minister Herbert Asquith ruled against further aircraft construction at Farnborough (which the Secretary of State for War, Richard Haldane, considered had been conducted in an amateurish and unscientific way).

The upshot was that Cody and his fellow constructor, John Dunne, were dismissed and Capper's responsibilities were restricted to balloons and airships, before in 1910 he returned to main-line engineering duties. Cody continued to demonstrate his

Nulli Secundus, the first Army airship. (Author's collection)

F. McWade and Colonel Capper (right) in the car of the smaller Army airship Baby. (Royal Aeronautical Society/National Aerospace Library)

Samuel Cody's first flight, 16 October 1908. (Author's collection)

genius by constructing and flying aircraft in a private capacity, and the committee's short-sightedness towards aircraft was revealed when six months later Louis Bleriot flew across the English Channel. This proved the first occasion when Farnborough's senior management was at odds with the British military and political establishment over the construction of aircraft. The second, which occurred during the First World War, resulted from Richard Haldane's choice of Mervyn O'Gorman, a charismatic civilian engineer who replaced Capper in order to implement a more scientific method for aeronautical research and development at Farnborough.[2] O'Gorman, who was second only to Cody among Farnborough's characters, and who undoubtedly wielded more power, set out to make Farnborough a unique research centre that would again design and produce aircraft.

His presence was soon felt when the Factory began to maintain and repair aircraft used by the Balloon School (itself about to evolve into the Army Air Battalion before becoming the Royal Flying Corps in 1912).

O'Gorman recruited aircraft designer F.M. Green, followed by the outstanding Geoffrey de Havilland when he purchased de Havilland's first successful aeroplane. Under the mantle of reconstruction, O'Gorman took advantage of de Havilland's and Green's skills to design and build planes of their own. In April 1911 Farnborough

Mervyn O'Gorman. (Royal
Aeronautical Society/National
Aerospace Library)

The headquarters of the Royal Flying Corps at Farnborough. (Author's
collection)

Removing an engine from an Army aircraft at Farnborough. (Author's collection)

obtained partial recognition as a production facility when it was renamed the Royal Aircraft Factory.

Although in 1912 Cody won the competition to build the most suitable aircraft for the embryonic Royal Flying Corps, the Factory's B.E.2 was generally considered to be by far the better aircraft although, being Factory built, it was barred from the competition. Even so, the Factory was given to understand the B.E.2 would constitute the main support for the RFC's aircraft, and following research work by Farnborough scientist E.T. Busk (supervised closely by O'Gorman), the B.E.2c was developed into the first inherently stable aircraft, of which 2,000 were built by outside firms. Other factory designs followed, including the B.E.8 and the outstanding S.E.5.

In his search for excellence O'Gorman also fearlessly recruited the country's best scientists and engineers, and established specialist departments in physics, chemistry, engine metallurgy and wireless, while from 1913, inspection methods were developed for both aircraft and their accessories. In 1914 this process was elevated into a department where the accessories examined included petrol flow meters, tautness meters, clinometers, anemometers, pressure heads, cockpit lighting, etc.[3] This was a time of rapid expansion for the Factory and by late 1916 its workforce had increased to more than 5,000, including some 3,000 women. O'Gorman's confident and wide ranging initiatives including aircraft construction were virtually bound to bring adverse criticisms, including the accusation that the Factory deliberately set

Early military aircraft flying over Farnborough Common. (Author's collection)

Airship and aeroplane sheds at Farnborough. (Author's collection)

out to undermine private constructors and unashamedly pirated other people's ideas. One trenchant critic was Charles Grey, the opinionated but powerful editor of *The Aeroplane*, who believed he represented the aviation industry. He had inadvertently been refused entry to the Factory and never forgave the slight. His criticisms were abetted by private aircraft constructors, including Frederick Handley Page and 'Tommy' Sopwith, who wanted their own models adopted by the RFC.

Following attacks in the House of Commons, a committee of inquiry was set up under Sir Richard Burbridge, which concluded that in future the Factory should confine its activities to the research and development aspects of aeronautics rather than engaging in the production of aircraft, even experimental prototypes. Turning his fire directly on O'Gorman, Burbridge decided that the Factory's Superintendent should possess special business experience and administrative capacity, qualifications that were never on O'Gorman's CV, although he was unquestionably a highly gifted executive. As O'Gorman had completed his initial seven-year term as superintendent, it was decided he should be transferred to assume the relatively innocuous appointment of consulting engineer to the Director General of Military Aeronautics at the War Office. At a stroke, Farnborough's aircraft design and production facilities were ended and O'Gorman neutralised. Henceforth, Farnborough's role would be to act as a research centre for the aviation industry, primarily to examine and report on equipment submitted to it, although it was also expected to carry out original

The Royal Aircraft Factory, Farnborough. (Author's collection)

research of its own. To this end all those engaged in the design and production of aircraft were straightaway reallocated to private industry, where their combined earnings quickly rose to £42,000 a year compared with the total of £6,000 a year they had received at the Factory.

O'Gorman was replaced as Superintendent by Henry Fowler, formally chief mechanical engineer of the Midland Railway, who, whatever his administrative capacity, had no aeronautical experience but who in 1917 took on the additional role of Assistant Director General of Aircraft Production. Apart from supervising the reorganisation of the factory and masterminding a very successful visit by King George V, Fowler was directly concerned with the air industry's production of the factory-designed S.E.5, of which no fewer than 5,205 were built. Within seventeen months Henry Fowler was awarded a knighthood for services to aviation and the munitions industry, thereby giving Mervyn O'Gorman legitimate grounds for wondering if there could be a curse on Farnborough's outstanding sons such as Templer, Cody and himself.

Six months later the Factory was renamed the Royal Aircraft Establishment to avoid confusion with the newly formed Royal Air Force (RAF), and to confirm its move away from the designing and building of aircraft to concentrating wholly on the functions of research and testing. The path was thus set for its contributions during the interwar period when Fowler was succeeded as Superintendent by W. Sidney Smith, a 52-year-old graduate engineer who already had experience as an inspector for dangerous trades at the War Office. He would remain in post for ten years and his task of developing the RAE into an acclaimed research centre coincided with fierce retrenchment following the war, when its 5,000 employees were quickly reduced to a fifth and Treasury grants were reduced proportionately. Despite the cutbacks, Sidney Smith continued to emphasise the aeronautical responsibilities of O'Gorman's original departments and added extra ones concerned with the latest technological developments. The familiar research departments of aerodynamics, engine experimental, physics and instruments, metallurgical, mechanical test and chemical and fabric were joined in 1922 by others in wireless and photographic, air worthiness and contracts. Sidney Smith also continued with Farnborough's trade school for apprentices in aeronautical engineering.

In 1924, as part of the countrywide retrenchment a committee under Air Commodore F.C. Halahan re-examined the RAE's establishment with a view to further cost savings, which he saw as attainable by defining the RAE's research functions more accurately. Henceforth, he recommended they should be directed towards:

a)   experimental and development work on aeroplanes and engines
b)   testing of experimental instruments and accessories
c)   flying instrument development for which there was little commercial demand

d) investigating failures within aircraft and components

e) liaising with industrial contractors for research purposes

f) carrying out technical supervision during the construction of experimental machines

g) approving the design and stressing of new aeroplanes and the issue of airworthiness certificates

h) issuing technical publications where applicable.[4]

These declared functions were so close to the previous ones that they suggested a strong element of window dressing and despite the Halahan Committee's attempts to make the research areas more specific, under Sidney Smith the RAE's outstanding scientists were left to work upon their favoured areas of research whether they entirely fitted Halahan's definitions or not.

However serious the staff and material shortages, much excellent work was carried out by such as Dr F.A. Lindemann, G.H. Norman, Dr A.A. Griffith, H. Glauert, L.C. Bygrave, I.J. Gerard and E.J.H. Lynam.[5]

Lindemann, for instance, investigated the seemingly intractable problem of aircraft spinning by flying and spinning obsolete aircraft over a Camera Obscura; Norman inherited and extended the work on light alloy pistons, cylinder heads and barrels; Griffith wrote a brilliant report in 1926 on 'An Aerodynamic Theory of Turbo Design'; Glauert became outstanding for his knowledge of aerodynamics and was Farnborough's first Fellow of the Royal Society; Bygrave was the originator of bomb ballistic research; Gerrard developed a method of full-scale testing of aeroplanes; and Lynam made great strides with his work on the variable pitch propeller.

It was a measure of the enthusiasm and dedication of Farnborough's scientists that from the early interwar years onwards they willingly took enormous risks with their experiments and a number lost their lives in the process. At the end of the war the Advisory Committee on Aeronautics had, for instance, highly praised F. Lindemann, H. Glauert and R.C. Harris for their experimental flying 'during which their disregard for personal danger was no less admirable than that of their fellow officers in the field'.[6] Three years after the war Major Norman, a notable and inventive engineer at Farnborough, actually set fire to his S.E.5 fighter while it was in flight so that he could be sure of new fire-extinguishing apparatus. After one test he overturned on landing, and although his injuries did not seem dangerous at the time, he collapsed and died later in the year.[7]

Sidney Smith retired in 1928 to be succeeded by A.H. Hall, who held a First-Class honours degree in Cambridge University's Mechanical Tripos. Hall had previously supervised the Government's airship programme at Cardington and, while he did not possess O'Gorman's charisma, he ably led the RAE at a time of expansion and development in which it prepared for its destined role in the Second World War as a leading research and test facility, investigating every aspect of aeronautical science. Under Hall, for instance, the RAE's department of aerodynamics led by the outstanding Hermann Glauert and George Douglas delivered ground-breaking results. Their main contribution came with the construction of wind tunnels, particularly the one of 1929 that had a working section fully 24ft in diameter and was housed in the Establishment's massive Q121 building, which could test not only propellers and scale models but complete aircraft. The test specimens were positioned in front of its fan by heavy cranes and the delicate balancing equipment used to make the test measurements was located in the building's tall tower, which became a local landmark.[8] In 1939 the building of a 4,000hp wind tunnel began, capable of testing scale model aircraft of 6ft wingspan and speeds of up to 600mph, and in pressures varying from one sixth to four times atmospheric pressure.[9]

By the beginning of the war new functions were being carried out. Methods of calculating the drag of wings were developed by H.B. Squire and A.D. Young, and experimental work on the effect of surface roughness continued during the early years of the Second World War, with particular reference to camouflage paints.[10] In 1938 the instrument and photographic department was responsible for constructing an air position indicator in latitude and longitude, the first automatic dead reckoning navigation equipment to be used in the war by both Bomber and Coastal Commands. It went on to develop a PX night camera using a type of photo-electronically operated shutter and a trailer capable of developing and printing air photographs.[11]

In June 1937 the Air Ministry approached the armament department to develop an incendiary bomb as a matter of the highest priority. Continuous day and night work for a period of approximately

A.H. Hall, Superintendent of the RAE. (FAST)

three weeks resulted in finalising the basic pattern and ballistic characteristics of such a weapon, which formed the prototype of the 4lb incendiary bomb so extensively used in the Second World War.

In November 1938 authority was received to develop a gyroscopic aerial predictor gun sight, which was introduced into both the RAF and the USAF during the war.

At about the same time Farnborough's experimental wireless department developed a complete system of air and ground VHF short-range radio telephone communication equipment that was in operational use during the Battle of Britain.

The engine experimental department was by no means left behind for by 1939 it had developed improved sparking plugs capable of operating reliably with leaded fuels and high engine boost pressures where aluminium oxide was used as an insulator instead of the mica formerly employed.[12] It also conducted work on the prevention of icing in aero-engine carburettors and the prevention of vapour locking up fuel systems under altitude conditions.[13]

Being Farnborough, it would never be without its quirkier investigations, such as the formation in 1938 of a camouflage department that developed a method of utilising old bus tyres suitably shredded for runway camouflage applications – only to have it abandoned due to 'a shortage of rubber and substitute wood chips'.[14]

Following the transfer of scientists from Bawdsey, radar work was started early in the war with the cleaning up of the 'chain stations' and erecting new ones for the south and west coasts, including ones capable of tracking low-flying aircraft.[15]

Such increasing responsibilities were reflected in Farnborough's staff levels. While until 1934 the number of senior scientific and technical staff had remained below 250, during the four years from 1934 to 1938 they rose steadily from 346 to 369 then 448 and 553. The outbreak of war brought rapid expansion and the total workforce rose to some 6,000.[16]

In retrospect, although the 1908 Defence Committee's decision against aeroplanes led to the dismissal of Samuel Cody and the loss of his renowned powers, the decision of the 1916 Burbridge Committee that once and for all ended the RAE's involvement with aeroplane design and production enabled it to develop into the renowned RAE of the future. Whereas the combination of outstanding designer Geoffrey de Havilland and his chief Mervyn O'Gorman led to great strides being made in aircraft construction that compared favourably with the private firms, this was not sure to continue under lesser men. In any case, the interwar years saw a private aircraft industry produce the aeroplanes required by the Air Ministry, some of which were to prove of outstanding quality. By the same token, with Farnborough relieved of the design and production of aircraft, Henry Fowler could develop O'Gorman's previous departments into most effective research and inspection facilities for both the civil air industry and the RAF. Under his successor A.H. Hall, Farnborough's tradition of original and independent thinking endured, if in a less confrontational way than before. By giving his scientists remarkably free rein to pursue their favoured researches, he attracted a generation of sometimes awkward, but in the main dedicated and strong-minded, 'boffins' who took Farnborough to ascending levels of scientific achievement. However, with such latitude along with notable advances there were likely to be blind spots and unmemorable investigations. How fourteen years were allowed to pass after A.A. Griffith's brilliant paper on the theory of turbine design before the emergence of the RAE's first axial-flow gas turbine is hard to believe, although Griffith's animosity toward Frank Whittle's competing design should never be forgotten. For whatever reasons it meant that the opportunity for a British jet fighter to dominate the skies during the early part of the Second World War was lost. However, it was only to be expected that following the war a new generation of Farnborough scientists should seize the immense opportunities to help develop the supersonic Concorde.

Whatever the lost chances and the earlier maulings by Government committees that proved so unjust to Farnborough's early sons, the Establishment progressed. During the interwar period under less high-profile leaders it carried out the testing of new aircraft and their systems using equipment unavailable to the private companies.

By such measures together with inventions such as the glycol engine cooler for advanced interceptors, and the early development of VHF radio, Farnborough helped to move the home nation to the forefront of current aviation developments.

PART 4

RACE FOR LOST TIME
1938–40

POST-MUNICH: CLOSING THE GAP

Despite the concerted efforts of Swinton, Freeman and others in modernising and expanding the RAF, when Neville Chamberlain met Adolf Hitler at Munich on 29–30 September 1938 to discuss Germany's reoccupation of the Sudetenland there were still most serious deficiencies in both the RAF's Bomber and Fighter Commands. In the case of Fighter Command, out of its twenty-nine mobilisable squadrons and their 406 aircraft, instead of the 688 considered necessary to meet any anticipated German attacks, only five were equipped with Hurricanes (seventy aircraft) and only one (19 Squadron at Duxford) had received its Spitfires (fourteen aircraft). With the exception of such Hurricanes and Spitfires the British fighters had little or no margin of speed over the German bombers, and even the Hurricanes were limited to fighting up to 15,000ft. The position with the reserve forces was worse still: out of a total of 2,500 reserve pilots only about 200 were fit to go into their service units immediately.[1] In the circumstances, if Chamberlain had failed at Munich and if during September 1938 Germany had in fact launched a lightning attack on Czechoslovakia under its contingency plan Case Green, France's treaty with that country would have obliged it to intervene, following which (according to the British Foreign Secretary, Lord Halifax) Britain would have been forced in by political necessity.[2] That it did not said much for the determination of an appeasing Prime Minister who was by no means a committed supporter of air power.

To stand any chance of success, Munich required a change of mind on the part of Hitler, who was determined to destroy Czechoslovakia at once, although majority opinion in Germany was against provoking a premature war against France and Britain (whom they realised were soon likely to be supported by the United States). If the Germans had moved on to mounting an air attack on Britain, Austin Hopkinson, the private secretary to Sir Thomas Inskip, believed that 'our air force would have been wiped out in three weeks and our pilots would have gone to certain death'.[3] Whether with Germany yet to gain control of the coastal air fields facing Britain this forecast was unduly pessimistic or not, Prime Minister Neville Chamberlain's personal role in the Munich crisis was fundamentally important to his nation's survival.

In fact, it was only through a random twist of fate that Chamberlain was Britain's political leader at Munich. While he came from a great political family where his father Joseph, while never becoming Prime Minister, had been a giant on the late Victorian political scene and his half-brother, Austen, six years Neville's senior, was

Chancellor of the Exchequer in 1925 at the time of the Locarno Treaty,[4] Neville was never intended for political life. He studied metallurgy in preparation for a business career in which after early major problems he succeeded in establishing himself as a leading figure, both in the industrial life of Birmingham and also as an exemplary employer.[5]

His belated entry into public life came in 1918, and he went on to show notable political strengths as a reforming and influential Minister of Health from 1924–29 before becoming Chancellor of the Exchequer from 1931–37, where he was committed to bringing about the country's economic recovery after the period of the slump.

Such were his abilities as Chancellor that he was widely considered as a future Prime Minister long before taking over from Stanley Baldwin in 1937; he soon revealed his core beliefs by attempting to reshape British foreign policy by confronting the increased threats to European peace through a policy of appeasing or pacifying Europe 'by trading territorial concessions both there and in colonial Africa for firm restrictions on the growth of German (and Italian) military power'[6]. However cleverly conceived and however much he hoped it would avoid war, it undoubtedly represented a policy of weakness against ruthless opponents. As Keith Feiling, Chamberlain's eminent biographer, observed:

> (Chamberlain) would never accept war as inevitable abroad nor at home nor would he do anything to bring it nearer nor leave anything undone that might stave it off, if Germany could be convinced not merely that her abuse of force would be instantly resisted, but that she would get consideration for any rational demand by way of peace.[7]

For Chamberlain's policy to work, Hitler, who naturally favoured war, needed to be convinced that any use of force on Germany's part would be widely condemned at a time when the British armed services were far from ready for conflict. This was all the more unlikely when it was widely known among politicians such as Halifax and Simon that Chamberlain was determined war should never be allowed to happen again: its destruction and human loss were unjustifiable and peace was always the proper state of affairs.

This thinking was evident when, as Chancellor, he agreed to the number of RAF Squadrons committed for home defence being raised from twenty to thirty-eight.[8] Yet, with the need for the nation's economic recovery foremost in his mind, he also scaled down the RAF's share of the defence budget to £50 million over a five-year period before in February 1936 giving his approval to an extension of the RAF rearmament programme under Scheme F.

However serious this proved for RAF expansion plans, when faced with an immediate German invasion of the Sudetenland, Chamberlain still believed he could resolve the crisis through his personal intervention, by meeting Hitler man-to-man. His determination to seize the initiative was evident when he proposed to go to Germany by air, having never flown before except on a short day trip. A message was accordingly sent to Hitler on 13 September 1938, announcing Chamberlain's intention of travelling to Germany the next day, and a somewhat startled Führer agreed to meet him at Berchtesgaden. During their meeting Chamberlain was so eager to reach an agreement that he made little attempt to support the Czech cause, and after two hours he had assented to the transfer of extensive territory in the Sudetenland to Germany.

On returning to London the next morning he succeeded in gaining his Cabinet's agreement before consulting with the French and Czechoslovak governments over ceding the territory. France agreed and Czechoslovakia followed suit after the utmost pressure from the other two, whereupon Chamberlain returned to Germany for a second meeting with Hitler on 22 September at the Hotel Dreesen in Godesburg.

There Chamberlain proposed an international commission to implement the transfer of the territory when to his dismay Hitler raised the bar, saying that he would allow no further delay and that German forces would start occupying the Sudeten areas by 28 September, three days before the scheduled agreement. Despite written objections from Chamberlain, Hitler would not be moved, and when the British Prime Minister returned home to give the news to his Cabinet, many believed the limits of concession had been reached, and that war with Germany was inevitable. This seemed more certain still when the French rejected the latest Godesberg terms.

Lord Halifax, a strong appeaser and contender for Prime Minister at the beginning of the Second World War. (Author's collection)

Chamberlain, however, still refused to give up hope and he sent to Germany his special ambassador, Sir Horace Wilson, who made a final appeal for fresh negotiations and warned Hitler that if he attacked Czechoslovakia and France became engaged in hostilities against Germany, Britain would be obliged to follow.

In Britain general mobilisation was scheduled for Wednesday 28 September, with the country apparently prepared to go into a near suicidal war, but on the morning of the 28th Chamberlain sent Hitler a telegram again offering to go to Germany. At noon, two hours before the British deadline, his persistence finally succeeded, with Hitler accepting Mussolini's proposal for further mediation.

That afternoon Chamberlain was addressing a specially convened House of Commons to inform them of the situation, when at 3.30 p.m. the news came through that Hitler had invited Chamberlain, Mussolini and the French Prime Minister Edouard Deladier to meet him at Munich. When Chamberlain told the House he had agreed to go it erupted in a burst of enthusiastic applause.

At Munich the diplomatic temperature fell when Germany agreed to accept a somewhat smaller area of land and spread the handover across a ten-day period, but although the immediate crisis had been resolved Chamberlain was far from satisfied.

Chamberlain departs for talks with Hitler. (Mary Evans Picture Library)

An American Lockheed 14 Super Electra used by Neville Chamberlain when flying to Munich. (Royal Aeronautical Society/National Aerospace Library)

Despite his country's military shortcomings, on the following morning he requested a private talk with Hitler that ended with them signing a joint communiqué in which they undertook to continue their efforts to remove possible sources of difference, and continue to ensure the peace of Europe that Chamberlain believed was a preliminary to the general European settlement, for which he had aimed since becoming Prime Minister.

On Chamberlain's return from Munich he was greeted by thousands of well-wishers, applauding him and casting flowers before his vehicle, which took more than an hour and a half to make the short journey from Heston Airport to London. In the capital the man who was believed to have saved Europe from a repetition of the Great War joined the King and Queen on the balcony of Buckingham Palace.

It was unquestionably the high point of his career but with Hitler's predictable failure to honour the promises made at Munich the euphoria could not last and opposition to appeasement grew, within both the Cabinet and the House of Commons. Even so, Chamberlain remained convinced that Hitler would keep his word until on 15 March 1939 (six months after Munich) German armies occupied the remainder of Czechoslovakia, an act that apparently struck Chamberlain with the suddenness of a clap of thunder in a blue summer's sky.[9]

When the German forces entered Prague to complete the dismemberment of Czechoslovakia and went on to force its provinces of Bohemia and Moravia to become Reich protectorates, Chamberlain finally realised it was impossible to deal with the Nazi regime as he had hoped and decided that such aggression had to be met by armed deterrence rather than his earlier policy of appeasement.

On 31 March 1939, in answer to a 'planted' question in the House of Commons, Chamberlain declared:

> I now have to inform the House that ... in the event of any action which closely threatened Polish independence ... His Majesty's Government would feel themselves bound at once to lend the Polish Government all support in their power.[10]

Such a threat required equal or superior force over one's opponent and, however strong and unequivocal his stand over Poland, Britain possessed neither the military means nor the air power to support it. When Chamberlain upgraded the UK's guarantees towards Poland 'into a formal reciprocal alliance,' Hitler postponed his attack for just one week but remained determined not to back down again whatever Chamberlain's assertions. As he remarked to his generals, 'our enemies are small worms, I saw them at Munich' where Chamberlain 'as an arch capitalist bourgeois with his deceptive umbrella

Winston Churchill returns to power. (Author's collection)

had taken him for a ride' and whose 'one and only object in undertaking the trip was to gain time'.[11]

While Chamberlain's intention went far beyond gaining time, this in fact is what he achieved, for it was not until 1 September 1939 that Hitler's armies attacked Poland. The British ultimatum having brought no response from Germany, Chamberlain was obliged to tell the House of Commons that: 'This country is at war with Germany.' He admitted 'everything that I have worked for, everything that I have hoped for, everything that I have believed in during my public life has crashed into ruins'.[12]

Chamberlain formed a war Cabinet in which Churchill returned to the Admiralty and presided over the military co-ordination committee while Chamberlain concentrated on home affairs. Some nine months later, on 10 May 1940, Hitler's forces attacked the Low Counties and France simultaneously, when the RAF's aeroplanes were shown to be outclassed.

Two months later Chamberlain was diagnosed with cancer of the large bowel and, after resigning from public life on 3 October, he died on 9 November. He remains a highly controversial figure who was later vilified in publications such as *Guilty Men* (published in 1940)[13] and *The Appeasers*[14] by Martin Gilbert and Richard Gott. Yet, whatever their criticisms, none of them could deny his ruthless pursuit of power: Ernest May concluded that, except possibly for Margaret Thatcher, no peacetime British Prime Minister has been so strong-willed, almost tyrannical.[15] When this coincided with his inability to form human relationships (he only shared his innermost thoughts with his sisters) and his need to be flattered, he presented an unattractive figure. However, such inflexibility and his strong sense of public and private duty helps to explain how he rated Hitler's act of signing the Munich agreement more highly than the dictator did himself and failed to understand someone who, as Professor Donald Watt pointed out, 'willed, wanted, craved war and the destruction of war'.[16]

As Prime Minister, Chamberlain undoubtedly exercised great influence over the RAF. Apart from favouring limited rearmament measures for aviation, he dismissed Lord Swinton, the brilliant Secretary of State for Air, and replaced him with the outwardly unimpressive Kingsley Wood. Previously he had appointed Sir Thomas Inskip as a co-ordinator between the three services, believing he 'would excite no enthusiasm but he would involve us in no fresh perplexities'.[17]

Both Kingsley Wood and Inskip would confound his expectations and their achievements continued beyond the temporary success of his diplomacy at Munich and the vital breathing space it brought, which he acknowledged on 26 May 1939 when he commented that: 'Whatever the outcome, it is clear as daylight that, if we had had to fight in 1938, the results would have been far worse.'[18]

However it was obtained, Munich gave the British people a further period in which to realise, however reluctantly, that war could not be avoided, as well as all three armed services the opportunity to undertake urgent modernisation programmes, without which the RAF for one would surely have been rapidly hounded from the skies. It was therefore during the year following Munich, together with the additional months of the phoney war, that the most glaring imbalances between the RAF and the German Luftwaffe were reduced.

So much depended here on the senior figures in the Air Ministry, Sir Kingsley Wood, who became Secretary of State for Air in May 1938; his Chief of the Air Staff Sir Cyril Newall, who held the post from September 1937 until 1940; and Air Marshal Wilfrid Freeman, the Ministry's Director for Research and Development, who in June 1938 added aircraft production to his already immense responsibilities.

Arguably Kingsley Wood's main contribution was in supporting the radical reforms instituted by Freeman for the RAF's modernisation and growth, which he acknowledged in his Cabinet paper of 25 October 1938, where he observed that at the time of Munich 'we had less than one week's notice behind the squadrons'.[19] The proposals for rearmament were contained in Scheme M, which was designed to replace all previous ones, and looked forward to a time three years later when all the bombers would be heavy and the fighters all metal single-engined interceptors.

Sir Kingsley Wood, (left) Secretary of State for Air, is greeted by Mr Scott-Paine when inspecting an armoured target boat for the RAF at Hythe, Southampton. (Royal Aeronautical Society/National Aerospace Library)

Sir John Slessor, Head of the RAF Plans Branch, believed Scheme M represented 'the collective thought and experience of the Air Staff as a whole under Sir Cyril Newall guided by the genius of Wilfrid Freeman as Air Member for Research and Development'.[20] Slessor cited the central role played by Freeman and the extent of his further reforms affecting the RAF's first-line reserves when he instituted drastic extensions to the training facilities, both for regulars and for the newly formed Volunteer Reserve. In the case of their aircraft, Slessor referred to Freeman's initiative of supplying 100 octane fuel to ensure the highest possible performance, while markedly increasing their numbers through his policy of subcontracting and working with existing aircraft firms and other great engineering organisations such as Harland and Wolff, John Brown and Vickers-Armstrongs to boost production.[21]

With German attacks expected on the British mainland, Scheme M gave precedence to the build-up of Fighter Command, which by April 1940 was expected to have a first-line strength of 640 planes as well as adequate reserves, a total scheduled to reach 800 (although Dowding as Head of Fighter Command would start the Battle of Britain with far less). Scheme M also approved a strike force of new heavy bombers that would go into large-scale production 'off the drawing board'. As a result it was estimated that by March 1942 this would produce 1,360 first-line aircraft plus 300 reserves, while it was hoped to produce 228 'heavies' – if not the four-engined models of the future – by as early as April 1939.

After the war Winston Churchill evaluated the services' plans for the build-up, concluding 'that in the case of the RAF the calculations for ground support had followed the correct lines and in fact proved justified in the later years of the war when the air strength had grown ten – or twenty – fold'.[22] This was undoubted praise for those in charge of policy at this time.

Of these, in spite of his subsequent whole-hearted support for Freeman's work, Kingsley Wood did not make a good start as Air Minister by admitting to not knowing one end of an aeroplane from another, and by his unimpressive physique – short and plump with a thin high voice and never speaking in public without manuscript notes. Air historian Montgomery Hyde went as far as to say that he was the least imaginative and most uninspiring of the pre-war Air Ministers: 'slow-thinking and slow moving, over cautious and prone to get bogged down in detail.'[23] He cited Churchill's frustration at Kingsley Wood's dilatoriness in reacting to experiments proposed by the Air Defence Research Committee, and his conclusion that the minister embodied in himself 'a form of departmentalism very vicious to England'.[24]

In fact, while Kingsley Wood could never compete with Churchill's mercurial and rapid powers of thought, his past record was solid enough, for prior to entering Parliament he had established a successful law practice before becoming a reforming Postmaster General and a competent Minister of Health. In both instances he proved energetic, thorough and, most important of all, 'willing to listen to advice and take up necessary decisions which he would maintain in both Cabinet and in Parliament'.[25]

As a one-time secretary of Neville Chamberlain it was understandable that he should (against widespread opposition in the RAF) accept the Treasury's arguments that if more fighters were required, the increasing bomber programme should be slowed to alleviate strain on the economy, although when major technical problems affected the delivery of new aircraft he showed himself quite prepared to follow Wilfrid Freeman's advice and confront the powerful Society of British Aircraft Constructors and tell it to put out 35 per cent of its production to sub-contractors.[26] This helped achieve the massive increases in production, without which 'the professional aircraft industry even when augmented by the so-called shadow factories … would not, in fact, be able to make good its forecasts'.[27]

Kingsley Wood was fully aware that Freeman planned to have the central assembly shops of large firms such as Vickers fed by a flow of components from sub-contractors working to a reduced number of designs and to combine companies into 'production groups' where more limited types of aircraft could be made. In March 1939 he told the House of Commons that 'the organisation of the aircraft industry on this basis will, I think, facilitate large scale planning and ordering, it will also … reduce the dislocation which might result in wartime if by any reason one of the manufacturing units was unable to continue in production.'[28] Such central direction had not yet been practised in Germany and its remarkable effects soon appeared in the production figures, for while in 1936 the industry had produced fewer than 2,000 aeroplanes, by 1939 the total had risen to 8,000.[29]

Kingsley Wood also faced the problem of the aircraft industry allegedly making excess profits. This thorny issue had arisen during the previous war and this time a pernickety Air Ministry calculated that if its existing pricing of contracts was not modified the average rate of profit would be 21 per cent rather than the official maximum of 15 per cent. After a series of consultations the constructors agreed to forego a third of their profits, in spite of which Kingsley Wood retained good personal relations with Sir Charles Bruce-Gordon, the Chairman of the Society of British Aircraft Constructors.

Kingsley Wood undoubtedly took his responsibilities seriously and by the spring of 1940 the strains of coping with such issues together with the reform of the Air Ministry's repair organisation, which had attracted repeated criticisms both in the Press and in Parliament, left him exhausted, and he temporarily surrendered his post to the previous Air Minister, Sir 'Sam' Hoare. In fact, he never returned, for Churchill's candidate Sir Archibald Sinclair was appointed in his place. In spite of low initial expectations and his relatively short period in office, Kingsley Wood loyally supported Freeman's sweeping proposals, many of which had been laid down by Swinton, with the result that during 1939 fighter production was three and a half times greater than in 1938 while bomber production was three times greater overall.[30]

It was ironic that at such a critical time in its development, the underrated Secretary of State for Air should be assisted by Cyril Newall, Chief of the Air Staff, who in his previous post as Air Member for Supply and Organisation was widely considered to have reached the limits of his capability. From all accounts he was undoubtedly lucky to have been strongly recommended for promotion by Swinton, although as the son of a general he had an immaculate military background.

Newall joined the RFC in 1914 at a time of massive expansion and by 1917 he had been appointed commander of a long-distance bombing wing at Ochey in the south of France that was committed to attacking Germany. In spite of the relatively light damage it inflicted, he became convinced that its effect on morale had been devastating. This led him to become a firm disciple of Trenchard, who was convinced that the possession of a powerful bombing force would deter an aggressor. Newall apparently clung to this belief until after the Germans had occupied the French coast, although by this time he recognised that the RAF's bomber force was, as yet, incapable of causing serious injury to Germany. In resisting the growing emphasis on fighters (and dive bombers) he even queried the effectiveness of the Luftwaffe's ground support operations during the Spanish Civil War – although he was realistic enough to support orders from Freeman for Hurricanes and Spitfires and to sponsor an aircraft repair organisation. Apart from such possible lack of judgement, Newall was hampered by being entirely lacking in Staff experience. He was also by no means a charismatic figure: Sir John Slessor, who worked closely with him, believed that in spite of an outwardly self-confident manner he was in fact rather reserved, self-effacing and difficult to know, although those who did came to have great confidence in him.

Newall was destined to attract conflicting assessments. At the beginning of the war he was accustomed to working long days at his Air Ministry desk and to spend proportionately little time inspecting his units. He was given the use of an underground cell beneath his office, where he both worked and slept at nights, and according to the critical Sholto Douglas (a future Marshal of the RAF) he became an absolute bag of nerves.[31] However, Sir John Slessor painted a far different picture, describing them having supper in Jermyn Street talking about such subjects as fishing, fox hunting and their children, before going back to work far into the night. Other question marks subsequently appeared over Newall's judgement when in 1940 he sacked the able Ludlow-Hewitt as head of Bomber Command and even attempted to remove Dowding as head of Fighter Command before being blocked by Churchill. During the same year severe criticisms surfaced in a memorandum from Wing Commander Edgar Kingston-McCloughry (a member of the Air Ministry's Directorate of War Organisation) in which Kingston-McCloughry accused him of being a weak link in the nation's defences where 'his mental capacity was inadequate, his practical experience was limited, his character and personality were weak and he lacked judgement and foresight'.[32]

Whatever the justice of such blistering observations, Newall appeared incapable of galvanising the Air Ministry as Churchill required, and with Trenchard and

Sir Cyril Newall (left) as CAS inspecting a Fairey Battle light bomber in France accompanied by Lord Londonderry. (Imperial War Museum)

Salmond cynically joining his critics, Churchill replaced him with Charles Portal on 25 October 1940. By then he had been Chief of the Air Staff during three vital years and, in a book on the Royal Air Force's high commanders[33] written half a century later, sycophantic RAF historian Air Commodore Henry Probert highly rated Newall's work through 1938 and 1939, without which he maintained the RAF would have been more ill-placed to fight. Ronald Clark, Tizard's official biographer, was also mildly positive, believing that circulating the knowledge about radar acquired during the Biggin Hill tests 'owed more to Newall than anyone else'.[34]

Quite the most detailed references to Newall's work appear in Sir John Slessor's book of part history and part autobiography *The Central Blue*,[35] where he maintained that, whereas Newall was 'the last man to claim great intellectual qualities (he) was sound, level-headed and decisive'[36] and he backed Dowding over refusing to send extra fighter squadrons to bolster up a lost cause in France. The sympathetic Slessor went further, believing that 'after about five of the most arduous years that any senior officer has ever had to face, he had earned the gratitude of the people of Britain as the prime architect of the wartime Air Force'.[37]

In contrast, Vincent Orange in his submission to the *Dictionary of National Biography* joined those with a very low estimate of Newall's powers, writing that he 'was even-tempered and had a ready smile and pleasant voice: he was at his best in small gatherings, where he listened more than he spoke.'[38]

Following his dismissal things became no clearer, for Newall was made Governor General of New Zealand, where he remained until 1946; after his return to the UK he never wrote about his wartime experiences nor gave any assessment of them to others.

For such reasons it is fair to conclude that, whatever their achievements, the RAF's two most senior political and military figures immediately before the Second World War, however committed and conscientious, appeared far from brilliant. It was therefore of the utmost importance that at such a time the Air Ministry had two other outstanding men in senior supporting roles, namely Wilfrid Freeman, with his encompassing responsibilities for research, development and aircraft production, and Hugh Dowding, with his legendary achievements at Fighter Command following his earlier time as Air Member for Research and Development.

Providing the sinews of war is bound to be less dramatic than using weapons in conflict, but in a lecture to the Royal Air Force Historical Society in 1986, Professor R.V. Jones told his listeners: 'If I had to single out the Senior Air Officer who has had the least recognition from posterity for the magnitude of his contributions (towards the preparation of the RAF for the Second World War) it would have to be Wilfrid Freeman.'[39] The opinion of so eminent an authority warrants the greatest respect, although it also raises the question that if so brilliant, why did Freeman not reach the highest rank? In possible explanation, air commentator Sebastian Ritchie, while fully acknowledging that Freeman had a notably alert and active mind and insisted upon quality in all his endeavours, believed he 'could be cynical and intolerant when dealing with less capable men'.[40] However, Ritchie subsequently appeared to contradict himself by citing one of Freeman's contemporaries, who remembered him as a cultured, civilised man with a warm and human understanding.[41] This latter view was supported by G.P. Bulman, a senior civil servant who, unlike Ritchie, worked closely with Freeman and saw him as 'a visionary but one who endeavoured to make his dreams effective ... a wonderful boss though sometimes I could have killed him ... beyond doubt he was the most inspiring man I ever served.'[42]

Freeman's failure to become Chief of the Air Staff was less likely to have been due to any shortcomings in human relationships than to the break-up of his marriage, which was taken most seriously in the RAF at the time, especially if it was followed by a subsequent highly charged divorce and re-marriage to someone twenty-two years his junior. As a result he was told he would have to retire at 47 after relinquishing command of the RAF Staff College, only for his career to be rescued by Lord Swinton, who so highly valued his abilities.

Freeman's profile was undoubtedly impressive. In 1914 he accompanied the RFC's first contingent to France, where he was awarded one of its first MCs at the Battle of Neuve Chapelle, and in fact he had always been considered a future candidate for Chief of the Air Staff. In 1917, as a Lieutenant-Colonel, he took part in the battles of Arras and Cambrai and also fought during the last German offensive of 1918. Following the war he occupied a number of increasingly senior training appointments before commanding the RAF Staff College and then in April 1936, as Swinton planned, assuming the post of Air Member for Research and Development. As such he took direct responsibility for the most important developments of the time, namely for aircraft progressing to all-metal throughout, the acceptance of the iconic Rolls-Royce Merlin engine and the installation of a radar defence system.

In such areas, Freeman's decision-making proved remarkably sound. He favoured the Spitfire when others wanted to stay with the 'safer' Hurricane, and initiated the development of four-engined bombers such as the Handley Page Halifax, the Short Stirling and the Avro Manchester, which became the Lancaster. In the spring of 1938 he also came to control aircraft production.

Freeman's biographer, Anthony Furse, believed he was entrusted with 'one of the most awesome responsibilities ever given to a serving officer',[43] with air commentator Harald Penrose going even further to suggest that 'no burden except that of Prime Minister could have been greater'.[44]

The need for large-scale production meant him increasing the labour force from 60,000 in September 1938 to well over

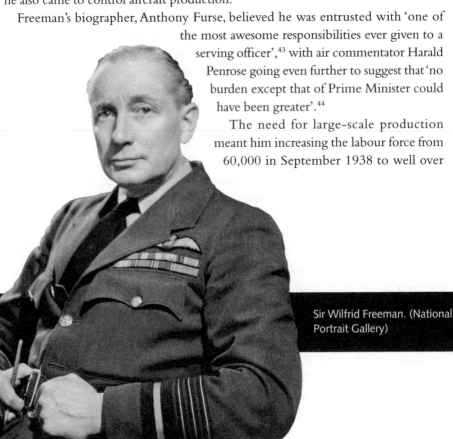

Sir Wilfrid Freeman. (National Portrait Gallery)

180,000 by January 1939 as well as broadening the base of aircraft production by contracting out at least 35 per cent to general engineering firms including Ford and General Electric.

By the end of that year he had gone further still with his grouping of engineering companies, and by encouraging Lord Nuffield to start building and equipping a massive shadow factory at Castle Bromwich for the production of Spitfires. To obtain the aluminium for their airframes Freeman went to Canada and ordered 60 per cent of the total Canadian output.

By early 1939 his plans for four-engined bombers massively increased the need for aero engines and Freeman recommended a second factory for Merlins being set up at Hillington near Glasgow, capable of producing 500 a month, with four more factories established to produce Bristol engines. To achieve their maximum performance these engines needed 100-octane fuel, and when Freeman discovered that Germany produced 970,000 tons of such fuel while Britain produced only 125,000 tons, he proposed making up the shortfall by creating large hydrogenation plants both in the UK and in Trinidad.[45]

Unlike Ellington and others, Freeman understood the pressing need for an effective repair and maintenance organisation to support the production of new aircraft. Although his first proposal was blocked by Ellington, Newall formed a Maintenance Command and by March 1940 both Rolls-Royce and Bristol were able to set up dispersed repair facilities.

Freeman's flair and drive for innovation continued with his ordering of the de Havilland Mosquito, widely seen as Freeman's folly but unquestionably one of the outstanding combat aircraft of the Second World War, while in 1940 he went on to order the American single-engined Mustang fighter that, when fitted with the Merlin engine, proved so decisive in protecting American bombers on daylight raids over Germany.

Despite stormy relations between Freeman and Lord Beaverbrook, whom Winston Churchill appointed over him to speed up aircraft production in a new ministry of that name, Beaverbrook graciously acknowledged that more than any other person Freeman gave the Royal Air Force the machines whose superior quality won the battles during the summer of 1940.

Freeman's skills were retained when he was made Vice-Chief of the Air Staff to Portal, who relied heavily on his advice, and although he retired from the RAF in 1942 he stayed on as chief executive at the Ministry of Aircraft Production, before in 1945 becoming a baronet and director of Courtaulds, the textile manufacturer.[46]

———————•◆•———————

Freeman was undoubtedly a one-off, a shooting star, who within the Air Ministry's politico/military system at this time assumed the crowning responsibility for providing superior aircraft against would-be attackers, a contribution that underpinned the battlefield heroics of the aircrews and their supporting staff, about whom so much has rightly been written. As for the numbers required, by September 1939, 8 million cu.ft of productive floor space had been created, with plans to double this to 19 million in 1941. Such extra capacity would not be fully used for another two years but Freeman laid down a structure for expansion far superior to that of Germany.

While his achievements depended on whole-hearted support from Kingsley Wood and Newall (who shouldered the problems associated with the day-to-day running of the service), it was Freeman with his unshakable confidence, speed of decision-making and above all, his wisdom, who after years of neglect and gross shortages of funds most enabled the RAF to move from a position of near total inferiority at Munich to one where under Dowding's strong direction and with the use of information provided by its electronic defence system it was afforded a genuine chance of countering the massed German assaults.

BRITISH CIVIL AVIATION: SIR JOHN REITH – TOWARDS INCORPORATION

The widespread concern, if not anger, in Britain over the state of its civil aviation peaked on 17 November 1937 when conservative MP and ex-pilot Robert Perkins ended his list of serious charges against the Air Ministry and Imperial Airways in particular by calling for the head of the Secretary of State for Air on a charger.[1] Although in twentieth century Britain this could have been no more than a hollow request, Lord Swinton remained in office for just a further six months, and Perkins achieved his main objective of gaining agreement for a Parliamentary Inquiry that was given the widest terms of reference. It was decided that this should be headed by the influential Lord Cadman, former chairman of the Anglo–Persian Oil Company.[2] To assist him Cadman had Sir Frederick Marquis (later Lord Woolton), Mr Harrison Hughes of the Suez Canal Company and Mr Bowen, retired General Secretary of the Union of Postal Workers.

Cadman acted quickly: after two months of interviews of witnesses, many of which took part 'in camera', the committee issued its report to Parliament in February 1938. The main attention was paid to the deficiencies of Imperial's air services within Europe despite almost 90 per cent of Imperial's flying time being spent on Empire services. In fact, civil aviation within Britain had already been examined by the Maybury Committee, which reported in January 1937 concerning the lack of air traffic control and radio facilities and the need to license airlines on specific routes.

Due to what Cadman perceived as previous neglect he recommended the appointment of an additional Under-Secretary of State with sole responsibility for civil aviation. This official would be expected to help the department correlate its activities with military aviation more effectively – which he mistakenly saw as another side of a single coin – and initiate more vigorous forward planning and research through a director of aeronautical production.

Although Imperial Airways made a submission of thirty-two pages, buttressed by a further thirty-two pages of appendices, refuting the charges made previously by Robert Perkins, this was substantially ignored.[3] With future war on the agenda, Cadman declared it a matter of national importance to establish as soon as possible first-class air services between London and all the principal capitals of Europe. To achieve this the committee recommended that air services be concentrated in a small number of well-founded and substantial organisations: Imperial Airways should be responsible for the development of the Empire air routes with British Airways concentrating on Europe and South America, while a new joint company would concern itself with the London–Paris runs. Under no circumstances should an external route be operated by more than one British company.

Recommending routes was one thing but they could not be operated without suitable aircraft and in this respect Cadman stated outright that there was not a 'medium sized airliner of British construction comparable to leading foreign types'.[4] To help remedy this it recommended that the development and provision of suitable transport aircraft for both civil and military purposes should be the concern of a further committee that was expected to make proposals for the longer term. Cadman believed that implementing his proposals was bound to require greater finance and recommended that Imperial and British Airways should be organised on a scale appropriate to their increased responsibilities, with a doubling of central subsidies from £1.5 million to £3 million. This the Government accepted, although it decided to divert some £100,000 to support internal air services.

Sir John Reith. (National Portrait Gallery)

Having found both the range of Imperial Airways services and its aircraft wanting, it was no surprise that the committee should hold the management responsible, particularly the Chairman who traditionally had never given his whole time to the organisation and internal management of the company. It demanded immediate reform with the appointment of a full-time Chairman assisted by two full-time directors.

Further defects were identified in the firm's management relations that were particularly directed towards its long-time Managing Director, George Woods Humphery, with recommendations for his dismissal.

The report pulled no punches:

In particular, not only has [the company] failed to co-operate fully with the Air Ministry, but it has been intolerant of suggestion and unyielding in negotiation. Internally its attitude in staff matters has left much to be desired. It appears to us that the Managing Director of the Company – presumably with the acquiescence of the Board – has taken a commercial view of his responsibilities that was too narrow ... and this may well involve some change in directing personnel.[5]

Cadman not only believed the company's Chairman should be full-time but, unlike Geddes, he should be willing to negotiate with representatives of its employees.

Speaking in the House of Commons on 16 March 1938, the Prime Minister, Neville Chamberlain, declared that: 'We have, in fact accepted practically everything of importance in the report.'[6] Whether this was correct or not it undoubtedly marked closer governmental involvement in civil aviation, with Imperial Airways accepting a full-time Chairman and implementing the practice of collective bargaining.[7] In the event, despite the Prime Minister's confident statement, it proved far easier to grant an increased subsidy than identify a new chairman for such a heavily criticised company. The post was offered to the previous CAS of the RAF Sir John Salmond, who rapidly declined, as did a string of others.

Chamberlain finally approached the Director General of the BBC Sir John Reith, who accepted with some reluctance. Reith did not know he was far from being the first choice and in any case he had harboured the hope that after leaving the BBC he would obtain a senior post at the War Office.

Whatever the circumstances, the appointment brought another remarkable Scot into aviation who, while quite different from Geddes, was every bit as confident, much better at personal presentation and equally, if not more, ambitious. Such attributes were soon to bring about a U-turn in Government policy towards civil aviation and developments far beyond those anticipated by the Cadman Committee.

As the youngest child of the Rev. Dr George Reith, a Free Church Minister from Stonehaven in Kincardineshire, John was sent at 15 to Gresham's School in Norfolk. However, despite doing well in German and Latin and distinguishing himself on the sports field (he grew to be 6ft 6in tall), his father concluded he was not academic and should take an apprenticeship with the North British Locomotive Company, where he relieved the tedium by pursuing military interests. By 1911 he had been granted a Territorial Army commission in the 5th Scottish Rifles and soon after the beginning of the First World War he was posted to the Western Front as a transport officer. He was already acquiring a reputation for 'prickliness' and after a disagreement with his adjutant he transferred to the Royal Engineers, with whom he was wounded in the left cheek by a sniper at Loos, which he always believed was a divine deliverance from an early death.

For the rest of the war he was never in comparable danger and on demobilisation the ultra-energetic and supremely confident Reith was appointed general manager of Beardmore, the Glasgow engineering firm, where he received a salary of £1,200 together with a bonus on output. At Beardmore he set about imposing much needed discipline by installing a time clock and ordering all foremen to wear their symbolic bowler hats, while at the same time organising football matches and dances for the workforce. The extent of his success was seen when the senior convenor, who presented him with a wedding gift on behalf of the company, paid him the following tribute: 'It is only by having gentlemen like Mr Reith to guide and direct the work and take an interest in the welfare of the workers, that we can hope to see the dawn of a brighter day, when the dark industrial clouds have passed away.'[8]

Having sorted out the one-time major problems at Beardmore, Reith started looking further afield and he answered an advertisement in the Morning Post for the general managership of the British Broadcasting Company in London. During the interview the panel failed to ask him many questions – something he considered fortunate for he hadn't the remotest idea what broadcasting was: 'And if I had tried it I should probably have found difficulty in discovering anyone who knew.'[9] He was offered the post upon which he felt sure 'there was some high work for me in the world'. His confidence was not misplaced for he stayed for more than fifteen years and in that time he turned the BBC into a national institution.

During May 1923, when the Sykes Committee was enquiring into the company's role, he showed his core political beliefs by declaring that broadcasting 'should be conducted as a public service and under a public corporation constitution'.[10] Three years later, as a result of the recommendations of the Crawford Committee, the BBC received its first Royal Charter for a period of ten years and, as the 37-year-old Reith wanted, it became the British Broadcasting Corporation. Reith enjoyed creative independence to broadcast a moderate amount of controversial material provided it was 'of high quality and distributed with scrupulous fairness' and he became the Corporation's first Director General. On being awarded a knighthood he believed it was rather less than his due for: 'A KG would not have been too much for what I have done.'[11] To be made a Knight of the Garter was to receive the most prestigious British Order of Chivalry and such a comment typified Reith's endless high expectations. Yet, while he was already well known for his autocracy, he undoubtedly captured the affection and loyalty of most of the BBC's employees and achieved a notable success for the corporation when he persuaded George V to make the sovereign's first Christmas Broadcast during December 1932, which was heard all over the country.

Whatever such achievements, he had already grown restless and entered into discussions about his future with Prime Minister Stanley Baldwin before Baldwin's successor Neville Chamberlain offered him the chairmanship of Imperial Airways. With the several charges currently being brought against the company its directors had little choice but to accept him despite Reith's inclination for state ownership, which he had demonstrated at the BBC. True to form, during his first week he voiced the belief that: 'Imperial Airways should henceforth be regarded as a public service company,' a belief he would soon spell out more clearly.

Even so, after his time at the BBC where he had come to be treated with reverential respect and his counsel was sought by monarchs and prime ministers alike, it was hardly surprising that he should find Imperial Airways profoundly uncongenial. This was evident from the entry in his diary describing his first visit to the company on 1 June 1938 that revealed as much about himself as the nature of the company:

> I was brought to the door of an old furniture depository behind Victoria Station. It was Imperial Airways, a plate on the wall said so. Inside were some counters, luggage on the floor, a few people standing about – a booking office evidently. I enquired of a young man behind one of the counters where the head office was. He pointed to a dark and narrow staircase; up there, he said. The managing-director's office? Second floor, he thought. Having ascended thither I went along a passage also dark and narrow, between wooden partitions, peering at the doors and wondering which to try first. Here it was – a bit of paper with 'Managing Director' written thereon. From Broadcasting House, to this. And the first decision demanded of me was an indication of what had happened to me otherwise. Would I approve the expenditure of £238 on passengers' lavatories at Croydon?[12]

There was much for Reith to do beyond the micro-management of lavatories and in reality he was rather less ignorant about Imperial Airways than his diary entry suggested. This was evident in the previous March when he had written in his diary that: 'Imperial Airways is getting bigger and bigger and must be an interesting show to run',[13] while some six months later he had met Imperial's Managing Director Woods Humphery, for whom he had previously acted as best man at his wedding.

Over lunch Reith had quizzed Woods Humphery about the company, to be told that it needed a capable public relations figure but the Board (with Geddes at its head) had refused to authorise such an appointment. At this time Woods Humphery also insisted that Imperial Airways did not need a full-time chairman because there was simply not enough for him to do. Their ideas were radically different, with Woods Humphery believing his prime responsibilities were to his shareholders, although he could hardly have suspected that if Reith became the full-time Chairman there would be no place for him as Managing Director. In fairness to Reith, after being appointed chairman by the Prime Minister he went to Imperial's acting chairman, Sir George Beharrell, and told him that there could be no restriction of his authority from a managing director.

For all Woods Humphery's martinet qualities the staff at Imperial Airways deplored his enforced resignation, with *The Observer* acknowledging that: 'Mr Woods Humphery was charged with making commercial aviation pay and he came nearer to succeeding than anyone else in the world.'[14] Yet in light of the criticisms from the Cadman Committee, and with Reith as Imperial's chairman, he had to go. Other pressing staff matters for the new chairman included the need to appoint a director of personnel and the creation of new pay scales upon which the pilots and other staff would be consulted.

Above all, new aircraft were urgently required and the need became more pressing when the company's latest Ensigns were withdrawn for major modifications, for which disruption Armstrong Whitworth subsequently paid the considerable sum of £42,500 in compensation.

For Reith, whose ignorance of air transport was counterbalanced by his knowledge of public corporations, his most important task was to move the stock-holders out of the company. He argued that: 'There was an impropriety in subsidies at one end and high dividends at the other, here the dividend motive was in my view, incompatible with the public service motive, here it seemed to have operated to the prejudice of efficiency and contentment.'[15] Such ideas meant that Imperial Airways as founded by Hambling and modified by Cadman was bound to disappear.

Whatever the challenges facing him, Reith quickly regretted leaving the BBC and he soon made it clear that 'he wanted – and deserved – a more stimulating job than running Imperial Airways'.[16] His conviction that his new post would be of a temporary nature was evident when he took a two-room flat in London at just seven guineas a week overlooking a slum tenement, 'very rackety and dirty'. This, if anything, increased the urgency at which he worked, and by the end of August he had gained the Air Ministry's informal approval for the amalgamation of Imperial and British Airways into a single corporation, which Reith named the British Overseas Aircraft Corporation (BOAC). By now he already felt confident enough to inform Parliament that he had only accepted the chairmanship of Imperial Airways on the understanding that it would be nationalised.

Under his energetic supervision things progressed rapidly and he took advantage of the unworkable proposals of the Cadman Committee about promoting a joint venture between Imperial Airways and British Airways on the London–Paris route to emphasise the need for full amalgamation. In the process he apparently stiffened the resolve of Kingsley Wood, the Secretary of State for Air, who appeared to be wavering during October 1938, and he showed strong disapproval when the Chairman and Managing Director of British Airways, the Hon. Clive Pearson and Major McCrindle, wanted to retain two separate airways within the corporation. The consent of the British Airways board to amalgamation came in August 1938, with that of Imperial following on 10 October of that year. (Under the scheme, Imperial Airways's shareholders were to be paid 32s 9d per £1 share and those of British Airways' 15s 9d per £1 share in compensation.)

By the autumn of 1938 the two Boards were seeking a new chief executive to work under Reith (who had assumed the title of Director General as he had at the BBC). They selected Leslie Runciman, who not only held directorships at Lloyds Bank and the LNER but was an air enthusiast (who) 'had raised and commanded the Durham squadron of the Auxiliary Air Force'.[17] More important still, he met Reith's requirement for a man with 'high administrative and commercial calibre'[18] who would give him increased weight in forcing his ideas on Clive Pearson and Ronald McCrindle of British Airways.

On 19 November *The Times* gave its approval of Runciman's appointment on the grounds that it 'satisfied the requirement that an energetic man with wide and up-to-date experience in aviation matters should be included in the management'[19] – although in fact the most important consideration was that he would not oppose Reith.

The paper quaintly referred to the corporation as 'not a condemnation of private enterprise nor a condonation of bureaucracy' and, presumably with Imperial's problems over its aircraft in mind, vigorously supported its creation, maintaining that for the safety of the Empire the development of civil aviation must 'enable it to maintain its power of production and of progressive improvement in design. That recommendation, so imperfectly followed in the past, must be the chapter of the new corporation'.[20]

In a mere four months Reith had made amazing progress, and just as he had with the BBC, he hoped to limit Government interference with his plans. By 10 July 1939 the second reading of what was called the British Overseas Airways Corporation Bill passed through Parliament. During its drafting Reith had drawn heavily on his BBC experience and typically he declared himself angry that the Secretary of State for Air, Kingsley Wood, was 'taking all the credit for the Airways Bill and also for the Civil Aviation Planning committee which was of course *entirely* my idea. Self-seeking little cad.'[21]

This seemed less than fair for, although he had strong conservative beliefs, Kingsley Wood spoke powerfully in support, declaring that 'it is more efficient and will make for greater progress to concentrate our available assistance in one large organisation and rely mainly on international competition to provide the necessary stimulus for progress and efficiency'.[22] (Increased financial provision was to come in the form of a subsidy of up to £3,900,000 a year until 1953.)

Kingsley Wood ended with a summary of the Bill's massive benefits: 'It will enable adequate finance to be employed in reasonable terms and long range plans to be projected and also that it will assist us to obtain aircraft in keeping with the high engineering achievements of this country',[23] the lack of which had slowed the advance of British civil aviation so far. During the same debate, Harold Balfour, the Under-Secretary of State supported his chief by maintaining it was his belief that in the course of two or three years, when it had made up the leeway, Britain would lead the world in civil aviation.

Despite such brave words, the Bill did not become law until 4 August 1939, at the outbreak of war, when the need was to construct bombers rather than civil aircraft. Any opportunity to realise Reith's dream of making up any leeway in building civil aeroplanes ended when all further work on Short and Fairey landplanes was cancelled, and no new air routes could be established until the cessation of hostilities.

Between 1932–37 British civil aviation had been dominated by Geddes, with his concept for Imperial Airways to salvage the wreckage of the four previously existing companies that had been operating in competition,[24] and to establish air services throughout the Empire and promote the carriage of mail by *efficiently husbanding its slender resources even occasionally and controversially returning dividends to its shareholders and loyally supporting the British aircraft industry*.[25] Despite this, in the last sixteen months before the war the forward vision was unquestionably Reith's.

Tragically, in spite of his massive contributions towards the formation of BOAC, the Corporation had no opportunity to show how it might have outperformed its predecessors, for it did not officially start operating until 1 April 1940, seven months after the outbreak of a war that had brought a halt to all civil aircraft production.[26] Although a committee under the chairmanship of noted early aviator and politician Lord Brabazon would sit from 1942 until the end of the war considering the future types of British airliners – including stop-gap adaptations of military aircraft – the war years were most difficult for the directors of BOAC. To continue operating – often under most difficult conditions – they were compelled to use ageing aircraft or rely on replacements from the United States.

Sir Kingsley Wood acknowledged the dramatic change brought about by the war in the House of Commons on 7 March 1940:

I wish I could say more about civil aviation. I have been disappointed that the war has meant such a blow to the plans which we had made so carefully during the last few months before war broke out. It has been a tremendous disappointment to me and to members of my Department, but, anxious as I am about what the position may be at the end of the war, I do feel that it is my duty to put first things first, and to put every ounce that we can into our military effort. After all everything depends upon that, for if that goes civil aviation and everything also goes too.[27]

After some five years of war, British aircraft designers would face a new world where aircraft technology had improved out of all recognition[28] with the jet age beckoning.

How far BOAC might have fared differently during the war under the ferocious leadership of Sir John Reith is impossible to say for he left BOAC at the beginning of the war in search of the new post he believed his abilities warranted, leaving Clive Pearson to succeed him as Chairman of a Corporation with a wholly unsatisfactory capital structure, plus the additional need to re-establish air communications with British forces overseas.[29] When the call came for Reith it was to the Ministry of Information with a seat in the House of Commons. Characteristically this fell well below his expectations but, following the appointment of a national Government, he was moved sideways to become Commissioner of Works and Public Buildings with a seat in the House of Lords. There he found himself unable to make any significant contribution and following a Government reshuffle he was dismissed by Churchill, finally working for the Admiralty in the modest capacity of a Naval captain (RNVR) preparing for the D-Day invasion.

Reith never forgave Churchill for what he saw as the destruction of his career, and in 1946 he wrote to him in both anger and desperation: 'You could have used me in a way and to an extent you never realised.' Instead, Reith saw himself deserted and 'eyeless in Gaza' like his blind hero Samson, without even the consolation Samson had in knowing it was his own fault.[30]

For Reith, who lived on until 1971, nothing could remotely equal his time at the BBC and it is doubtful whether he ever fully appreciated the opportunities open to him with British aviation, where in addition to masterminding the negotiations for combining Imperial with British Airways into a new corporation, he was still handling 'the day to day problems of running an international airline'[31] where he was in charge of eleven stations, with 3,600 staff and seventy-seven aircraft, as well as eight associated companies and twelve subsidiaries.

If the war had not come so soon, or if he had returned to BOAC as he might reputedly have done in 1943,[32] Reith's achievements for British aviation could conceivably still have been prodigious – although they were unlikely to have satisfied the ceaseless ambitions of such a complex yet dynamic man.

HUGH DOWDING AND THE TEST OF ARMS

In spite of the RAF's plans for modernisation and expansion through its Schemes A to M, it was during the year following Munich that it began to receive the planes so badly needed to match a resurgent German Luftwaffe.

Even so, on the declaration of the Second World War, Germany enjoyed clear if not overwhelming numerical superiority over the joint British and French air forces. Germany had 4,320 first-line aircraft compared with the Allies' 3,335 (Britain 1,660, France 1,735), with the German reserve totalling 4,900 to the Allies' 3,800 (Britain 2,200, France 1,600). In the case of the RAF's manpower levels, although it had expanded from a low point of 30,000 officers and airmen in 1934 (supported by a regular reserve of 9,400) to a total of 186,000 by 1 September 1939, this was still well below its complement in 1918.[1]

The Luftwaffe's premier fighter, the Me Bf 109E. (Digital image by Paul H. Vickers)

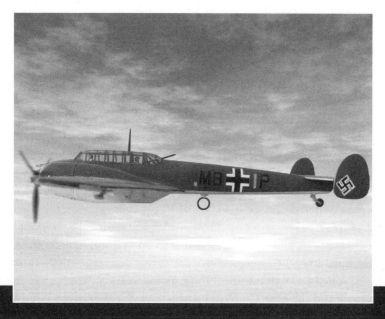

The Luftwaffe's Me Bf 110. (Digital image by Paul H. Vickers)

Things quickly became worse when the French were taken by surprise by the German advance into their country and their air force played a smaller part than its numbers warranted. In any case, by the time the Germans began their air attacks on Britain, France had been effectively overrun.

In such circumstances massed German air attacks designed to pave the way for an invasion of Britain appeared to have strong chances of success. That this did not happen owed much to two things: the enduring pattern of English history in which a leader emerged who would excel against all odds and the fact that the material balance proved less in the Luftwaffe's favour than was first believed.

Apart from comparative strengths the calibre of the two sides' equipment was also of prime importance. Air historian Montgomery Hyde, for instance, was sure that although unquestionably smaller, the superb quality of the RAF equipment was crucial. In reality it was not this simple for, while not denying the high calibre of the RAF's two most famous fighters, the German Me Bf 109 was comparable in performance and superior at over 20,000 cu.ft. The Germans not only possessed superior numbers (including their bombing fleets), but their crews had already taken part in successful campaigns and in experienced hands such larger numbers could be reasonably expected to compensate for some inferiorities in their aircraft.

In fact, their numerical superiority during the autumn of 1940 would prove lower than expected. By the time of the attacks on Britain, the rapid succession of campaigns in Poland, Norway and, most of all, France had taken their toll, especially as such losses were not entirely made good.

Whatever the costs, they had unquestionably been successful. The air operations over Poland commencing on 1 September 1939 played a major part in the surrender of the Polish land forces just sixteen days later (followed by the withdrawal of the surviving ninety-eight Polish combat aircraft to Romania).[3] During the course of this campaign the Luftwaffe's casualties were relatively light: 285 aircraft were lost and 279 more suffered damage in excess of 10 per cent, with aircrew casualties of 539[4] and with every chance of these being made good during the six months before the next engagement. During the Luftwaffe's second campaign in Scandinavia and Norway in April 1940 the casualties were not all that different with 260 aircraft lost, 141 aircrew killed and 448 missing. However, the losses suffered in the campaign against France and the Low Countries that followed within days proved far more serious. Here a total of 2,065 aircraft were in opposition, of which 1,072 were from the RAF (643 of which were serviceable). In comparison, the Luftwaffe had a front-line strength of 3,984 combat aircraft compared with 4,320 in 1939, of which 2,877 were serviceable.

Over the six-week campaign highly effective support was given to the German Panzer divisions, although conflicting orders caused their failure to prevent the evacuation of Allied troops from Dunkirk between 27 May and 3 June. In the hard fighting against the British and French air forces the Luftwaffe's manpower casualties amounted to 6,658 including 4,417 aircrew, with its material losses totalling 28 per cent of its original aircraft strength: when damaged planes were included this rose to 36 per cent (1,428 destroyed, 488 damaged).

The Battle of Britain that followed on 5 August 1940 was unquestionably the sternest test of German air power so far, when the Luftwaffe was expected to counterbalance the superior British Royal Navy by giving air cover to the German invasion fleet while crossing the Channel. Prior to this it was required to carry out 'softening up' measures by attacking the British ports and, most important of all, by neutralising the RAF – destroying its infrastructure and driving its aircraft from the sky prior to an invasion scheduled for 15 September.[5]

The campaign opened just forty days after the Battle for France and in the short interim the Luftwaffe needed to rebuild its squadrons, many of which had been reduced to half strength. Simultaneously it had to move them forward about 1,000km to positions along the Channel and Atlantic coasts where supplies, including complex signal systems, had to be taken along roads and railways that it had already bombed. Such a tight schedule meant the Luftwaffe's earlier losses were yet to be made good; although by 13 August the numbers of German aircraft had only risen to 2,849, of which 1,344 were bombers, they were still markedly superior to their RAF opponent. Nevertheless, this was still some thousand less than in the earlier battle for France. Of these 79 per cent, 2,256 were serviceable – and in the all-important area of fighter planes the Luftwaffe had some 800 single-engined and 200 twin-engined fighters, together with 250 dive bombers. By July its fighter strength had risen to 1,100.[6]

Significantly, from now onwards, due to the intensity of the fighting and inadequacies in their production facilities, the Germans would fail to sustain such levels, let alone increase them.

Prior to the Battle of Britain the British losses mirrored those of the Germans, 169 planes in Norway and 645 during the French campaign, many of which were obsolescent, although of the 261 Hurricanes despatched from Britain to France (Dowding had refused to send over any Spitfires) only sixty-six returned. By

Max Aitken, Lord Beaverbrook. (Foto draaf ONB EKN End/ ANEFO National Archief Licentie-cc)

June 1940 such losses meant that the RAF's Fighter Command was reduced to 331 Spitfires and Hurricanes supported by 150 second-line machines of questionable value, but in contrast to the Germans, British fighter plane production now increased, leading to the command having a total of 639, including around 550 Hurricanes and Spitfires by the time of the Battle.[7]

Much of this remarkable achievement was due to a single individual, the ruthless and unorthodox press baron Max Aitkin, Lord Beaverbrook, appointed by Winston Churchill as Minister of Aircraft Production, whose civilian Repair Organisation alone contributed about a third of the fresh aircraft during the battle, although the dislocation he caused brought a corresponding fall in production towards the end of the year.[8]

This boost to British aircraft production that Churchill initiated contrasted with the actions of the German leader, Adolf Hitler, who believed that with the fall of France the shooting war was virtually over because a country with Britain's pacifist tendencies was sure to seek some political accommodation. As a result he rashly ordered demobilisation of some troops, decreased aircraft production and restarted aircraft exports.[9] Although this decision was quite quickly reversed it meant that from June to December 1940 British fighter production proved markedly superior.

Most importantly, in spite of German bombing, Spitfire production was maintained:

Spitfire Production 30 June–26 October 1940

Week ending	Number	Week ending	Number
26 June–6 July	32	31 Aug–7 Sept	36
6 July– 13 July	30	7 Sept–14 Sept	38
13 July–20 July	41	14 Sept–21 Sept	40
20 July–27 July	37	21 Sept–28 Sept	34
27 July–3 Aug	41	28 Sept–5 Oct	32
3 Aug–10 Aug	41	5 Oct–12 Oct	31
10 Aug–17 Aug	31	12 Oct–19 Oct	25
17 Aug–24 Aug	44	19 Oct–26 Oct	42
24 Aug–31 Aug	37		

Such an advantage was not repeated with replacement aircrews. During early 1940 Fighter Command lost many of its senior pilots flying both inferior aircraft and Hurricanes in France. For instance, in the case of 85 Hurricane Squadron, out of its normal establishment of eighteen pilots in the space of eleven days it lost eight killed or missing in action and six wounded.[10] (Its commanding officer was among those killed and Squadron Leader Peter Townsend was sent to rebuild it.) Such losses were rendered more serious because of the higher prestige given to bomber pilots during

Hermann Goering (far left), Commander of the German Luftwaffe. (Author's collection)

the interwar period, with the result that fighter squadrons had to rely on reservists with 25 per cent of its pilots coming from the Auxiliary Air Force and Volunteer Reserve. Other pilots arrived from the Fleet Air Arm or were on attachment from Bomber and Coastal commands, as well as 127 New Zealand and 112 Canadian pilots from the Commonwealth, while Czech, Belgian, French and Polish pilots arrived from occupied Europe eager to fight the Germans.

The newly qualified pilots from the flying schools were particularly vulnerable, having learned only the rudimentary rules of conflict, and by the end of October 1940 Douglas Evill (Fighter Command's Chief Staff Officer) believed the RAF was at its lowest ebb for operational pilots, but while undoubtedly serious a judicious rotation of squadrons prevented the situation from becoming critical.

While not enjoying the advantage of being joined by ready-trained pilots, the Luftwaffe also succeeded in achieving the remarkable increases required for its aircrew personnel. Between 30 September 1939 and 30 March 1940 the number of its first-line crews rose by 31 per cent from 3,593 to 4,727, with the number of fully operational aircrew rising 19 per cent from 3,312 to 3,941. These were remarkable results from a training organisation that had been severely disrupted at the beginning of the war by the need to move its schools to safer sites in eastern Germany, Austria and Czechoslovakia. A captured notebook from a young *Unteroffizer* who attended his flying school during March–April 1940 revealed the full range of instruction undertaken: from simple circuits, to long-range flights, medium- and low-level bombing, aerial gunnery and formation flying.[11]

The pattern diverged with the respective battlefield senior commanders. In the case of Hermann Goering, the Luftwaffe's vain and flamboyant commander, his earlier exploits as an air ace during the First World War when he was credited with twenty-two kills, coupled with the successes of the Polish and French campaigns, helped propel him into becoming *Reichsmarschall*, the most senior military rank and arguably also the most powerful military figure in all Germany.

In contrast, the British leader, the tall, somewhat remote and unsmiling figure of Air Chief Marshal Hugh Dowding, who had headed Fighter Command since its creation in 1936, never courted publicity and, while unquestionably deserving his place among senior RAF commanders during the inter-war period, appeared to lack the charisma suited for a command role in what would prove one of the most decisive battles in British history.

Sir Hugh Dowding, Head of RAF Fighter Command. (National Portrait Gallery)

Aerial commentators have varied widely in their assessments of him. Group Captain Teddy Haslam, head of the Air Historical Branch, saw him as an evangelical figure reminiscent of John Knox whose stern sense of duty, united with his complete competence in practical flying matters, made him a formidable advocate for his strongly held views. Haslam concluded that he was no easy compromiser, nor politician, and that he often aroused hostility, sometimes unwittingly, because his vision was intense but narrow.[12] Dowding's biographer, Vincent Orange, also pointed out his personal challenges, saying that for good or ill he was not a man to compromise, thereby provoking anger, exasperation, respect and devotion – sometimes all of these in a single day. Although well-read and with a dry wit, Orange believed he was too abstemious and intensely serious to be easy company, even off duty.[13] How then in the essentially fraternal atmosphere of service life Dowding came to be given such a role still intrigues commentators, although as a very senior officer he had already held other posts more highly regarded than Fighter Command.

Dowding had, in fact, never intended to make a career in the armed forces. Although his grandfather on his mother's side had been a senior officer in the Indian Army, it was Dowding's inability to learn Greek at Winchester College, effectively barring him from senior Civil Service or academic appointments, which led him to the less demanding option of seeking admission to the Royal Military Academy at Woolwich. From there he was rapidly posted to India, where apparently his first six years as a young officer proved the happiest in his life as he revelled in the many sporting opportunities interspersed with regimental exercises before the idyll ended with his return to England to further his career.

He was granted a year's leave (at a reduced salary) to prepare for the Staff College examination, during which time – in case he failed – he paid to take flying lessons at Brooklands. In fact, he received his pilot's certificate on 20 December 1913, the day he passed out of Staff College. His time there proved unremarkable, although he managed to take up skiing, an activity he pursued for the rest of his life for it gave him the physical challenges he relished without having to conform to the rules of team sports, which he found burdensome.

On the outbreak of war Dowding joined the Royal Flying Corps and spent his first three months at its Central Flying School. There he met Hugh Trenchard and John Salmond, two future Chiefs of the Air Staff, who did not warm to him (few men did), and after helping to form up squadrons for France he sought active service there. Trenchard agreed to accept him as an observer rather than as a pilot, and although Dowding subsequently acted as a pilot he never excelled in aerial combat, for which he was possibly too deliberate to succeed, although he was undoubtedly brave and a fine shot.

Back in England Dowding commanded a wireless experimental establishment, where he found the technology fascinating and claimed he was the first person in England, if not in the world, to listen to a wireless telephone message from the air.[14]

In July 1915 he returned to France to command 16 Squadron at Merville near Lille, where he appeared far less at ease. While strict and efficient he did not show up particularly well in human terms and his younger aircrew revived his nickname of 'Stuffy' gained during his Camberley days, for they felt it appeared to suit his older, more withdrawn and austere approach to flying duties.[15] During this time he had a serious brush with Trenchard, who sent his squadron the wrong replacement propellers. After trying them out Dowding objected and he was proved right about their unsuitability, a circumstance that did not endear him to 'Boom'. During another exchange between them he asked for squadrons that had suffered severe casualties to be replaced by reliefs from time to time, which caused Trenchard to brand him as a 'dismal Jimmy' obsessed by the fear of casualties. He sent him home (on promotion) but did not offer him another field appointment during what proved to be a longer war than anyone had expected.

After the war, Dowding showed Trenchard a better measure of his ability when he made a brilliant job of organising the RAF's showcase pageants at Hendon and in 1926 he was appointed Director of Training at the Air Ministry and made a member of the Air Council, before in 1930 becoming Air Member for Research and Development. In this capacity he was immediately called upon to issue an airworthiness certificate for the R101, the newly commissioned Government airship, on the basis of what would subsequently prove to have been highly optimistic technical reports. Although the subsequent inquiry blamed no one for the R101's tragic crash, it led Dowding to henceforth rely on his own judgement to a greater extent than ever before. As member for Research and Development he set himself to gain as much knowledge as he could about the vital new technical developments required in a future war, including all-metal monoplanes, heavy bombers, eight-gun armament for fighters and the radar defence system, where in all cases he showed both practicality and an enthusiasm for technology.

It was not until 1936 when he became head of the newly formed Fighter Command at the relatively late age of 54 that he finally gained the opportunity to apply his technical knowledge to active operations.

Seizing his opportunity during the next four years, he masterminded the redevelopment of the UK's air defences through the creation of new squadrons of Hurricanes and Spitfires, for which he established good landline and wireless communications by setting up operations rooms to process the information from newly constructed radar stations around the east and south coasts. He was also directly responsible for his fighters receiving such additional equipment as 'bullet-proof' windscreens, more powerful radios, armoured seats, constant-speed airscrews, self-sealing fuel tanks and an electronic device allowing radio operators to distinguish them from enemy fighters.[16]

When in 1937 Sir Cyril Newall became Chief of the Air Staff Dowding's hopes for the top job ended, and he was free to apply his rather narrow single-mindedness[17] to perfecting the country's fighter defences. To achieve this he was in no doubt that he needed enough squadrons to defend the home country against invasion, but although the Air Ministry had already agreed to a minimum of fifty-two for home defence the demands of the Norwegian and French campaigns reduced Dowding's Fighter Command to thirty-six. He resolved to do everything he could to bring his squadrons up to the required fifty-two and prevent any more from being sent overseas.

His concern was widely known and he was given permission to attend a Cabinet meeting on 15 May 1940, where it was anticipated that Winston Churchill (who had recently become Prime Minister and was a strong Francophile) would propose sending additional home squadrons to France. The meeting was held in the Prime Minister's office and Dowding was relegated to a wall seat beyond the main conference table, but so determined was he to convince the Prime Minister about the dangers of sending more Hurricanes abroad that at one stage he got to his feet and, taking a graph of projected fighter strength prepared that morning in his headquarters at Bentley Priory, he laid it directly in front of a glowering Churchill. While doing so he made the unforgiving remark 'that if the present rate of wastage continues for another fortnight we shall not have a single Hurricane left in France or this country'.[18] As he acknowledged later, he laid particular emphasis on 'or this country'.

His intervention proved a pivotal point at the meeting (and for his own career), for no one else seemed willing to take on the new pugnacious Prime Minister, who was convinced of the need to give a positive answer to France's desperate plea for help. In the event Dowding had every right to have expected support from both his Secretary of State for Air and his Chief of the Air Staff but this was not forthcoming: for Sir Archibald Sinclair had been in office just four days and as a strong supporter and firm friend of Churchill he was 'in his pocket', while Sir Cyril Newall had earlier been rebuffed by Churchill over an inconsequential matter and was studiously keeping silent.

Everything therefore depended on Dowding, whose brusque but utterly convincing initiative brought a volte face that Sir Ian Jacob, the Military Assistant Secretary, said was the only occasion in the whole war when the Prime Minister changed his mind after a firm decision had been reached. Dowding followed this up with a historic letter (presently occupying a prominent position in the RAF Officer Training College at Cranwell) in which he confirmed what he believed to be the dangers of sending further fighter planes out of Britain. At Downing Street, Dowding not only demonstrated personal courage but his own brand of clear-headedness and willingness to oppose generally accepted views, whether held by an all-powerful Prime Minister or not, and during the Battle of Britain he would show the same confidence by the studied deployment of his forces into separate groups with specific responsibilities.

In typical fashion, having laid down the principles of engagement, he left the actual conduct of the battle to his group commanders. This was particularly important for his second-in-command, Air Vice-Marshal Keith Park, whose No. 12 Group was responsible for the defence of London and south-east England. Each group relied on information provided by radar about the enemy's approaches, which was processed in Dowding's operation rooms. On the basis of this Dowding ordered attacks to be concentrated on the German bombers rather than seeking out the destructive fighters. Such tactics were by no means to the liking of some strong-willed subordinates nor understood by many at the Air Ministry but they succeeded, and were akin to the tactics of the Duke of Wellington, who preserved his infantry by making them lie down on the battlefield before they made a telling contribution.

Dowding also sought to preserve morale, during what proved an intense and costly battle, with the self-same tactics that Trenchard had refused to consider during the First World War, by ordering the rotation of squadrons and replacing those that had sustained heavy losses with others that had been less heavily involved. By such means Dowding endeavoured to preserve both his pilots and his aircraft for what he rightly anticipated would be the climax of the battle.

Such methods of battlefield command contrasted with that of his opponent Goering, for whereas Dowding believed in letting his commanders make their own decisions, Goering was quite prepared to intervene. For instance, during the heat of the battle, he called upon his senior commanders to leave their headquarters and make the long journey to his hunting estate 40 miles from Berlin in order to justify their conduct during the Luftwaffe's disappointing Eagle's Day attack.

The commanders' different profiles were also evident immediately prior to the battle when, in contrast to Dowding who took pains to spell out the dangers, Goering was if anything overconfident about his superior numbers of aircraft, despite his dive bombers and his Bf 110s being inferior to the most powerful British fighters. He agreed straightaway to Hitler's request to attack Britain, despite the unrealistically short time frame for moving his air fleets to the Channel coast, and failed to make sure that Hitler was aware of the interruptions to German military aircraft production[19] that were to prove so important in his inability to replace losses. As an opportunist, if not a chancer, Goering boasted he would destroy the Royal Air Force within four weeks without having decided on the actual course of his campaign.

Equally serious for the commander of a technical arm was Goering's lack of appetite for technical matters, compared with Dowding's, which tended to make him overconfident about his superior numbers of aircraft (whatever their deficiencies in certain cases) and the dedication and skills of his airmen to achieve results beyond their capabilities facing a determined enemy.[20] Goering also underestimated the vital need for good intelligence by putting the incompetent Joseph Schmidt in charge, which resulted in vital RAF installations not being identified, to faulty target selection and scant appreciation of the importance of British radar facilities. One serious result of such technical misunderstanding occurred while Goering was haranguing his commanders at his hunting lodge, when he made the appalling blunder of telling them he doubted whether there was any point in continuing the attacks on radar sites, 'in view of the fact that not one of these attacked has so far been put out of action'.[21] In fact, the installations had been seriously damaged and further bombing could conceivably have put the whole system out of commission.

All this led to Goering conducting the Battle of Britain in snatches and being too often subject to the initiatives of his opponent. This occurred for instance, when despite the RAF's best efforts, his attacks on their airfields and stations were achieving significant successes, only for him to switch his attacks to London. Similarly, when his bomber losses gave him cause for concern he ordered his fighters to fly alongside them, thereby sacrificing their capacity for speed and manoeuvrability and squandering their limited fuel capacity.[22]

In retrospect, whatever Dowding's undoubtedly superior tactics, the balance of force also went against the Luftwaffe: Goering's medium bombers were never sure of destroying their targets while from their bases at the cross-Channel ports his fighters lacked sufficient endurance to give the bombers continued protection or engage the opposing British fighters in prolonged conflict.

Remarkably, despite his successes in a battle that could have conceivably cost Britain the war, Dowding would join Lord Swinton and Wilfrid Freeman in arguably not receiving the credit he deserved. He was replaced at Fighter Command on 25 November 1940, less than two months after the battle, while the bombing of London remained a nightly occurrence. In fairness, from August 1938 until August 1940 he received five separate messages about the Air Ministry's intention to request his retirement on grounds of age, although following his brilliant achievements in September 1940 Newall indicated that he could remain in office indefinitely or in practical terms until his 60th birthday in April 1942. That Dowding was replaced so precipitately owed much to him delegating responsibility for the actual fighting to his group commanders, as well as not being fully aware of the clashes that developed between Keith Park, head of No. 11 Group, and his opposite number at No. 12 Group, Trafford Leigh Mallory.

These arose because Leigh Mallory, spurred on by his irrepressible Squadron Leader Douglas Bader, came to favour the use of squadrons in Big Wing formation (four squadrons or more) over Park's use of single or double squadrons that enjoyed the advantage of being able to rise and meet the German threats within an amazing four minutes, compared with the twenty minutes or so required for the Big Wings to become airborne and form up. Although during the Battle of Britain Dowding's and Park's tactics of relying on the skills of individual pilots and their aeroplanes' virtuosity (rather than bulldozing their way across the sky) succeeded in withstanding the main daylight attacks, support grew for Leigh Mallory's and Bader's more grandiose formations to match the heavier and better directed German daytime raids that were expected in 1941.

Arguably such new formations needed new blood to direct them and Dowding did not help himself remain in post by making little or no attempt to placate his long-time opponents in the Air Ministry. In fact, he vigorously opposed the Air Defence Committee's findings – valid and otherwise – published in September 1940 about the best ways of countering the successful German night bombing.[23] This had been chaired by John Salmond, the former CAS who was strongly critical of Dowding, as was the legendary but still interfering grandee Hugh Trenchard. Dowding fearlessly courted further trouble by paying open tribute to Lord Beaverbrook for his supply of vital fighters during the Battle of Britain, a man whose ruthless methods and 'stunts' caused him to be thoroughly unpopular within the Air Ministry.

Despite Winston Churchill's public belief that during the Battle of Britain Dowding had shown himself a genius in the art of war[24] he was succeeded in November by the Deputy Chief of the Air Staff Sholto Douglas, who favoured the use of large fighter forces, with Park being replaced by his arch critic Leigh Mallory. Following his dismissal Churchill persuaded Dowding to visit the United States on behalf of the Ministry of Aircraft Production, but predictably this proved unsuccessful as a result of Dowding's inclination to put forward his own views above others. On his return Churchill gave him the task of writing a detailed account of the Battle of Britain – and then suppressed its publication until 1946.

In 1943 Dowding finally had a barony conferred upon him, the first since Trenchard, for which he took the title of Bentley Priory, his old headquarters at Fighter Command. He was, however, never made a Marshal of the RAF, an honour given to both Sholto Douglas and Arthur Harris despite them failing to become Chiefs of the Air Staff. That Dowding was hurt by his treatment following the Battle of Britain was evident in a letter he subsequently sent to *The Times* that was published on 19 January 1970, in which he wrote 'the actions that were taken by others went far too deeply and if I may say so grievously imprinted on my mind for me ever to forget them'.

He found compensation in retirement through his deep interest in spiritualism and theology, and also in his second marriage thirty years after his first wife's death. He also derived immense pleasure from developing into a legend to his Battle of Britain pilots, becoming an ever-constant figure at their annual dinners.

Whatever such disfavour, Dowding knew that by advocating his own beliefs and disregarding what he viewed as cheap popularity he had outclassed his adversary, Goering, in the RAF's first and possibly last great air battle, and that under his direction his young fighter pilots had shown themselves capable of beating off the much-vaunted Luftwaffe's attacks. For a man with such a stern sense of duty there would always be the consolation that on this occasion he held his country's fortune in his hands and had not failed, while in their turn and in their inimitable style his pilots appreciated his true worth. As one of them (George Lacey) felt compelled to ask 'where would we have been if Stuffy had lost the battle?'

A demonstration of the continuing high regard for Dowding occurs every year at the border town of Moffatt where he was born. His birthday is commemorated in the municipal gardens before local dignitaries and townsfolk, with a senior RAF officer giving the dedication and, after Dowding's own words are played over the PA system, the spectators are treated to a flypast from the Battle of Britain Memorial Flight, where its Spitfire and Hurricane make low passes over the small township and the snarling notes of their Merlin engines fill the valley in which the town is situated.

ASSESSMENT

Whatever the pioneering achievements by British aviation during the interwar period, nothing surpassed the forging of weapon systems to defend the mother country from invasion in 1940 – although these came about 'scarcely before the chocks were pulled away'.[1] Despite the Air Ministry's restricted share of the early defence budgets it achieved a level of technical – if not numerical – superiority over the raiding Luftwaffe. In such a close and oscillating encounter two developments proved of vital importance. The Schneider Trophy contests gave a unique spur to a handful of outstanding aircraft designers and engineers towards making revolutionary improvements in aircraft design, and following the dismissal by the scientist Robert Watson-Watt of using shortwave electromagnetic radiation as a death ray, he drew attention to the still difficult but less unpromising problem of radio detection[2] that marked the commencement of work on radar, without which success in 1940 would have been impossible.

In the case of fighter aircraft, so much depended on their means of propulsion and here the British held the trump hand with their legendary Rolls-Royce Merlin developed from Henry Royce's R engine.[3] The Merlin, whose supercharged version developed an amazing 1,000hp (only to be doubled later), would be installed in the most influential British aircraft during the Second World War, including Spitfires and Hurricanes and the Lancaster and Mosquito bombers. No other engine would approach its production run of 160,000 units, of which 100,000 were produced in Britain.

In the war's opening stages, equipped with its Merlin engines, the Spitfire equalled the best German fighter (the Me Bf 109) except in the dive,[4] and the Merlin-powered Hurricane was not far behind, being more than a match for all German fighters except the Me Bf 109, even against which it was by no means outclassed. As a pair, the RAFs two interceptors had no equal. The German Bf 110 twin-engine fighter never complemented the 'star' Bf 109 in the way the Hurricane did the Spitfire.

Yet however potent, with their inferior numbers and awesome defence responsibilities, the British pilots could never have succeeded without radar.

Work on radar began with the formation of a five-man subcommittee at the Air Ministry under Professor Henry Tizard. This set out to develop a means of tracking incoming enemy bombers and their escorts through radio beams transmitted from the ground that could identify them and hopefully calculate their height, speed and numbers. Under Tizard's driving the committee worked at phenomenal speed from its base in Tizard's own flat in London's St James's Court. By May 1935, after erecting a 70ft mast, they tracked an aircraft at 17 miles distance. By July this had been extended to 40 miles and masts of 350ft came to be built with effective lines of communication to Fighter Command Headquarters.

On 4 August 1936 Tizard and the RAF pilots at Biggin Hill held joint tests to determine the best way of intercepting a formation of enemy bombers[5] with exciting results, and within a further two and a half years a complete chain of coastal transmitters and masts had been erected and RAF personnel trained in their use. On Friday 7 April 1939 the system was activated (to continue in use throughout the war) with ranges up to 100 miles. A year later this capability was extended to aircraft coming into formation above their aerodromes in France and Belgium.

Such outstanding progress was, for the most part, due to Tizard, who richly deserves a place among British aviation's most notable individuals during the interwar years. That he succeeded as he did was due to the high degree of cross-departmental co-operation that he developed between the air staff, their civil servants and the pilots involved. However able their scientists, with their outstanding work for instance, in rocket technology, the Nazis never established the same inter-relationship among them, with many of the finest leaving the country before the war. Equally important, although the two sides were at about the same stage with their radar work, the Germans failed to appreciate the key part it actually played during the initial attacks, unaccountably abandoning their bombing of the British installations and not attempting to jam its radio stations.

Although the British democratic tradition opened the door to questioning the role of the RAF and the gross neglect of British military aviation, when the doubters became convinced of the need for strong air forces against a militant Germany scientific advances were achieved at unrivalled speed. What was more, in spite of notable exceptions, Britain retained the technological advantages with which it entered the war.

In the case of civil aviation the process was far less satisfactory, with the challenges to British interests never as clear-cut nor given comparable priority. Following similar neglect during the first decade, it too relied on dedicated individuals to meet a host of recurring problems, and although much was achieved in pioneering air routes, the movement towards amalgamation and more focused services still had far to go by the commencement of the war.

That Britain did so well in 1940 owed everything to the effectiveness of the last-minute preparations between the wars. As for the individuals concerned, in the British tradition when facing great dangers, leaders emerged including some who proved uniquely well equipped to meet them. Apart from the most responsible position of all, where Winston Churchill, who had been much underestimated and widely suspected, made a magnificent wartime Prime Minister (and went on to lionise The Few), potent figures emerged in the RAF. These came with Wilfrid Freeman, who had been due to leave the service prematurely, and Hugh Dowding, who despite his wide technical knowledge and analytic qualities was not only near retirement but the antithesis of earlier RAF legendary figures. In civil aviation, while John Reith transformed things, there were too few planes and insufficient time to implement his reforms before the war. In military aviation, at least, following earlier sweeping disinterest such individuals not only proved capable of altering the course of anticipated developments but of moving things beyond any previous expectations in their country's favour to establish an enduring legend.

NOTES

Prologue

1   Reese, Peter, *The Men Who Gave Us Wings, British Aviation 1792–1914*, 2014.
2   Sir Harry M. Garner, 'Prophecy and Achievement in Aeronautics: Lecture to the Royal Aeronautical Society', 29 Mar 1952, *Journal of the Royal Aeronautical Society (JRAeS)*, vol. 56, 1952, p. 493.
3   ibid, p. 495.
4   Sir A.H. Roy Fedden, A Century of Progress in Aeronautics, Lecture to the Society of Engineers, May 1954, Trans of Society of Engineers, Sept 1954, p. 183.
5   Halford-MacLeod, Guy, *Born of Adversity, Britain's Airlines 1919–1963*, 2014, p. 7.
6   Penrose, Harald, *British Aviation, The Adventuring Years, 1920–1929*, 1973, pp. 1–2.
7   Montgomery Hyde, H., *British Air Policy Between the Wars, 1918–1939*, 1976, p. 490.

Chapter 1

1   *The Aeroplane*, 7 Jan 1920, vol. xviii, no. 1, Editorial.
2   Penrose, Harald, *British Aviation*, op cit, p. 20.
3   Higham, Robin, *Britain's Imperial Air Routes 1918 to 1939*, 1960, p. 40.
4   Hayward, Keith, *The British Aircraft Industry* 1989, p. 10.
5   Smith, Ron, *British Built Aircraft, Greater London*, 2002, p. 19.
6   ibid, p. 18.
7   Hayward, Keith, op cit, p. 12.
8   Reese, Peter, op cit, p. 164.
9   Official Brochure of The Aircraft Disposal Co. Ltd, p. 6.

10 ibid, p. 7.
11 ibid, p. 7.
12 James, Derek W., *Westland Aircraft Since 1915*, 1991, pp. 26–29.
13 ibid, pp. 202–209.
14 King, Peter, *Knights of the Air*, 1989, p. 63.
15 Barnes, C.H., *Handley Page Aircraft Since 1907*, 1976, p. 12.
16 JRAeS, vol. 68, Jul 1964, p. 433.
17 Centenary Pamphlet for Sir Frederick Handley Page issued to City University on Fri 15 Nov 1985, p. 4.
18 King, Peter, op cit, p. 225.
19 ibid, p. 225.
20 Barnes, C.H., op cit, p. 27.
21 King, Peter, op cit, p. 228.
22 Smith, Ron, op cit, p. 85.
23 King, Peter, op cit, p. 229.
24 ibid, p. 203.
25 Mason, Francis K., *Hawker Aircraft Since 1920*, pp. 1–2.
26 Sharp, Martin C., *D.H., A History of de Havilland*, 1982, p. 104.
27 King, Peter, op cit, p. 277.
28 Hayward Keith, op cit, p. 11.
29 JRAeS, vol. 63, p. 353.
30 King, Peter, op cit, p. 203.

Chapter 2

1 Jones H.A., *The War in the Air Being the Story of the Part Played in the Great War by the Royal Air Force*, 1937, Appendices, p. 10.
2 The Women's Royal Air Force was disbanded on 1 Apr 1920.
3 Bowyer, Chaz, *RAF Operations 1918–38*, 1988, pp. 17–18.
4 Montgomery Hyde, H., op cit, p. 57.
5 ibid, p. 45.
6 *London Gazette*, 1 Jan 1919.
7 Jones, H.A., op cit, vol. VI, app. IV, p. 19.
8 Sykes, Sir Frederick, *From Many Angles*, 1942, p. 266.
9 Boyle, Andrew, *Trenchard, Man of Vision*, op cit, p. 361.
10 ibid, p. 343.
11 Montgomery Hyde, H., op cit, 1976, p. 63.
12 ibid, p. 68.

13   ibid, p. 64, footnote 26.

14   This did not include the considerable wear and tear sustained by the aircraft involved.

15   Bowyer, Chaz, op cit, p. 24.

16   Boyle, Andrew, op cit, p. 348.

17   Havard, Cyril, *The Trenchard Touch*, 2000, p. 59.

18   Meilinger, Phillip S,. *Air War Theory and Practice*, p. 47.

19   ibid, p. 45.

20   ibid.

21   Allen, Wing Commander H.R., *The Legacy of Lord Trenchard*, 1972, pp. 51, 52.

22   ibid, p. 54.

23   Havard, Cyril, op cit, p. 70.

Chapter 3

1   Ord Hume, Arthur J.G., *British Commercial Aircraft*, 2003, pp. 22–23.

2   ibid, p. 22.

3   *Dictionary of National Biography*, vol. 54, p. 324.

4   Davis, Mick, *Airco The Aircraft Manufacturing Company*, 2001, p. 13.

5   *Dictionary of National Biography*, op cit, p. 325.

6   *The Aeroplane*, 5 Dec 1917, p. 1694.

7   ibid, p. 1694.

8   In 1919 French commercial airlines covered 21,800 miles, which in the following year would rise to 93,000 miles (*The Times*, 18 Dec 1920).

9   House of Commons Debates, 11 Mar 1920, vol. 126, col. 1622.

10   The Future of Aerial Transport, Pamphlet, Ministry of Reconstruction, 1919, p. 5.

11   op cit, p. 20.

12   Brindley, J.F., and Newton, G., *IATA Wings Across the World Since 1945*, 2009, p. 4.

13   Pudney, John, *The Seven Skies A Study of BOAC and its Forerunners Since 1919*, 1959, p. 50.

14   Handley Page, Frederick, Eleventh Brancker Memorial Lecture delivered in London on 15 Apr 1953.

15   Jackson, A.S., *Imperial Airways and the First British Airlines 1919–40*, 1955.

16   *Daily Mail*, 13 Oct 1920.

17   *The International History Review*, vol. 11 (2), May 1989, p. 224 [Robert L. McCormack, Missed Opportunities, Winston Churchill, the Air Ministry and Africa 1919–1921].

18 *Daily Mail*, 13 Oct 1920.

19 Higham, Robin, *Britain's Imperial Air Routes*, op cit, 1960, p. 34.

20 *The Aeroplane*, 13 Oct 1920, Editorial.

21 *The Times*, 15 Oct 1920.

22 G. Holt Thomas, *Aerial Transport*, 1920, p. 23.

23 ibid, p. vi.

24 Proceedings of the Third Air Conference, 6 and 7 Feb 1923, HMSO, 1923, p. 90.

25 Letter of Winston Churchill to David Lloyd George of 4 Jan 1921.

26 The International History Review, vol. 11 (2), May 1989, *Missed Opportunities: Winston Churchill, the Air Ministry and Africa 1919–1921*, p. 206.

27 ibid, p. 225.

28 ibid, p. 228.

29 Birkhead, E., Chapter 3, 'The Financial Failure of British Air Transport Companies, 1919–24', in *Air Transport* (J. Lyth, ed.), 1996, p. 14.

30 ibid, p. 15.

31 ibid, p. 18.

32 *Flight*, vol. 75, 1959, p. 112.

33 Higham, Robin, *Britain's Imperial Air Routes*, op cit, p. 64.

34 *Flight*, vol. 15, Jan–June 1923, p. 120.

35 Penrose, Harald, *Wings Across the World, An Illustrated History of British Airways*, 1980, p. 33.

36 Higham. Robin, *Britain's Imperial Air Routes*, op cit, p. 75.

37 Jackson A.S., op cit, p. 28.

38 Penrose, Harald, *Wings Across the World*, op cit, p. 34.

39 ibid, p. 51.

40 Hoare, Sir Samuel, *India by Air*, 1927, p. xvii.

41 Templewood, Viscount, Sir Samuel Hoare, *Empire of the Air*, 1957, p. 97.

42 ibid, pp. 289–291.

43 Pirie, Gordon, Air Empire, *British Imperial Civil Aviation, 1919–1939*, 2009, p. 73.

Chapter 4

1 Allen, Peter, *The 91 Before Lindbergh*, 1984, p. 33.

2 Burge, Squadron Leader C.G., *Encyclopaedia of Aviation 1935*, p. 318.

3 Wallace, Graham, *The Flight of Alcock and Brown, 14–15 June 1919*, 1955, p. 112.

4 ibid, p. 113.

5 Alcock, Sir John and Brown, Sir Arthur Whitten, *Our Transatlantic Flight*, 1969, p. 52.

7 Allen, Peter, op cit, p. 44.

8 There were conflicting theories about the problems, including one that suggested the open and closed controls for the radiator were wrong, or wrongly interpreted by Hawker.

9 Allen, Peter, op cit, p. 70.

10 Wallace, Graham, op cit, p. 234.

11 Allen, Peter, op cit, p. 70.

12 ibid, pp. 72–73.

13 Smith, Sir Ross, *14,000 Miles Through the Air*, 1922, p. 19.

14 Price, A. Grenfell, *The Skies Remember, The Story of Ross and Keith Smith*, 1969, p. 86.

15 Eustis, Nelson, *The Greatest Air Race*, 1969, p. 113.

16 Price, A. Grenfell, op cit, p. 89.

17 Smith, Ross, Account for *National Geographic Magazine,* March 1921; Semple, Clive, *Airway to the East 1918–20*, 2012, p. 203.

18 ibid, p. 25.

19 Semple, op cit, p. 208.

20 ibid, p. 232.

21 Hooper, Meredith, *Kangaroo Route, The Development of Commercial Flight between England and Australia*, 1985, p. 131.

Chapter 5

1 JRAeS, vol. 70 (661), Jan 1966, p. 268.

2 Details of which are given in Jackson, A.J., *De Havilland Aircraft*, 1987, pp. 10–11.

3 Havard, Cyril, op cit, p. 64.

4 Cobham, Sir Alan, *A Time to Fly*, 1978, p. 21.

5 ibid, p. 83.

6 ibid, p. 93.

7 ibid, p. 102.

8 ibid, p. 107.

9 Cobham, Sir Alan, *Australia and Back*, 1926, p. 6.

10 ibid, p. 21.

11 Cobham, Sir Alan, *A Time to Fly*, p. 2.

12 ibid, p. 154.

13 ibid, p. 170.

14   *The Times*, Cobham Obituary, 22 Oct 1973.

15   Wilkins, Harold T., 'Champion Air Woman Wins 8000 Mile Race', *Popular Mechanics*, Sep 1928, pp. 457, 459.

16   Pirie, Gordon, *Cultures and Caricatures of British Imperial Aviation*, 2012, p. 26.

17   Luff, David, *Amy Johnson, Enigma in the Sky*, 2002, p. 113.

18   ibid, p. 330.

19   *Dictionary of National Biography*, 2004, vol. III, p. 403.

20   *The Argus*, Melbourne, Victoria, 26 Jan 1930.

21   Chichester, Francis, *Solo to Sydney*, 1929.

22   Chichester, Francis, *The Lonely Sea and the Sky*, 1964, p. 107.

23   ibid, pp. 233–234.

24   Chichester, Francis, *Solo*, op cit, p. 207.

25   Sir Alan Cobham, Obituary, *Flight*, 25 Oct 1973, p. 688.

Chapter 6

1   Higham, Robin, *Britain's Imperial Air Routes*, op cit, p. 80.

2   Munson, Kenneth, *Pictorial History of BOAC and Imperial Airways* 1970, p. 21.

3   ibid, p. 21.

4   ibid, p. 80.

5   Allen, Peter, op cit, p. 77.

6   Higham, Robin, *The British Rigid Airship, 1908–1931. A Study in Warfare Policy* 1961, p. 122.

7   Brooks, Peter W., *Zeppelin: Rigid Airships 1893–1940*, pp. 121–123.

8   Swinfield, John, *Airship: Design, Development and Disaster*, 2012, pp. 83–84.

9   Robinson, Douglas H., *Giants in the Sky, A History of the Rigid Airship*, 1973, p. 181.

10   PRO 116/1915 ACNS to Amery, 22 Mar 1922.

11   Higham, Robin, *British Rigid Airship*, op cit, p. 251.

12   PRO PREM 1/51, 14 May 1924, Swinfield, p. 128.

13   ibid, p. 177.

14   ibid, p. 129.

15   Masefield, Sir Peter G., *To Ride the Storm*, 1982, p. 13.

16   Higham, Robin, *British Rigid Airship*, op cit, p. 199.

17   Robinson, Douglas, H., op cit, pp. 174–175.

18   Shute, Nevil, *Slide Rule*, 1954, p. 54.

19   Higham, Robin, *British Rigid Airship*, op cit, p. 285.

20   ibid, p. 297.

21   Report of the R101 Inquiry, March 1931, p. 71.

22 ibid, p. 75.

23 Macmillan Norman, *Sir Sefton Brancker*, 1935, p. 415.

24 Report of the R101 Inquiry, op cit, pp. 92–93.

25 ibid, p. 95.

26 ibid, p. 95.

27 Thomson, Lord C., *Air Facts and Fancies*, 1927, p. 18.

28 ibid, p. 18.

29 ibid, p. 112.

30 Swinfield, John, op cit, p. 271; The Grabowsky-Atherstone Log, 19 Jul 1930.

31 Leasor, James, *The Millionth Chance, A Story of the R101*, 1957, p. 34.

32 Shute, Nevil, op cit, pp. 130–139.

33 Masefield, Sir Peter G., op cit, p. 410.

34 *Dictionary of National Biography*, vol. 54, p. 498.

35 Montgomery Hyde, H., op cit, p. 267.

36 Morpurgo, J.E., *Barnes Wallis: A Biography*, p. 77.

Chapter 7

1 Pegram, Ralph, *Schneider Trophy Seaplanes and Flying Boats, Victors, Vanquished and Visions*, 2012, p. 9.

2 Barker, Ralph, *The Schneider Trophy Races*, 1981, p. 11.

3 Montgomery Hyde, H., op cit, p. 214.

4 Barker, Ralph, op cit, p. 244.

5 The full details of the winning nations and the speeds obtained are given in the table at the end of Chapter 7 on p. 125.

6 Bastow, Donald, *Henry Royce: Mechanic*, 1989, p. 10.

7 Pemberton, Sir Max, *The Life of Sir Henry Royce*, 1936, pp. 109–10.

8 Smith, G. Geoffrey, 'Sir Frederick Henry Royce – and his work', *War in Pictures*, Jan 1944, p. 14.

9 ibid, p. 15.

10 *Dictionary of National Biography*, vol. 48, p. 54.

11 Nixon, Frank, 'Aircraft engine development during the past half century', JRAeS, vol. 70 (661), Jan 1966, p. 150.

12 Bastow, Donald, op cit, p. 20.

13 Barker, Ralph, op cit, pp. 188–189.

14 Evernden, Ivan, 'Sir Henry Royce, Bart', JRAeS, vol. 60 (552), Dec 1956, p. 779.

15 Harvey-Bailey, Alec, *The Merlin in Perspective*, 1983, p. 8.

16 Evernden, Ivan, op cit, p. 781.

17 Sydney, E.Veale, Rolls and Royce, *The Aeroplane* 1904, p. 573.

18 Mitchell, Gordon, *R.J. Mitchell: Schooldays to Spitfire*, 2002, p. 31.

19 Shelton, John, *Schneider Trophy to Spitfire: the Design Career of R.J. Mitchell*, 2008, p. 17.

20 Eves, Edward, *The Schneider Trophy Story*, 2001, p. 102.

21 ibid, p. 115.

22 Mitchell, Gordon, op cit, p. 55.

23 ibid, p. 66.

24 ibid, p. 72.

25 Eves, Edward, op cit, p. 199.

26 Mitchell, Gordon, op cit, p. 100.

27 Shelton, John, op cit, p. 250.

28 *Dictionary of National Biography*, vol. 28, p. 299.

29 ibid, p. 251.

30 *Dictionary of National Biography*, vol. 28, p. 300.

31 Barker, Ralph, op cit, p. 220.

32 Mitchell, Gordon, op cit, p. 109.

33 ibid, p. 109.

34 ibid, p. 111.

35 Barker, Ralph, op cit, p. 245.

Chapter 8

1 Laffin, John, *Swifter than Eagles, A Biography of Marshal of the RAF, Sir John Salmond*, 1964, p. xi.

2 ibid.

3 Probert, Air Commodore Henry, *High Commanders of the Royal Air Force*, 1991, p. 8.

4 *Dictionary of National Biography*, vol. 48, p. 738.

5 ibid, p. 738.

6 Parker, Major S.E., unpublished manuscript on early days of the Royal Flying Corps, 1962, p. 24.

7 ibid.

8 Probert, Air Commodore Henry, op cit, p. 9.

9 ibid.

10 ibid, pp. 10–11.

11 Montgomery Hyde, H., op cit, p. 240.

12 ibid, p. 264.

13 Trenchard Papers IV/54/86.

14 Londonderry, The Marquess of, *Wings of Destiny*, 1943, p. 52.

15 ibid, p. 50.

16 *Dictionary of National Biography*, vol. 52, pp. 644–5.

17 Meilinger, Philip, op cit, p. 107.

18 ibid, p. 108.

19 ibid, pp. 112–113.

20 ibid, p. 113.

21 ibid, p. 114.

22 ibid, p. 115.

23 Cabinet Meeting Notes, 7 Mar 1933, AIR 8/158.

24 Philpott, Wing Commander Ian M., *The Royal Air Force 1930–39*, 2008, vol. II, p. 378.

25 Probert, Air Commodore Henry, op cit, p. 11.

Chapter 9

1 Imperial Defence Policy, Report of the Defence Requirements Committee, CAB 24/247/64 of 5/3/34, p. 4.

2 ibid, p .7.

3 ibid, p. 10.

4 Probert, Air Commodore Henry, op cit, p. 12.

5 ibid, p. 13.

6 Montgomery Hyde, H., op cit, p. 494; *Liddell Hart Memoirs*, vol. II, 1965 p. 193.

7 ibid, p. 495.

8 ibid, p. 494.

9 ibid, p. 494.

10 Furse, Anthony, *Wilfrid Freeman, The Genius Behind Allied Survival and Air Supremacy 1939–45*, 2000, p. 95.

11 de la Ferté, Air Chief Marshal Sir Philip Joubert, *The Third Service, the Story Behind the Royal Air Force*, 1955, p. 89.

12 *Dictionary of National Biography*, vol. 52, p. 647.

13 Montgomery Hyde, H., op cit, pp. 336–337.

14 ibid, p. 341.

15 *Dictionary of National Biography*, vol. 52, p. 645.

16 Montgomery Hyde, H., op cit, p. 343.

17 Churchill, Winston S., *The Second World War, Vol. 1, The Gathering Storm*, 1948, p. 100.

18 Dean, Sir Maurice, *The Royal Air Force and Two World Wars*, 1979, p. 56.

19 This was published on 17 Feb 1949.

20 By the beginning of the Second World War his breach with Winston Churchill was irrevocable and Londonderry's wartime responsibilities were restricted to acting as the regional commander of the Northern Ireland Air Training Corps.

21 Dean, Sir Maurice, op cit, p. 56.

22 Montgomery Hyde H., op cit, p. 350.

23 ibid.

24 *Dictionary of National Biography*, vol. 33, p. 989.

25 Furse, Anthony, op cit, p. 60.

26 ibid.

27 Swinton, The Earl of, *Sixty Years of Power*, 1966, p. 117.

28 ibid, p. 89.

29 Furse, Anthony, op cit, p. 81.

30 Details of Freeman's remarkable contributions are given in Chapter 14.

31 Swinton, The Earl of, op cit, p. 89.

32 Balchin, Nigel, *The Aircraft Builders, An Account of British Aircraft Production 1935–45*, 1947, pp. 15–16.

33 Furse, Anthony, op cit, p. 74.

34 Montgomery Hyde, H., op cit, p. 410.

35 ibid, p. 402.

36 Dean, Sir Maurice, op cit, p. 56.

37 Swinton, op cit, pp. 89–90.

38 ibid, p. 119.

39 Montgomery Hyde, H., op cit, p. 420.

40 ibid, app. VI, p. 516.

41 Swinton papers 174/2/8-9.

42 Swinton, The Earl of, *I Remember*, 1948, p. 117.

Chapter 10

1 A list of representative specifications and the resulting new aircraft during the 1920s and 1930s are listed in *Aeroplane* for November 2005, pp. 38–40.

2 Mason, Francis K., *Hawker Aircraft Since 1920*, 1991, p. 35.

3 Mitchell, Gordon, op cit, p. 133.

4 A monocoque fuselage was made by laying thin strips of wood over a mould contoured to the desired fuselage shape.

5 Montgomery Hyde, H., op cit, p. 419.

6 Jarrett, Philip (ed.), *Biplane to Monoplane, Aircraft Development 1919–1939*, 1997, p. 71.

7   ibid.

8   *Dictionary of National Biography*, vol. 38, p. 433.

9   Shelton, John, op cit, pp. 18–19.

10 ibid, p. 220.

11 Mitchell, Gordon, op. cit, p. 169.

12 Fozard, Dr John (ed.), *Sydney Camm and the Hurricane*, 1991, p. 101 (evidence of Dr P.B. Walker).

13 Penrose, Harald, *British Aviation, The Adventuring Years*, p. 285.

14 ibid, p. 44.

15 ibid, p. 16.

16 ibid, p. 16.

17 ibid, p. 97.

18 ibid, p. 59.

19 ibid, p. 58.

20 Lloyd, F.M.H., *Hurricane, The Story of a Great Fighter*, 1945, p. 22.

21 Fozard, Dr John, op cit, p. 42.

22 Lucas, Philip G., *A Hurricane History*, p. 160.

23 Chacksfield, John, *Sir Sydney Camm, From Carpenter to Chief Designer*, unpublished typescript, (National Aerospace Library).

24 Mitchell, Gordon, op. cit, p. 295.

25 ibid, p. 276.

26 Fozard, Dr John, op cit, p. 235.

Chapter 11

1   Quin-Harkin, A.J., *The Journal of Transport History*, 1st Series, vol. 1 (4), (1954), pp. 197–200.

2   Pirie, Gordon, *Air Empire, British Imperial Civil Aviation, 1919–39*, 2009, p. 238.

3   ibid, p. 75.

4   Geddes to Hoare, 5 Aug 1929, Templewood MSS, Oxford DNB 2004, vol. 21, p. 698.

5   Penrose, Harald, *Wings Across the World, An Illustrated History of British Airways*, 1980, p. 42.

6   ibid, p. 46.

7   Pirie, Gordon, op cit, p. 178.

8   Penrose, Harald, *Wings Across the World*, op cit, p. 57.

9   Bluffield, Robert, *Over Empire and Oceans, Pioneer Aviators and Adventurers*, 2014, p. 140.

10   ibid, p. 138.
11   Report of the Annual General Meeting of Imperial Airways for 1931, p. 13.
12   Penrose, Harald, *Wings Across the World*, op cit, p. 74.
13   Higham, Robin, *Britain's Imperial Air Routes, 1918–1939*, op cit, p. 347, Table IV.
14   Slade, J. Edouard, *The Pioneer Days of Aviation in Jersey*, vol. 1, 1965, p. 88.
15   Ord Hume, Arthur W.J.G., op cit, p.210.
16   Bluffield, Robert, op cit, pp. 145–146.
17   Report of the Annual General Meeting of Imperial Airways for 1933, p. 10.
18   ibid, p.15.
19   Report of the Annual General Meeting of Imperial Airways for 1934, pp. 13–14.
20   Bluffield, Robert, op cit, p. 149.
21   Report of the Annual General Meeting of Imperial Airways for 1935, p. 7.
22   Penrose, Harald, *Wings Across the World*, op cit, p. 98.
23   Report of the Annual General Meeting of Imperial Airways for 1936, p. 9.
24   Pirie, Gordon, op cit, p. 216.
25   Penrose, Harald, *Wings Across the World*, op cit, p. 101.
26   Report of the Annual General Meeting of Imperial Airways 1937, p. 5.
27   Knott, Richard, *Flying Boats of the Empire, The Rise and Fall of the Ships of the Sky*, 2011, p. 35.
28   Higham, Robin, *Britain's Imperial Air Routes*, op cit, p. 76.
29   Jackson, A.S., op cit, p. 49.
30   House of Commons Adjournment Debate of 28 Oct 1937.
31   Jackson, A.S., op cit, p. 121.
32   Halford-MacLeod, Guy, op cit, p. 116.

Chapter 12

1   Doyle, Neville, *The Triple Alliance, The Predecessors of the First British Airways*, 2001, p. 23.
2   *The Aeroplane*, 27 Oct 1937.
3   Doyle, Neville, op cit, p. 10.
4   ibid, p. 11.
5   ibid, p. 13.
6   ibid, p. 30.
7   ibid.
8   Courtenay, William, *Airman Friday*, 1938, p. 195.

9 Wickstead, Maurice, 'Edward Hillman: A Man and his Airline', *Air Pictorial*, Nov 1994, p. 505.
10 Doyle, Neville, op cit, p. 61.
11 ibid, p. 59, 60.
12 Wickstead, Maurice, op cit, pp. 505–506.
13 Penrose, Harald, *Wings Across the World*, op cit, p. 78.
14 Wickstead, Maurice, op cit, p. 549.
15 Doyle, Neville, op cit, p. 77.
16 Fresson, Captain E.E., *Air Road to the Isles*, 2008, p. 43.
17 Clegg, Peter V., *A Flying Start to the Day*, 1987, p. 19.
18 Dodds, Colin N., *The Story of the de Havilland Dragon Type*, 2005, p. 40.
19 Davies, R.E.G., *British Airways the Imperial Years*, 2005, p. 76.
20 Halford-MacLeod, op cit, p. 25.
21 HC Debate 10 Jul 1939, 5th series, vol. 349, col. 1918.

Chapter 13

1 Reese, Peter, *The Flying Cowboy*, 2006, p. 56.
2 Child, S. and Caunter. C.F., *A Historical Summary of the Royal Aircraft Factory and its Antecedents 1878–1918*, p. 11.
3 ibid, p. 18.
4 Caunter. C.F., *A Historical Summary of the Royal Aircraft Establishment 1914–1948*, p. 24.
5 Cooper, Peter J., *Forever Farnborough, Flying the Limits, 1904–1996*, p. 50.
6 Turnill, Reginald and Reed, Arthur, *Farnborough, The Story of RAE*, p. 44.
7 ibid, p. 46.
8 *Laboratory of the Air, An Account of the Royal Aircraft Establishment of the Ministry of Supply,*, Farnborough, HMSO 1948, p. 40.
9 Caunter, C.F., op cit, p. 106.
10 ibid, p. 101.
11 ibid, p. 102.
12 ibid, p. 108.
13 ibid, p. 107, 108.
14 ibid, p. 105.
15 ibid, p. 115.
16 ibid, p. 106.

Chapter 14

1 Montgomery Hyde, H., op cit, pp. 429–430.
2 Reynolds, David, *Summits: Six Meetings that Shaped the Twentieth Century*, 2007, p. 39.
3 Nicolson, Harold, *Diaries and Letters*, vol. 1, p. 381.
4 Whereby the Rhineland borders of France and Germany were guaranteed and Germany was brought into the League of Nations.
5 *Dictionary of National Biography*, vol. 10, pp. 936–937.
6 Reynolds, David, op cit, p. 42.
7 Feiling, Keith, *The Life of Neville Chamberlain*, 1946, p. 402.
8 ibid, p. 304.
9 Fuchser, Larry William, *Neville Chamberlain and Appeasement*, 1982, p. 173.
10 ibid, p. 178.
11 Reynolds, David, op cit, p. 93.
12 House of Commons Debates, 31 Mar 1939, vol. 2415.
13 The author Frank Owen went under the pseudonym of 'Cato'.
14 Gilbert, Martin and Gott, Richard, *The Appeasers*, 1963.
15 Orange, Vincent, *Churchill and his Airmen*, p. 110.
16 Watt, Donald Cameron, *How War Came*, 1989, p. 623.
17 Macleod, Ian, *Neville Chamberlain*, p. 193.
18 Feiling, Keith, op cit, p. 446.
19 Cabinet Paper 218 (38) Relative Air Strengths and Proposals for the Improvement of the Country's Position.
20 Slessor, Sir John, *The Central Blue, Recollections and Reflections*, 1956, p. 178.
21 ibid, p. 179.
22 Churchill, Winston S., *The Gathering Storm*, 1948, p. 426.
23 Montgomery Hyde, H., op cit, pp. 500–501.
24 ibid.
25 *Dictionary of National Biography*, vol. 60, p. 127.
26 Report for the Society of British Aircraft Construction for 1936 and Summary of Activities of the Society's Work for the seven-year period 1939–1946, pp. 1–2. (National Aerospace Library)
27 Montgomery Hyde, H., op cit, p. 424.
28 House of Commons Debates, 9 March 1939, vol. 344, cols 2391–2.
29 Summary of Activities of Society of British Aircraft Distribution Ltd, p. 1.
30 *Dictionary of National Biography*, vol. 60, 125, p. 6.
31 ibid, p. 563.

32 ibid.

33 Probert, Air Commodore Henry, op cit, p. 17.

34 Clark, Ronald W., *Tizard*, 1965, p. 168.

35 Slessor, Sir John, op cit, 1956.

36 ibid, p. 241.

37 ibid.

38 *Dictionary of National Biography*, op cit, p. 564.

39 Furse, Anthony, op cit, p. 7.

40 *Dictionary of National Biography*, vol. 20, p. 940.

41 ibid.

42 Furse, Anthony, op cit, p. 64.

43 ibid, p. 81.

44 ibid.

45 At the time most extensive use was made of 87-octane fuel.

46 Freeman was offered a peerage, which he refused, accepting a baronetcy instead.

Chapter 15

1 House of Commons Debates, 17 Nov 1937, vol. 329, p. 417.

2 *Air Transport* (Walker, Ronald, ed.) 1943, The Cadman Enquiry, Before and After, p. 41.

3 Report of the Committee of Inquiry into Civil Aviation and the Observations of HM Government thereon, HMSO 1938, 1-X111, pp. 3–33.

4 Montgomery Hyde, H., op cit, p. 434.

5 Report of the Committee of Enquiry, op cit, paragraphs 46, 47, pp. 15, 16.

6 House of Commons Debates, 16 Mar 1938, vol. 333, p. 441.

7 Montgomery Hyde, H., op cit, p. 435.

8 McIntyre, Ian, *The Expense of Glory, A Life of John Reith*, 1944, p. 103.

9 Reith, John, *Into the Wind, Summarized Diary*, 13 Dec 1922.

10 ibid, p. 90.

11 *Dictionary of National Biography*, vol. 46, p. 443.

12 Higham, Robin, *Britain's Imperial Air Routes 1918–1939*, op cit, p. 292.

13 Reith, John, op cit, 5 Mar 1937.

14 Jackson, A.S., op cit, p. 135.

15 Reith, John, op cit, p. 329.

16 Pudney, John, op cit, p. 133.

17 *Dictionary of National Biography*, vol. 48, pp. 128–129.

18 Bray, Winston, *The History of BOAC*, 1974, p. 10.
19 *The Times*, Nov 19 1938.
20 *The Times*, Nov 12 1938.
21 Reith, John, op cit, 15 and 19 Jun 1939.
22 *Imperial Airways Gazette*, Aug 1939, vol. II (8), pp. 4–5.
23 ibid, p. 7.
24 House of Commons Debates, 17 Mar 1936, vol. 310, p. 271.
25 Halford-MacLeod, Guy, op cit, p. 11.
26 *Dictionary of National Biography*, vol. 48, p. 445.
27 Halford-MacLeod, op cit, p. 41.
28 Munson, Kenneth, op cit, p. 52.
29 Higham, Robin, *Speedbird, The Complete History of BOAC*, 2013, p. 7.
30 McIntyre, Ian, op cit, p. 285.
31 ibid, p. 38.
32 Pudney, John, op cit, p. 207.

Chapter 16

1 Montgomery Hyde, H., op cit, app. VIII.
2 *Aeroplane*, July 2010, vol. 38 (7), pp. 51–53.
3 Hooton, E.R., *The Luftwaffe, A Study in Air Power 1933–1945*, 2010, p. 59.
4 ibid, p. 61.
5 ibid, p. 75.
6 Killen, John, *The Luftwaffe, A History*, 1967, p. 125.
7 Collinson. R.P.G., *Fight for the Skies, The Battle of Britain 1940*, 2013, p. 8.
8 British Aircraft Production Figures, Ministry of Supply Report No. 4 for the British, American, German and Japanese Aircraft Industries. (National Aerospace Library)
9 Vajda Ferenc, A. and Dancey, Peter, *German Aircraft Industry and Production 1933–1945*, p. 45
10 Bishop, Patrick, *Fighter Boys*, 2009, p. 169.
11 Hooton, E.R., *Phoenix Triumphant, The Rise and Rise of the Luftwaffe*, 1994, pp. 207–208.
12 *Dictionary of National Biography*, vol. 16, p.777
13 ibid.
14 Collier, Basil, *Leader of the Few*, 1957, p. 103.
15 May, Ernest R., *Strange Victory: Hitler's Conquest of France*, 2015, p.170.
16 Orange, Vincent, *Dowding of Fighter Command*, 2009, p. 90.
17 Collier, op cit, p. 84.

18 Wright, Robert, *Dowding and the Battle of Britain*, 1969, p. 104.

19 Orange, Vincent, op cit, p. 134.

20 Reese, Peter, *Target London, Bombing the Capital 1915–2005*, p. 83.

21 Killen, John, op cit, p. 135.

22 *Dictionary of National Biography*, 2004, vol. 16, p. 776.

23 Orange, Vincent, op cit, p. 10

24 ibid, p. 193.

Assessment

1 Clark, Ronald, W. *Tizard*, 1963, p. 419.

2 Bragg, Michael, *RDFI, The Location of Aircraft by Radio Methods 1935–1945*, 2002, p. 25.

3 Ernest Hives was responsible for developing Henry Royce's first engine, the Eagle, followed by a long list of successful engines culminating in the Merlin.

4 Harvey Bailey, Alec, *The Merlin in Perspective – The Combat Years*, 1995, p. 136.

5 *Dictionary of National Biography*, vol. 54, p. 855.

SELECT BIBLIOGRAPHY

Papers and Miscellaneous Official Publications

Air Conference, 12–14 October 1920, press cuttings, Air Ministry Publication, (National Aerospace Library).

Baker, G.S., 'Flying Boats, The Forms and Dimensions of their Hulls', paper read at the North East Coast Institution of Engineers and Shipbuilders, 27 February 1920.

Broke-Smith, Brigadier P.W.L., 'The History of Early British Aeronautics', pamphlet reprinted by Litho from the Royal Engineers Journal (National Aerospace Library).

Centenary pamphlet for Sir Frederick Handley Page, issued to the City University, Friday 15 November 1985 (National Aerospace Library).

Chacksfield, John, *Sir Sydney Camm, From Carpenter to Chief Designer*, manuscript (unpublished typescript) (National Aerospace Library).

'Disposition of Officers at Stations of Royal Naval Air Service', paper, 25 March 1918 (National Aerospace Library).

Ellam, C., 'The British Heavy Bomber', paper presented at a joint meeting with the RAeS at the Science Museum London on 11 December 1996, *Transactions of the Newcomen Society*, vol. 68, 1996–1997.

Hilton, Dr W.F., 'British Aeronautical Research Facilities', Centenary Journal of the RAeS, 1866–1966, pp. 103–107.

Institution of Civil Engineers, 'Construction and Maintenance of Flying Stations, 1924' (National Aerospace Library).

Lucas, Philip G., 'A Hurricane', paper delivered to the Hatfield Branch of the RAeS, 1972 (National Aerospace Library).

McCormack, Robert L., 'Winston Churchill's Missed Opportunities for Overflying Africa', *Canadian Journal of African Studies*, vol. X, No. 1, 1976, pp. 87–105.

'Ministry of Aircraft Production, 1939–1945', pamphlet (National Aerospace Library).

Minute Book, The Society of British Aircraft Constructors Ltd, CAC Committee October 1934–September 1941 (National Aerospace Library).

'The Air Way', official handbook describing the activities of Imperial Airways (National Aerospace Library).

'The Future of Aerial Transport', pamphlet, Ministry of Reconstruction, 1919.

'The Second World War, 1939–1945 Royal Air Force Flying Training', vol. 1, Policy and Planning, 1952, Air Ministry Publication.

White Smith, H. (Chairman of the Society of British Aircraft Constructors), 'Aeroplane and Seaplane Efficiency', Conference on Air Transport, Friday 25 February 1921 at Olympia.

Woods Humphery, G.E., 'A review of Air Transport', 16 February 1933, (National Aerospace Library).

Reports

Report of the Airworthiness Authorities on R101 as modified by the addition of a new bay, Air Ministry Document AD (O) of 7 May 1931. (National Aerospace Library).

Report of the Committee of Inquiry into Civil Aviation and the observations of HM Government thereon HMSO, 1938.

Reports of Imperial Airways Annual General Meetings, 1933–1938 (National Aerospace Library).

Report of the Proceedings of the Air Conference 1920 with Appendices, HMSO [Cmd 1157], 1920.

Report of the Proceedings of the Second Air Conference held on 6–7 Feb. 1923, HMSO, 1923.

Report of the R101 Inquiry Presented by the Secretary of State for Air to Parliament by Command of His Majesty, March 1931, HMSO, 1931.

Report on the Royal Aircraft Establishment, 1878–1918, Aero 2150 by S. Child and C.F. Caunter, 1947 (National Aerospace Library).

Report on the Royal Aircraft Establishment 1918–1948, Aero 2150 A by C.F. Caunter, 1949 (National Aerospace Library).

Magazines

Air Pictorial

Flight

ICARE revue de l'aviation, La Coupe Schneider, 1913–1931

Imperial Airways Gazette, 1929–1939

Journal of the RAeS

The Aeroplane, 1918–1940

Books

Alcock, Sir John and Brown, Sir Arthur Whitten, *Our Transatlantic Flight*, 1919.

Allen, Peter, *The 91 Before Lindbergh*, 1984.

Andrews, C.F. and Morgan, E.B., *Vickers Aircraft Since 1908*, 1988.

Armstrong, William, *Pioneer Pilot*, 1952.

Balchin, Nigel, *The Aircraft Builders, An Account of British Aircraft Production 1935–1945*, 1947.

Barker, Ralph, *The Schneider Trophy Races*, 1971.

Barnes, C.H., *Handley Page Aircraft Since 1907*, 1976.

Bastow, Donald, *Henry Royce – Mechanic*, 1989.

Batten, Jean, *Alone in the Sky*, 1979.

Bishop, William A., *Winged Peace, The Air Age, its birth, its future and its impact in terms of progress or devastation*, 1944.

Bluffield, Robert, *Imperial Airways, The Birth of the British Airline Industry 1914–1940*, 2009.

—— *Over Empires and Oceans Pioneers Aviators and Adventurers Forging the International Air Routes, 1918–1939*, 2014.

Boughton, Terence, *The Story of the British Light Aeroplane*, 1963.

Bowyer, Chaz, *RAF Operations*, 1918–1938, 1988.

Bowyer, Michael J.F., *Aircraft for the Few, The RAF's Fighters and Bombers of 1940*, 1991.

Boyle, Andrew, *Trenchard Man of Vision*, 1962.

Bragg, Michael, *RDFI, The Location of Aircraft by Radio Methods, 1935–1945*, 2002.

Brindley, J.F., and Newton, G., *IATA, Wings Across the World Since 1945*, 2009.

Brittain, Sir Harry, *By Air*, 1933.

——*Wings of Speed*, 1934.

Brooks, Peter W., *Zeppelin, Rigid Airships 1893–1940*, 1992.

Bruce, the Rt Hon Mrs, Victor, *The Bluebird's Flight*, 1931.

Budiansky, Stephen, *Air Power, From Kitty Hawk to Gulf War II, A History of the People, Ideas and Machines that Transformed War in the Century of Flight*, 2003.

Burge, Squadron Leader C.G., *Encyclopaedia of Aviation*, 1935.

Butler, Ewan and Young, Gordon, *Marshal Without Glory, The Troubled Life of Herman Goering*, 1951.

Cairncross, Sir Alec, *Planning in Wartime Aircraft Production in Britain, Germany and the USA*, 1991.

Chichester, Francis, *Solo to Sydney*, 1929.

—— *Seaplane Solo*, 1933.

—— *The Lonely Sea and the Sky*, 1964.

—— *Alone over the Tasman Sea*, 1966.

—— *Ride on the Wind*, 1980.

Clegg, Peter V., *A Flying Start to the Day*, 1986.
—— *Flying Against the Elements*, 1987.
—— *Rivals in the North*, 1988.
—— *Sword in the Sky*, 1990.
—— *Wings over the Glens*, 1995.
—— *Avro Test-Pilots Since 1907*, 1997.
Clydesdale, The Marquess of and McIntyre, D.F., *The Pilot's Book of Everest*, 1936.
Cobham, Sir Alan, *Australia and Back*, 1926.
—— *My Flight to the Cape and Back*, 1926.
—— *Twenty Thousand Miles in a Flying Boat*, 1928.
—— *A Time to Fly*, 1978.
—— *To the Ends of the Earth, Memoirs of a Pioneering Aviator*, 2007.
Cole, Lance, *Secrets of the Spitfire, The Story of Beverley Shenstone the Man Who Perfected the Elliptical Wing*, 2012.
Cooper, John Cobb, *Explorations in Aerospace*, 1968.
Cooper, Peter J., *Forever Farnborough, Flying to the Limits 1904–1996*, 1996.
—— *Farnborough 100 Years of British Aviation*, 2006.
Courtenay, William, *Airman Friday*, 1938.
Cox, Sebastian and Gray, Peter (eds), *Air Power History Turning Points from Kitty Hawk to Kosovo*, 2012.
Cruddas, Colin, *Those Fabulous Flying Years, Joy Riding and Flying Circuses between the Wars*, 2003.
—— *Highways to the Empire, Long Distance Flying between the Wars*, 2006.
Davies, R.E.G., *Rebels and Reformers of the Airways*, 1987.
—— *British Airways, An Airline and its Aircraft, vol. 1, 1919–1939, The Imperial Years*, 2005.
Davis, Mick, *Airco The Aircraft Manufacturing Company*, 2001.
Dean, Sir Maurice, *The Royal Air Force and Two World Wars*, 1979.
Dennis, Richard, *Farnborough's Jets, An Account of Early Jet Engine Research at the Royal Aircraft Establishment, Farnborough and at Pyestock*, 1999.
—— *Royal Aircraft Establishment at War*, 2008.
Dodds, Colin N., *The Story of the de Havilland Dragon Types*, 2005.
Douglas-Hamilton, James, *Roof of the World, Man's First Flight over Everest*, 1983.
Doyle, Neville, *The Triple Alliance, The Predecessors of the First British Airways*, 2001.
Duggan, John and Meyer, Henry Lord, *Airships in International Affairs 1890–1940*, 2001.
Eustis, Nelson, *The Greatest Air Race, England–Australia, 1919*, 1969.
Eves, Edward, *The Schneider Trophy Story*, 2001.
Fozzard, Dr John W., (Editor), *Sydney Camm and the Hurricane*, 1991.
Fresson, Captain E.E., *Air Road to the Isles*, 2008.
Fuchser, Larry William, *Neville Chamberlain and Appeasement, A Study in the Politics of History*, 1982.

Furse, Anthony, *Wilfrid Freeman, The Genius Behind Allied Survival and Air Supremacy 1939 to 1945*, 2000.

Grahame-White, Claude and Harper H., *Our First Airways*, 1919.

Grierson, John, *Jet Flight*, 1946.

Groves, Brigadier-General P.R.C., *Our Future in the Air, A Study of the Vital Question of British Air Power*, 1922.

Halford-MacLeod, Guy, *Born of Adversity Britain's Airlines 1919–1963*, 2014.

Handley Page, Sir Frederick, *The Wings of Commerce, Aircraft Disposal Co Ltd.*, London, 1920.

Hartcup, Guy, *The Challenge of War, Scientific and Engineering Contributions to World War Two*, 1970.

Harvey-Bailey, Alec, *The Merlin in Perspective*, 1995.

Havard, Cyril, *The Trenchard Touch*, 2000.

Hayward, Keith, *The British Aircraft Industry*, 1989.

Hearne, R.P., *Airships in Peace and War*, 1909.

Heath, Lady and Wolf Murray, Stella, *Women and Flying*, 1929.

Higham, Robin, *Britain's Imperial Air Routes, 1918–1939, The Story of Britain's Overseas Airlines*, 1960.

—— *The British Rigid Airship, 1908–1931, A Study in Weapons Policy*, 1961.

—— *The Military Intellectuals in Britain, 1918–1939*, 1966.

—— *A Handbook on Air Ministry Organisation*, 2001.

Hoare, Sir Samuel, Viscount Templewood, *Empire of the Air, The Advent of the Air Age, 1922–1929*, 1957.

Holt, Thomas G., *Aerial Transport*, 1920.

Hooper, Meredith, *Kangaroo Route, The Development of Commercial Flight between England and Australia*, 1985.

Hooton, E.R., *Phoenix Triumphant, The Rise and Rise of the Luftwaffe*, 1984.

—— *The Luftwaffe, A Study in Air Power, 1933–1945*, 2010.

Hutchinson, Iain, *The Flight of the Starling, The Story of Scottish Pioneer Aviator, Captain Eric Starling*, 1992.

Jackson, A.J., *De Havilland Aircraft Since 1909*, 1987.

—— *Avro Aircraft Since 1908*, 1990.

—— *Imperial Airways, First British Airlines, 1919–1940*, 1995.

Jackson, Robert, *Airships in Peace and War*, 1971.

Johnson, Amy, *Sky Roads of the World*, 1939.

Jones, Glyn, *The Jet Pioneers, The Birth of Jet Powered Flight*, 1989.

Kilduff, Peter, *Herman Göring: Fighter Ace*, 2010.

King, Peter, *Knights of the Air, The Life and Times of the Extraordinary Pioneers who first built British Aeroplanes*, 1989.

Klaas, M.D., *Last of the Flying Clippers, The Boeing B-314 story*, 1997.

Knott, Richard C., *The American Flying Boat – An Illustrated History*, 1979.

—— *Flying Boats of the Empire, The Rise and Fall of the Ships of the Sky*, 2011.

Latham, Colin and Stubbs, Anne (Editors), *The Birth of British Radar, The Memoirs of Arnold 'Skip' Wilkins*, 2006.

Leasor, James, *The Millionth Chance, The Story of the R101*, 1957.

Lloyd, F.M.H., *Hurricane, the Story of a Great Fighter*, 1945.

Loftin, Laurence K. (Jnr), *Quest for Performance, The Evolution of Modern Aircraft*, 1985.

Lomax, Judy, *Women in the Air*, 1986.

Londonderry, The Marquess of, *Wings of Destiny*, 1943.

Lovell, Mary S., *Straight on Till Morning, The Biography of Beryl Markham*, 1987.

Luff, David, *Amy Johnson, Enigma in the Sky*, 2002.

Macmillan, Captain Norman, *The Air Travellers' Guide to Europe*, 1929.

—— *Sir Sefton Brancker*, 1935.

Masefield, Sir Peter G., *To Ride the Storm*, 1982.

Mason, Francis K., *The British Bomber Since 1914*, 1994.

Meilinger, Philip S. (Editor), *The Paths of Heaven, The Evolution of Airpower Theory*, 1997.

—— *Air War Theory and Practice*, 2003.

Meyer, Henry Cord, *Airshipmen, Businessmen and Politics, 1899–1940*, 1991.

Mitchell, Gordon, *R.J. Mitchell, Schooldays to Spitfire*, 1997.

Mondey, David, *The Schneider Trophy*, 1975.

Montgomery Hyde, H., *British Air Policy Between the Wars, 1918–1939*, 1976.

Morpurgo, J.E., *Barnes Wallis, A Biography*, 1972.

Mousseau, Jacques, *Conquering The Skies, 1903–1933*, 2003.

Munson, Kenneth, *Pictorial History of BOAC and Imperial Airways*, 1970.

Murray, Iain, *Bouncing Bomb Man, The Science of Sir Barnes Wallis*, 2009.

Naughton, Lindie, *Lady Icarus: The Life of Irish Aviator Lady Mary Heath*, 2006.

Orange, Vincent, *Churchill and his Airmen, Relationships, Intrigue and Policy Making, 1914–1945*, 2013.

Ord-Hume, Arthur, J.G., *British Light Aeroplanes, Their Evolution, Development and Perfection, 1920–1940*, 2000.

—— *British Commercial Aircraft, Their Evolution, Development and Perfection 1920–1940*, 2003.

—— *Flying in Pre-War Skies, Private and Club Aviation, 1920–1939*, 2014.

—— *Scotland's Aviation History*, 2014.

Pegram, Ralph, *Schneider Trophy, Seaplanes and Flying Boats, Victors, Vanquished and Visions*, 2012.

Pemberton, Sir Max, *The Life of Sir Henry Royce*, 1986.

Penrose, Harald, *British Aviation, The Great War and Armistice 1915–1919*, 1969.

—— *British Aviation, The Adventuring Years, 1920–1929*, 1973.

—— *British Aviation, Ominous Skies, 1935–1939*, 1980.

—— *Wings Across the World, An Illustrated History of British Airways*, 1980.

Philpott, Wing Commander Ian M., *The Royal Air Force, An Encyclopedia of the Interwar Years, vol. II, Rearmament 1930 to 1939*, 2008.

Pirie, Gordon, *Air Empire, British Imperial Civil Aviation 1919–1939*, 2009.

—— *Cultures and Caricatures of British Imperial Aviation*, 2012.

Price, A. Grenfell, *The Skies Remember, The Story of Ross and Keith Smith*, 1969.

Probert, Henry (Air Commodore), *High Commanders of the Royal Air Force*, 1905.

Pudney, John, *The Seven Skies, A Study of BOAC and its Forerunners Since 1919*, 1959.

Reader, W. J., *Architect of Air Power, The Life of the First Viscount Weir*, 1968.

Reid, Ian, *Britain's First Air Show, Doncaster Racecourse, 100 Anniversary Edition 1909–2009*, 2009.

Reynolds, David, *Summits: Six Meetings that Shaped the Twentieth Century*, 2007.

Ritchie, Sebastian, *Industry and Air Power, The Expansion of British Aircraft Production, 1935–1941*, 1997.

Roussel, Mike, *Spitfire's Forgotten Designer, The Career of Supermarine's Joe Smith*, 2013.

Semple, Clive, *Airway to the East, 1918–1920 and the Collapse of No. 1 Aerial Route RAF*, 2012.

Shelton, John, *Schneider Trophy to Spitfire, The Design Career of R.J. Mitchell*, 2008.

Sinnott, Colin, *The RAF and Aircraft Design, 1923–1939*, 2001.

Slade, J. Edouard, *The Pioneer Days of Aviation in Jersey, vol. 1*, 1965.

Slessor, Sir John, *The Central Blue*, 1956.

Smith, Ron, *British Built Aircraft: Greater London*, 2002.

Smith, Sir Ross, *14,000 Miles Through the Air*, 1922.

Smith, W.L., *Air Transport Operations*, 1931.

Swinfield, John, *Airship Design, Development and Disaster*, 2012.

Sykes, Sir Frederick, *From Many Angles*, 1942.

Tangye, Nigel (Editor) *The Air is our Concern, A Critical Study of England's Future in Aviation*, 1935.

Thetford, Owen, *Aircraft of the Royal Air Force Since 1918*, 1988.

Turnill, Reginald and Reed, Arthur, *Farnborough, The Story of the RAE*, 1980.

Vajda, Ferenc, A. and Dancey, Peter, *German Aircraft Industry and Production, 1933–1945*, 1998.

Vann, Frank, *Willy Messerschmitt, First Full Biography of an Aeronautical Genius*, 1993.

Wallace, Graham, *The Flight of Alcock and Brown, 14–15 June 1919*, 1955.

Webb, Denis le P., *Never a Dull Moment at Supermarine, A Personal History*, 2001.

Webster, Sir Charles and Frankland, Noble, *History of the Second World War, The Strategic Air Offensive Against Germany, 1939–1945*, 1961.

White, Ian, *The History of Air Intercept Radar and the British Nightfighters, 1935–1959*, 2007.

Widmer, Emil, J., *Military Observation Balloons, (Captive and Free)*, 1917.

Wohl, Robert, *The Spectacle of Flight, Aviation and the Western Imagination, 1920–1950*, 2005.

Worcester, Richard, *Roots of British Air Policy*, 1966.

Zimmerman, David, *Britain's Shield, Radar and the Defeat of the Luftwaffe*, 2001.

INDEX

Page numbers in *italics* denote illustrations

You may also be interested in …

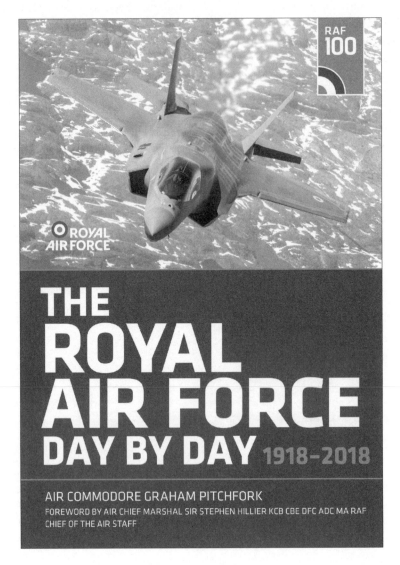

978 0 7509 79733

'He has produced a page-turner.' – Air Vice-Marshal Nigel Baldwin CB CBE

THE RAF IN
100 OBJECTS

PETER JACOBS

FOREWORD BY AIR VICE-MARSHAL
NIGEL BALDWIN CB CBE

978 0 7509 65361

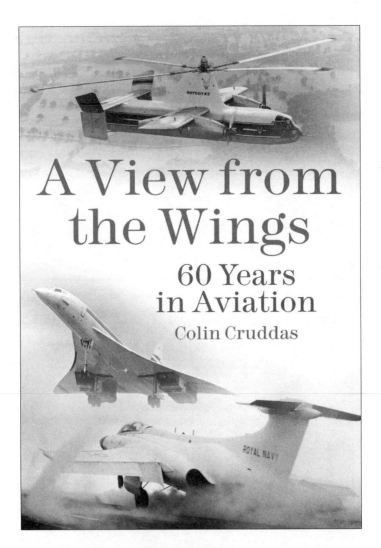

A View from the Wings

60 Years in Aviation

Colin Cruddas

978 0 7524 77480

The History Press
The destination for history
www.thehistorypress.co.uk